More Than Listening

NASPA
Student Affairs Administrators
in Higher Education

Ruth Harper, Nona L. Wilson, and Associates

More Than Listening

*A Casebook for Using Counseling Skills
in Student Affairs Work*

NASPA

Student Affairs Administrators
in Higher Education

More Than Listening: A Casebook for Using Counseling Skills in Student Affairs Work

Published by NASPA – Student Affairs Administrators in Higher Education
1875 Connecticut Ave., NW
Suite 418
Washington, DC 20009
www.naspa.org

Additional copies may be purchased by contacting the NASPA publications department at 301-638-1749 or visiting http://bookstore.naspa.org.

NASPA does not discriminate on the basis of race, color, national origin, religion, sex, age, gender identity, gender expression, affectional or sexual orientation, or disability in any of its policies, programs, and services.

Library of Congress Control Number: 2009941835
ISBN 978-0-931654-63-3
Printed and bound in the United States of America
FIRST EDITION

Cover artwork "Tea Cup Blue" by Jeff Stevenson, www.jeffstevenson.com. Reproduced with permission.

Table of Contents

ACKNOWLEDGMENTS

Ruth Harper and Nona Wilson wish to recognize the case study contributors: experienced student affairs professionals from throughout the United States and Canada who serve in a variety of roles. In several instances, these associates contributed the student development responses to the scenarios they created. In others, they collaborated with the lead authors, who wrote the counseling responses.

Early encouragement for this project came from NASPA Executive Director Gwen Dungy and from Rick Roberts, chair of the department of counseling and student development at Eastern Illinois University. The authors also wish to acknowledge the contributions of Melissa Dahne, director of publications for NASPA, whose support, flexibility, and resourcefulness have been instrumental throughout the production of this book.

Important feedback on the text was obtained from four external reviewers, whose sharp questions and thoughtful commentary informed the final version in many ways. Thanks go to Anne Blackhurst, dean of graduate studies and research at Minnesota State University Mankato; Gregory Eells, director of counseling and psychological services at Cornell University; Mimi Benjamin, associate director for faculty programs at Cornell University; and

Kevin Gaw, director of university career services at Georgia State University.

In addition, several South Dakota State University students edited, checked sources and facts, and reacted to the case studies. Thanks to Joe Cooper, Adam Dahlke, Amy Danielson, Ryan Knigge, Sylvia Lozada, Janel Magnus, Emily Noem, Nicole Spry, Kellie Van Gerpen, and Yanchun Xu. Finally, thank you to Larry Rogers, Margaret Harper-Rogers, and Jay Trenhaile for their ongoing edits and critiques.

INTRODUCTION

Ruth Harper and Nona L. Wilson

The range and intensity of personal growth and development occurring for college students, regardless of their ages, are readily observable to everyone working in student affairs. The cumulative force and forward momentum of all that potential are awe inspiring and invigorating. The opportunity to support—up close, every day—human potential is, in large measure, what draws people to the profession. Yet, while it is true that the outcomes of this growth and development are rewarding, the process itself often can be distressing. Encountering demands that are beyond one's current ability or understanding, and striving to meet those demands, is not easy. The growing edge of experience (be it emotional, physical, cognitive, or spiritual) is tender, often rife with uncertainty, hesitation, and mistakes, as well as moments of exhilaration. With distance and perspective, the process is interesting, but in the moment—in the act of growing—it may be uncomfortable. And that's just typical development, the fits and starts that are expected as students try something new and discover their way through trial and error.

When expected development is complicated by too many demands at once or demands that far outpace current ability, or when support is insufficient, the process is not just uncomfortable, it can be overwhelming. This is particularly true when mental health issues or significant developmental concerns intersect with or complicate developmental tasks.

Although younger professionals might not remember when the kind of attention to mental health issues that currently characterizes campus life was lacking, the landmark studies that first documented significant increases in the incidence and severity of mental health concerns at college counseling centers began appearing less than a decade ago (e.g., Benton, Robertson, Tseng, Newton, & Benton, 2003; Gallagher, 2001; Gallagher, Zhang, & Taylor, 2003). Since then, recognition of how pervasive and pressing such issues are has come at a strong and steady pace. The evidence of significant mental health issues—across the full spectrum of concerns—is as troubling as it is undeniable on most campuses today.

Overview of Mental Health Concerns on Campus

Many factors contribute to the rising numbers of college students with mental health challenges. In the past, many such students did not consider postsecondary education possible. Today—as a result of early diagnosis, more effective treatment, and federal laws that prohibit discrimination against otherwise qualified people with disabilities—colleges and universities are seeing a greater variety of students who may need modifications or support in both academic and nonacademic arenas (Dickerson, 2006). As a result, "more schools [are] seeing the mental health of students as part of the overall education mission" (Eells, 2008, p. 47).

Before this recognition and the attendant changes in higher education, students with developmental challenges that can interfere with learning (e.g., autism spectrum disorders, learning disabilities, attention deficit disorders) might never have attempted to earn a college degree. Academic advisors, residence hall directors, student activities coordinators, and student affairs professionals in every role are now working with students who live with concerns and conditions rarely encountered or acknowledged in higher education venues 25 years ago. For example, "colleges and universities have seen a striking increase in the number of matriculated students diagnosed with Asperger's disorder" (Osfield & Junco, 2006, p. 176). Community colleges, in particular, are experiencing rising enrollments of students with autism spectrum disorders; those with Asperger's may be socially unprepared as well as "especially vulnerable sexually and emotionally" (Moore, 2006, para. 10). Students with serious, chronic mental illness, such as bipolar disorder or obsessive-compulsive disorder, form another small but growing population in higher education.

Though student affairs professionals have long dealt with the symptoms and consequences of depression and anxiety among students, recent surveys conducted by the American College Health Association (ACHA) and the National College Health Assessment (NCHA) confirm widespread self-reported symptoms of depression and other mental or emotional distress among college students. Almost 50% of students, when asked, said they felt "hopeless" at least once during the previous year; one third felt "so depressed that it was difficult to function"; and nearly 90% felt "overwhelmed by all you had to do" (ACHA/NCHA, 2009, p. 13). In addition, approximately 60% said they were "very sad" or "very lonely" in the past 12 months (p. 14). Kadison and DiGeronimo (2004) note that "the chances are almost one in two" that a college student will experience debilitating depression, and there is a "one in ten" chance a student will "seriously consider suicide" (p. 1).

Alan Glass, MD, director of student health and counseling at Washington University and a member of the ACHA board of directors, identifies depression and suicide as the largest mental health concerns on campus, requiring more and more resources (ACHA/NCHA, 2009, para. 4). Similarly, Twenge (2006) notes that "the average college student in the 1990s was more anxious than 85% of students in the 1950s and 71% of students in the 1970s" (p. 107); also, "one out of three college freshmen reported feeling 'frequently overwhelmed' in 2001, twice as many as in the 1980s" (p. 109). It is unclear whether the number of students with depression and anxiety has actually increased or if students today are simply more willing to acknowledge and disclose such concerns. However, there is no doubt that many students who identity depression and anxiety as concerns, and who feel unable at times to cope, are now attending institutions of postsecondary education.

College counseling centers confirm the unsettling portrait of an increasingly seriously distressed college student population. The 2003 National Survey of College Counseling Center Directors reports that 81.4% of such centers saw students with more serious psychological concerns than they did in the previous five years (Gallagher et al., 2003). Approximately 24% of students seeking services from campus counseling centers are taking psychotropic medications (Eells, 2008, p. 31).

Students with serious psychological conditions, however, are only part of the complex picture of college student mental health. Many students contend with less diagnostically severe, but nonetheless troubling, concerns. Fram (2008) found students struggling with concentration, motivation, and sleep issues, noting that "most say they have been agitated, worried, too tired to work" (para. 5). The transition to college itself is filled with potential stressors: "learning to live more independently, handle finances, maintain academic standards and integrity, and adjust to a new social life" (Brougham, Zail, Mendoza, & Miller, 2009). When these issues become overwhelming, students struggle to manage, with varying degrees of success.

The millennial generation is "disproportionately affected" by the current economic crisis; they face "unemployment at a rate more than 8% higher than the national average, suffer under a crushing average of $27,000 in student loans, $2,000 in credit card debt, and a health care crisis that leaves 30% of them without any insurance" (Simmons & Enista, 2009, para. 2). Many students owe significantly larger sums in education-related loans. Often, young adults do not understand how interest on loans is figured, how to calculate the size of monthly repayments after graduation, or the accumulating cost of credit card purchases not paid off at the end of the month (Doss, 2006). Additionally, many family college savings funds have been hit hard by stock market instability, and some students are being urged by their parents to find less expensive schools closer to home or even to delay their entry into college (Schevitz, 2008). This situation adds pressure to students who are already uncertain about how they will afford a college education or handle their debt loads after graduation.

Clearly, there is a significant demand for professional mental health services on campus. The standards of the International Association of Counseling Services (IACS), which accredits college counseling centers, specifies that "every effort should be made to maintain minimum staffing ratios of one F.T.E. (full-time equivalent) professional staff member (excluding trainees) to every 1,000 to 1,500 students, depending on services offered and other campus mental health agencies" (IACS, 2000, para. 3). Despite the growing need and an accepted standard for meeting it, few colleges or universities are able to devote additional resources to mental health services and support for students. In fact, "in the face of increasing severity, complexity, and quantity of mental health cases, counseling center staff have seen zero growth in resources or reduced budgets" (Cooper, 2006, p. 152). Likewise, Kadison and DiGeronimo (2004) note, "Nationwide, budget cuts are causing many departments in colleges and universities to cut . . . mental health positions" (p. 165).

Limited staffing means that college counselors are spending more time responding to students in crisis and to critical incidents. Fewer resources can be devoted to screening, prevention, educational, and outreach efforts on campus—activities that might have broader impact for more students. Operating in this manner is not the best way to serve students and can lead to higher rates of burnout and ineffectiveness among counseling professionals (Kadison & DiGeronimo, 2004).

Impact on Student Affairs Professionals

Although mental health issues have always been present to some degree among college students, their current prevalence, along with the convergence of increasing demand and decreasing resources, represents an important challenge to student affairs administrators. Approximately 40 years have passed since campuses abandoned the *in loco parentis* approach to their relationships with students and began treating students as adults—as mature, independent decision makers (Benton & Benton, 2006). But today's 18- to -24-year-olds may hold a more ambivalent view about their status as adults (Arnett, 2004). They, along with their often highly involved parents, may have elevated, sometimes unrealistic, expectations for care, service, and accommodation of mental health issues. On a day-to-day basis, responding to such expectations most often falls to advisors, residence hall directors, and others in student affairs. Many staff members—such as those in academic advising, financial aid, student retention programs, residence halls, and intercollegiate athletics—find themselves dealing quite regularly with students in crisis, as well as students in need of steady support and monitoring. But few of these professionals have educational or experiential backgrounds in counseling or mental health services.

Professional Preparation Programs

At one time, the majority of student affairs professional preparation programs resided in graduate programs in counseling or educational psychology (Reynolds, 2009). However, over the past 25 years or so, more and more student affairs practitioners are graduates of programs in higher educational administration or business administration, or hold "another master's degree" (Kretovics, 2002, p. 918). The Council for the Advancement of Standards (CAS), known as "the preeminent force for promoting standards in student affairs" (CAS, n.d., para. 1), does not mention counseling knowledge or skills as competencies needed or desirable for entry-level professionals in student affairs. Kretovics (2002) cites "noticeable disagreement as to what academic discipline was most appropriate" (p. 912) for prospective student affairs professionals and says that while "demonstrated helping skills" rank third on the list, "counseling coursework" ranks 13th (p. 916). Kretovics states the obvious dilemma: "If counseling classes are not taught, where will graduates learn these skills?" (p. 918). He recommends that "counseling skills, even as basic as listening and reflection, should be included in student affairs curricula and be taught by properly trained counselors and counselor educators" (p. 918).

Although Kretovics maintains that counseling skills are implied in the CAS area of professional studies, this interpretation may be generous, given that counseling skills are not specifically included in the CAS guidelines. Reynolds (2009) agrees with Kretovics' position but notes, "Student affairs preparation programs often do not address mental health issues in the curriculum . . . . It appears that much of the education about college students' mental health issues occurs as part of on-the-job training" (p. 47).

Thus, preparation programs that are not counseling-related, though superb in many other ways, may not provide adequate training in the helping skills that today's student affairs practice demands. Current options in many counseling programs often are not ideal either, offering curricula that are far too clinical or not well integrated with student affairs research and practice. The Council for the Accreditation of Counseling and Related Educational Programs (CACREP, n.d.) has established standards in two specializations related to student affairs: (1) college counseling and student development and (2) student affairs professional practice. So far, neither of these specialization standards reflects input from NASPA or ACPA (Barrett, 2005, para. 18); therefore, such standards may not be fully aligned with current student affairs professional practice and expectations.

This is the predicament: At the same time we face a heightened need to integrate student affairs practice and helping skills, training programs are bifurcating. Prospective graduate students have excellent options for locating strong student affairs/higher education programs or strong counseling programs, but they may find it harder to identify preparation programs that purposefully integrate the two in ways that make sense of student affairs practice. Despite its roots in the vocational guidance movement (Evans, Forney, & Guido-DeBrito, 1998, p. 6) and a traditionally holistic concern for students, the profession of student affairs now leaves many practitioners somewhat unprepared to meet the needs of today's students. Many of the key documents that professionalized and greatly strengthened the field of student affairs do not explicitly address the mental health concerns that now occupy a lot of time and energy on the part of student affairs staff. These documents include *The Student Learning Imperative* (American College Personnel Association, 1996); *Principles of Good Practice for Student Affairs* (ACPA, NASPA, 1997); and *Learning Reconsidered* (Keeling, 2004). Yet with adequate—sometimes even minimal—help, students with mental health challenges can learn, succeed, and excel in college.

Why This Book?

This book seeks to help bridge the knowledge gap that student affairs staff members may experience when they deal with students who have mental health concerns. It provides a model for how both student development and counseling theories can inform and enhance student affairs practice. The goals of this book include:

- Summarize and explicate basic concepts of selected theories of counseling and college student development.

- Illustrate effective use of these theoretical frameworks through a variety of case study scenarios in student affairs settings across a range of institutional and functional venues.

- Provide integrative responses to case studies that combine key ideas from both counseling and student development theories to help student affairs practitioners holistically conceptualize and deal with student mental health issues.

- Offer key insights to student affairs professionals on how to collaborate with mental health professionals in campus-based counseling centers or community-based mental health services.

- Discuss important factors related to diversity, professional ethics, campus safety, and consultation.

The book is organized as follows. Chapter 1 provides an overview of several theories of college student development. Three widely used theories of counseling are presented in chapter 2—Person-Centered (student-centered), Solution-Focused, and Cognitive-Behavioral Therapy—as well as a brief introduction to mindfulness and acceptance. Chapters 3 through 12 offer a series of case studies based on composites of situations typically handled by student affairs professionals. These case studies were contributed by seasoned student affairs professionals, many of whom are deeply involved in NASPA Knowledge Communities. Each scenario is followed by two theory-based responses: one drawing on student development theories and student affairs practice and the other grounded in counseling theory and suggesting or modeling practical helping skills. Chapter 13 provides information about how to work effectively with mental health professionals, and outlines signs and signals that can help identify students who need assistance. The final chapter (14) offers three short case studies for reflection, application, and discussion, in the hope that readers will pursue the opportunity to practice what is presented throughout the volume.

The Goal of the Book

The goal of this book is to contribute to the ongoing discussion about how student affairs professionals can best help students in crisis and those with mental health issues. The ideas presented here may seem controversial to some people. Mental health professionals have legitimate concerns about protecting students from helpers who are not fully qualified or who may overstep their roles. For the same reasons, student affairs staff members, especially those who are supervising inexperienced staff, may be reluctant to encourage them to explore counseling theories and skills. We share those concerns. We believe, however, that strong helping skills not only enhance student affairs professionals' ability to provide the best assistance but can also help them identify and communicate the boundaries of their roles. This book promotes the notion that counseling-based ideas and techniques can enhance the effectiveness of student affairs professionals in their supportive and educational roles with all students, including those who have psychological concerns.

References

American College Health Association (ACHA). (2009). *American College Health Association-National College Health Assessment II: Reference Group Executive Summary, Fall 2008.* Baltimore: Author.

American College Personnel Association. (1996). *The student learning imperative: Implications for student affairs.* Alexandria, VA: author.

American College Personnel Association / National Association for Student Personnel Administrators. (1997). Principles of good practice for student affairs. Retrieved November 2, 2008, from *www.acpa.nche.edu/pgp/princip8.htm*

Arnett, J. J. (2004). *Emerging adulthood: The winding road from the late teens through the twenties.* New York: Oxford University Press.

Barratt, W. (2005). *Selecting a student affairs graduate program.* Retrieved October 20, 2008, from www.myacpa.org/c12/selecting.htm

Benton, S. A., & Benton, S. L. (Eds.). (2006). *College student mental health: Effective services and strategies across campus.* Washington, DC: NASPA.

Benton, S., Robertson, J., Tseng, W., Newton, F., & Benton, S. (2003). Changes in counseling center client problems across 13 years. *Professional Psychology Research and Practice, 34,* 66–72.

Brougham, R. R., Zail, C. M., Mendoza, C. M., & Miller, J. R. (2009). Stress, sex differences, and coping strategies among college students. *Current Psychology, 28,* 85–97.

Cooper, S. E. (2006). Counseling and mental health services. In S. A. Benton & S. L. Benton (Eds.). *College student mental health: Effective services and strategies across campus* (pp. 151–167). Washington, DC: NASPA.

Council for the Accreditation of Counseling and Related Educational Programs (CACREP). (n.d.). *2009 standards.* Retrieved August 15, 2009, from www.cacrep.org/2009standards.pdf

Council for the Advancement of Standards in Higher Education. (n.d.). *General standards 08rev*. Retrieved August 15, 2009, from www.cas.edu/index.html

Dickerson, D. (2006). Legal issues for campus administrators, faculty, and staff. In Benton, S. A., & Benton, S. L. (Eds.), *College student mental health: Effective strategies and services across campus*. Washington, DC: NASPA.

Doss, J. A. (2006). *The financial knowledge of first year college students: Implications for curriculum development*. Unpublished master's thesis, South Dakota State University, Brookings.

Eells, G. (2008). *College mental health 2008: Key issues for counseling*. (Webinar). Retrieved April 28, 2008, from www.paper-clip.com

Evans, N. J., Forney, D. S, & Guido-DiBrito, F. (1998). *Student development in college: Theory, research, and practice*. San Francisco: Jossey-Bass.

Fram, A. (2008, March 18). *For many college students, stress hurts motivation, attention, AP-mtvu poll says*. Retrieved April 15, 2009, from www.signonsandiego. com/news/eduation/20080318-0808-collegepoll-stress.html

Gallagher, R. P. (2001). *National survey of college counseling center directors 2001*. Washington, DC: International Association of Counseling Services.

Gallagher, R. P., Zhang, B., & Taylor, R. (2003). *National survey of counseling directors*. Alexandria, VA: International Association of Counseling Centers. International Association of Counseling Services (IACS). (2000). *Accreditation standards for university and college counseling centers*. Retrieved December 1, 2008, from www.iacsinc.org/Accreditation%20 Standards.htm

International Association of Counseling Services. (2000). *IACS statement regarding staff to student ratios*. Retrieved July 20, 2009, from www.iacsinc.org/Statement Regarding Ratios.html

Kadison, R., & DiGeronimo, T. F. (2004). *College of the overwhelmed: The campus mental health crisis and what to do about it*. San Francisco: Jossey-Bass.

Keeling, R. (Ed.). (2004). *Learning reconsidered: A campus-wide focus on the student experience*. Washington, DC: NASPA/ACPA.

Kretovics, M. (2002). Entry-level competencies: What student affairs administrators consider when screening candidates. *Journal of College Student Development, 43*(6), 912–920.

Moore, A. S. (2006, November 5). A dream not denied: Students on the spectrum. *New York Times*. Retrieved November 3, 2008, from nytimes. com/2006/11/05/education/edlife/traits.html

Osfield, K. J., & Junco, R. (2006). Support services for students with mental health disabilities. In S. A. Benton & S. L. Benton (Eds.), *College student mental health: Effective services and strategies across campus* (pp. 169–188). Washington, DC: NASPA.

Reynolds, A. L. (2009). *Helping college students: Developing essential support skills for student affairs practice*. San Francisco: Jossey-Bass.

Schevitz, T. (2008, October 15). Economic crisis upsets students' college plans. *San Francisco Chronicle*. Retrieved October 15, 2008, from www.sfgate. com/cgi-bin/article.cgi?f=/c/a/2008/10/15/MNSG13DJRB.DTL

Simmons, R., & Enista, M. (2009). *The most powerful generation in America*. Retrieved July 20, 2009, from huffingtonpost.com/russell-simmons/the-most-powerful-generat_b_230311.html

Twenge, J. M. (2006). *Generation me: Why today's young Americans are more confident, assertive, entitled—and more miserable than ever before*. New York: Free Press.

CHAPTER 1

Theories of College Student Development
An Overview

Ruth Harper

There are no homogeneous groups that speak in one voice with only one perspective, and our theories and practice must honor this reality (Pope, Reynolds, & Mueller, 2004, p. 40).

The case studies in this book will introduce you to Ellie, a student with autism who is learning about life in a residence hall; Hodekki, a traditional American Indian student who is far from home and extremely lonely; Justyna, an immigrant student who is questioning her sexual orientation and jeopardizing her scholarship by not attending classes; Victoria, who wants to be her whole self—Mexican, White, Jewish, bisexual; and many others.

Today's students are not the students Chickering (1969) studied as he developed his well-known vectors of college student development. Nor are they the population that informed Kohlberg (1976) as he searched for the ways young adults develop into moral beings. While contemporary college students still develop competence, relationships, and purpose, and determine the values and principles that will guide their lives, they do so in ways uniquely their own. Almost all have instant access not only to their friends and families but also to worldwide events in real time.

Those who study college students today draw on the work of scholars such as Chickering and Kohlberg, but they also look to the work of Reynolds (2009) and Abes, Jones, & McEwen (2007), among others, to help reconceptualize and reconsider the developmental issues of far more diverse students and the layered aspects of their individual identities. Most, if not all, readers of this book are likely to be at least somewhat familiar with these important sources and with some excellent overviews of foundational theories of college student development and their various applications (e.g., Evans, Forney, & Guido-DiBrito, 1998; Komives, Woodard, et al., 1996; Moore, 1992; Pascarella & Terenzini, 2005).

This chapter offers a brief synopsis of major theories to those who may not have studied student development. (In fact, readers with significant background in student development theory may wish to skip this chapter.) Bachelor's-level residence hall directors and admissions recruiters, as well as those who enter the student affairs profession through less traditional means (e.g., master's degrees in disciplines such as English or sociology), may find this material new and enlightening.

This broad overview is intended to reflect the fact that college students today are diverse in all ways imaginable and develop in complex, messy, multilayered ways, rather than in discrete, time-ordered sequences that can be "managed" by college professionals. As Pascarella and Terenzini emphasize in their enormously useful compendium of related research, "Student growth along any one dimension is often highly related to, and perhaps even dependent on, growth along other dimensions" (2005, p. 7). And, as Blackhurst (2008) notes:

> While it is possible to identify common themes in the backgrounds and characteristics of student populations, each student is a unique variation on those themes. We're quick to acknowledge that the labels don't apply to everyone, but we often miss the much more important point that they don't really describe anyone. If the labels have value at all, it is in their ability to focus our attention on the particular cultural

and societal forces that shape the students who come to our campuses—and on how we might need to alter our educational . . . practices as a result. (p. 6)

The case studies in this book clearly illustrate the complicated, fascinating nature of the lives of contemporary college students, particularly those who experience crisis or live with mental health concerns. Not all theories raised in the case studies are presented in this chapter; resources listed after each scenario direct the reader to more information. Likewise, not all theories described here will appear in the case studies. However, these theories can serve as frameworks for considering and conceptualizing the student situations in this book. As you read about the theories, keep in mind the students you work with today—students like Ellie, Hodekki, Justyna, and Victoria. And remember that "our theories and practice must honor this (rich, diverse, and individually unique) reality" (Pope et al., 2004, p. 40).

Foundational Theories

Any attempt to offer a condensed introduction to student development theory must begin with several caveats. First, we do not cover many important, even essential, theories because of time and space constraints. Second, our descriptions of the theories that *are* included will, of necessity, be far less nuanced and well developed than is optimal. Despite these built-in limitations, we present the basic theories of college student development that we think are most relevant to the reader and to the case studies that follow. In some cases, our work with current college students will suggest new ways in which the theories can be applied, stretched, or even questioned. It is not within the purview of this chapter or book to critically evaluate any theory; rather, we want to link widely used theories to today's practice of student affairs administration.

Names immediately associated with the psychosocial and identity development of college students include Chickering and Reisser (1993), Marcia (1966), and Josselson (1987). Within the realm of cognitive-structural theories, Perry (1981), Kohlberg (1976), and Gilligan (1982) are widely acknowledged, as are

Baxter Magolda (1999, 2001), Belenky, Clinchy, Goldberger, and Tarule (1986), and King and Kitchener (1994). Perhaps sparked by Sanford's early (1967) ideas regarding the key roles of challenge and support in student development, the importance of how students interact with their college environments has been established in decades of research by Alexander Astin (1984) and others.

In this chapter, we will explicate only one or two theories in each area. And we will present new ways to consider and apply these theories in light of the emerging needs and issues of today's students. As Coomes & DeBard (2004) noted, "This generation of students and their attitudes, beliefs, and behaviors will require student affairs practitioners to adopt new learning and service strategies, rethink student development theories, and modify educational environments" (p. 1).

Chickering and Reisser, Marcia, and Josselson

Arthur Chickering remains one of the most widely cited theorists in the field. His original seven-vector model of student development (1969) is a cornerstone of professional thinking in student affairs. Based on work with mostly male students at Goddard College in the 1960s, Chickering's conceptualization also drew on assessments, student journals, and studies at a few other colleges. The vectors (so named to convey the dynamic notions of both direction and magnitude) offer a fluid and comprehensive way of looking at how students grow in college (Chickering, 1969, p. 8). This model includes "emotional, interpersonal, ethical, and intellectual aspects of development" (Evans et al., 1998, p. 38).

Chickering and Reisser revised and reordered the elements of this model in 1993 to reflect the increasing diversity of the American college student body. While still not fully inclusive, the updated version incorporates the perspectives of nontraditional students, women, and students of color to a greater extent than did the original work. The seven vectors are:

1. Developing competence

2. Managing emotions

3. Moving through autonomy toward interdependence

4. Developing mature interpersonal relationships

5. Establishing identity

6. Developing purpose

7. Developing integrity

Developing Competence

Within this domain lie the diverse areas of intellectual, interpersonal, and physical competencies. Intellectual competence relates directly to being able to succeed academically by "mastering content, gaining intellectual and aesthetic sophistication, and, most important, building a repertoire of skills to comprehend, analyze, and synthesize" ideas encountered both within and beyond the college classroom (Chickering & Reisser, 1993, p. 45).

Intellectual competence, reflected most often in subject matter knowledge, is what most faculty members value in students. Student affairs professionals also address this central aspect of student development in their innumerable methods of engaging students in learning activities, both formal and informal. Working with living-learning communities, advising undeclared or undecided students, and creating supplemental instruction and tutoring services are only a few examples of how student affairs professionals enhance student learning and intellectual development.

Students today arrive at college with a broad range of academic preparation, from severely inadequate to superb; in addition, many have learning disabilities and mental health concerns such as clinical depression or an anxiety disorder that can interfere with learning. As a result of early diagnosis and better interventions in K–12 settings, as well as the push toward inclusion from the Americans with Disabilities Act (ADA), students who in the past might never have considered college are now attending in ever-increasing numbers (National Alliance on Mental Illness, 2009).

Other educational venues, particularly distance education and online courses, affect student learning and require new and different kinds of support. Institutions such as the University of Phoenix, which enrolls more than 400,000 students internationally (Just the Facts, 2009), serve nontraditional adult learners, some of whom are place-bound and most of whom have other major life roles (e.g., employee, parent, community leader) that compete with their identity as a student. Student affairs professionals in such programs work with many students they may never meet face-to-face.

Interpersonal competence, in this model, addresses far more than simple social skills. It includes active listening, appropriate self-disclosure, respectful discussion, productive group membership, and confidence among and empathy toward peers (Chickering & Reisser, 1993).

Helping students build relationships and community is a traditionally important and central role for student affairs practitioners; however, in the past, most postsecondary settings were fairly homogeneous compared with today's campuses. Much of students' social lives now exist online, where, until recently, student affairs professionals did not go (Junco & Timm, 2008). Contexts and social rules for engagement have shifted significantly.

Physical competencies refer to wellness activities, broadly defined. These include highly visible intercollegiate and intramural athletic efforts as well as creative endeavors that engage the student through activities such as dance, pottery making, or even installing insulation in a Habitat for Humanity house (Chickering & Reisser, 1993, p. 72). Strange (2004) notes that Millennial students, although healthy in many ways, "bring with them higher incidences of asthma, obesity, and attention deficit hyperactivity disorder" (p. 53). Clearly, there is important work for student affairs professionals to do in this area.

Managing Emotions

All human beings experience emotions, both positive and negative. At times, the same emotion (say, anxiety) can be positive (motivating a student to prepare well for an exam) or negative (triggering a panic attack), depending on the extent to which the emotion is experienced and the student's ability to process and manage it. Anxiety disorders are a part of life for 13.2% of college students, according to a recent American

College Health Association/National College Health Association (ACHA/NCHA) survey (ACHA/NCHA, 2009, p. 4). Development in the affective area is vital, as students often live in close quarters in residence halls or apartments; they also interact regularly with peers and others in the college and community (physical and virtual).

As we shall see throughout the case studies in this book, many of today's college students experience debilitating levels of anxiety and depression (Kadison & DiGeronimo, 2004). The issues addressed in this vector of managing emotions, in contrast to those involved in achieving competence, can be intensely personal. Rarely are they the focus of curricular or co-curricular programs, yet the skills involved are crucial to personal and college success. Chickering and Reisser refer to the "toxic" emotions of "fear and anxiety, anger leading to aggression, depression, guilt, and shame, and dysfunctional sexual or romantic attraction" (1993, pp. 90–91). Writing 16 years ago, these authors did not foresee the issues of cyberstalking, self-harming (e.g., cutting, burning), or epidemic levels of clinical depression among students today.

Moving Through Autonomy Toward Interdependence

In their 1993 revision, Chickering and Reisser took a new approach to the vector previously termed "autonomy." While they continued to emphasize the need for college students to achieve a certain independence of thought and self-reliance in terms of approval and goal setting, the vector now recognizes that not all cultures value a Western, largely male manner of achieving independence. The use of the word *interdependence* acknowledges that people must, to some extent, rely on others and, in turn, be reliable.

The revised concept enables more understanding and respect for gender and cultural differences. A new wrinkle in the fabric of interdependence is the phenomenon of overinvolved parents (Wilson, 2004, p. 66). NASPA's recently launched Knowledge Community on Parent and Family Relations is a useful resource for student affairs professionals who seek to take advantage of parental interest in their students while also helping students and families find healthy ways to allow their relationships to evolve (www.naspa.org/kc/pfr/default.cfm).

Progress in this vector can be difficult to define, let alone measure. Today's students are more difficult to "type," as their families of origin embrace myriad ways of "being normal." Given ready means for frequent communication and many patterns of family interaction, students should be encouraged to define for themselves the frequency and type of contact with home that is necessary and desirable. Many students call every day just to check in; others may do so out of urgent emotional need. The concept of what constitutes healthy individuation has been affected by technology, changing family norms, and growing recognition of diversity.

Developing Mature Interpersonal Relationships

This vector focuses on the need to affirm differences among people and nurture intimacy. The high school student who has "300 good friends" becomes the college student who (although he or she might still have hundreds of friends on Facebook) interacts meaningfully with a much smaller number of close companions on an everyday basis (Heiberger & Harper, 2008). Chickering and Reisser state, "Students develop mature intimacy when the relationship is valued for itself, when both persons can be whole and authentic, when love and loyalty allow for growth and experimentation" (1993, p. 161). So while peers at large and parents in particular still exert influence, students who can create and sustain mature interpersonal relationships enjoy time alone as well as in trusting, stable, supportive friendships and partnerships.

As students text and Tweet uncounted times each day, the natures of communication and relationship are changing. "Community" can be an active Facebook group as readily as a traditional student organization or hall council—and the two are not mutually exclusive. Student affairs professionals must recognize that students "network with each other using technology as much as, if not more than, face-to-face communication" (Heiberger & Harper, 2008, p. 19) and must intentionally use technology to increase student involvement and build relationships. For example, "Facebook gives [students] opportunities to learn about and self-select into programs and services beneficial to them"—but only if the programs and services are on Facebook (Heiberger & Harper, 2008, p. 32). Whether Facebook remains the dominant social network does not matter; what matters is that student affairs professionals seek to appropriately connect with students in the ways students connect with each other.

Students with certain disabilities may be especially prone to delays in the development of social and emotional maturity. Without being condescending or judgmental, student affairs professionals will understand that they have a supportive, even instructional role to play with some students in the area of social development. This issue is addressed in depth in the case study of Ellie, a student with an autism spectrum disorder.

Establishing Identity

Chickering and Reisser (1993, p. 173) acknowledge that this vector could be the developmental umbrella under which the other vectors fall. It involves competencies, relationships, and acceptance of self and others. Identity, in the long run, also includes purpose (career) and integrity (life values).

In the second edition of *Education and Identity* (1993), the authors incorporate the ideas of James Marcia (1966). Building on the work of Erik Erikson, Marcia identified four possible states of identity development. We will use the example of a traditional first-year student dealing with the death of a close friend to illustrate these states.

The first state is ***identity diffusion***, in which no crisis has been experienced and no commitment has been made. At this stage, the student in our example will not have experienced the death of a friend and may not have been required to cope with or contemplate the impact of such an event. Death may be of no immediate concern to this student.

The second state, according to Marcia, is ***foreclosure***, a time when no crisis is experienced, but commitments to certain ideas are made. Relating this to the illustration, the student will not have dealt with a death but may have strong beliefs or opinions, often based on the teaching of parents or a particular church, regarding what happens when a person dies. These beliefs, at this stage, are untested.

The third state is ***moratorium***, a challenging time when the student is experiencing a crisis and is flailing about, attempting to come to terms with something overwhelming. When the student is confronted with a tragic reality—a friend who dies through suicide, a car accident, or from an illness—he or she can be hard-pressed to make sense or meaning of the event, even with strongly held beliefs. The student, overwhelmed by grief, may try to cope via healthy (e.g., counseling, reading, talking with others) or unhealthy (e.g., substance abuse, social isolation) means. This process may become a search for an effective way of managing emotions and perhaps exploring new ways of trying to understand the ultimate realities of life and death.

The fourth state is ***identity achievement***, when the crisis has been experienced and survived, and commitments to meaningful ways of coping or understanding have been made. The student in the example will have endured the death of a close friend and found solace in fulfilling activities, such as prayer, meditation, journaling, or working on a memorial service or tribute. Some students leave long messages on the Facebook page of a deceased friend. Others comfort each other in small groups, telling stories and sharing anecdotes about the person who died.

Ruthellen Josselson (1987) based her work with undergraduate women on Marcia's work, incorporating the concepts of crisis and commitment to career choice as well as religious/political philosophy. Josselson's pathways to identity for women include: Foreclosures (Purveyors of the Heritage), Identity Achievements (Pavers of the Way), Moratoriums (Daughters of the Crisis), and Identity Diffusions (Lost and Sometimes Found). Josselson concluded that these pathways are greatly influenced by the nature of the relationships in their lives.

Chickering and Reisser (1993) further expanded the notion of identity to include "comfort" in the areas of physical appearance, gender and sexual orientation, sense of self in social/cultural/historical context, personal roles and lifestyle—in other words, a clarified sense of self obtained through feedback from trusted others, self-acceptance and self-esteem, and personal integration. As Evans and colleagues note, "This vector now acknowledges differences in identity development based on gender, ethnicity, and sexual orientation" (1998, p. 169)—a very important addition to the concept of identity development that has led to emerging models (introduced later in this chapter) that focus on these factors.

Technology can affect identity development, too. Through the ability to create an online alter ego, for example, students can put forward misleading or distorted self-images. Reality does not necessarily have to match what is on Face-book or other social networking sites. Blogs, anonymous and otherwise, allow students to express points of view without "owning" them. Virtual worlds that allow users to interact within a three-dimensional environment can be used to enhance student development by supporting learning—or they can interfere with such development by encouraging a rich fantasy life (Junco & Timm, 2008, p. 11). Many colleges use a platform called Second Life to let students "explore identity, including body image, gender, and ethnicity through development of their virtual self (called an avatar)" (p. 11).

Developing Purpose

Career goals fall into this vector, as do commitments to avocational interests and key social relationships. Political party affiliation, membership in student or-ganizations related to an academic major or hobby—these represent intentional choices based on a student's interests and strengths. Investment of personal time and energy can result in clarified goals and values (Chickering & Reisser, 1993).

Students today develop purpose through, for example, courses, mentor-ing relationships with both faculty and staff members, service learning, in-ternships, study abroad, volunteer work, and part-time jobs, much as they did in the past. However, career development specialists and advisors have a tougher task in a world with a rapidly changing workplace, a somewhat un-stable economy, the ever-increasing number of career changes during an adult lifetime, and a global market. Rather than focusing only on the traditional model of interests, aptitudes, and values, students will need to cultivate adapt-ability for future success. It will be important to help students discern their purpose, career and otherwise, from nonlinear, multidirectional perspectives that include their values and their decision-making styles (Duys, Ward, Max-well, & Eaton-Comerford, 2008). The recent phenomenon of parallel streams of development reflects the evolving priorities of a college junior who may be simultaneously contemplating graduate school, Teach for America, and learn-ing a specific skill, such as phlebotomy, at a technical institute.

Developing Integrity

The final vector, integrity, is closely related to the previous two, developing identity and purpose. Students' values are challenged during college, typically becoming more liberal, altruistic, and humanitarian (Pascarella & Terenzini, 2005). Students often identify "turning points" or "aha moments," when new values and beliefs suddenly click and feel right in the context of major life decisions (Chickering & Reisser, 1993, p. 240). These moments can be related to Carl Rogers's notion of congruence (explained further in chapter 2), which has to do with the integration or fit of important ideas with the self, both alone and in the world (Chickering & Reisser, 1993, p. 253). A student may say, "I was one of those people who used to say 'just get a job' when I thought about the unemployed. Then I interned with CityServe and learned what poverty is really about." According to Parker Palmer (2004), congruence or integrity has many names:

> Thomas Merton called it true self. Buddhists call it original nature or big self. Quakers call it the inner teacher or the inner light. Hasidic Jews call it a spark of the divine. Humanists call it identity and integrity. In popular parlance, people often call it soul. (p. 33)

Chickering and Reisser's psychosocial model tracks students' development from figuring out basic information (like where their classes meet) to, for example, the regular practice of meditation. As a guide to program development in student affairs, the vectors provide a useful and comprehensive framework for intentional interventions. While this model's impact on research and practice in student personnel work is enormous, using it with today's students will require thoughtful adaptation of many of its core concepts.

Schlossberg's Transition Theory

Another very useful way to conceptualize work with college students was created by Nancy Schlossberg (1981, 1984; Schlossberg, Waters, & Goodman, 1995). Although originally conceived as a method for counseling older adults or nontraditional-aged students, her ideas have been successfully applied to college students of all description in a variety of higher education settings (Evans et al., 1998, p. 108). Schlossberg's transition theory, with its examination of the "timing, duration, spacing, and ordering of life events," draws directly on the role of environment in overall student development (Komives et al., 1996, p. 171).

Just knowing that a person is experiencing a particular transition (for example, a student entering college) provides little information of value, Schlossberg would argue. Yet almost all colleges plan extensive orientation programs designed to meet the needs of new students. Consider who that entering student might be: an 18-year-old American Indian female moving from a South Dakota reservation to an urban private liberal arts college; a 20-year-old White male who has worked for two years in the Detroit auto industry before being laid off and enrolling at the local community college to pursue a new career direction; a 44-year-old White woman who has left an abusive relationship in an isolated rural setting, moving with three young children to a nearby city and taking classes at the state's land grant university; a gay African-American male honors graduate of a private preparatory school who studied for a year in India between finishing high school and entering an Ivy League college. Starting college will be a quite different experience for each of these four students.

Transition theory asks student affairs professionals to look deeply into what type of transition college is for the individual. A transition, as defined by Schlossberg and colleagues, is "any event, or non-event, that results in changed relationships, routines, assumptions, and roles" (1995, p. 27). With regard to the four students described above, the transition to college life will affect their relationships, routines, assumptions, and roles in powerful and sharply contrasting ways. The type, context, and impact of the transition have an effect on how the individual experiences that transition. In most cases, an honors student who has lived abroad is well prepared, both academically and socially, to move into residence hall life, select appropriate courses, become involved in student activities, and thrive in a competitive college setting. Certainly, there will be new routines and relationships, but they will probably be similar to those the student has already experienced and mastered. Compare this to the impact of entering college as a survivor of physical and emotional abuse, a woman who has recently moved away from danger but also is now separated from most sources of support.

Schlossberg and colleagues (1995) described "the four S's": situation, self, support, and strategies (Evans et al., 1998, p. 113) to help understand the scope and impact of a particular transition. The example of the American Indian student—we'll call her Laurel—can be used to explore these aspects of coping with transition.

Situation

In terms of situation, Laurel is **on time** with her transition; that is, she is entering college as an 18-year-old who has just graduated from high school. In that sense, it is a "normal" transition. She feels pretty much in control of her decision, although there was moderate pressure from family and friends to follow an older cousin to this college. There will definitely be many role changes for Laurel in the days ahead. From being a school and community leader at home, a known high school athlete and scholar in a uniquely supportive extended family environment, Laurel will become one of relatively few Native people on her private college campus. She knows she's capable, but will people at college look at her and automatically assume that she is in need of academic support services? And what if Laurel does need help with academics for the first time in her life?

The **duration** of the transition is hard for Laurel to fully grasp. On one hand, she knows she can always go home. On the other, she has seen that some people she knows who have gone away to college are different when they return to the reservation. They are treated differently, too, sometimes even within the family, as if others now think that education makes them better or even "too good" to hang out with or trust. This possibility worries Laurel more than she cares to admit.

Does she have **previous experience with a similar transition**? No, and in Laurel's case, there is the historical overlay of tragedy and oppression associated with "going away to school." The boarding school experience is not a footnote in an American history book to her; it is her aunt's actual life. There are still active Indian boarding schools in her home state. When the admissions recruiter from the private college tells Laurel's family that Laurel should move far from family and culture to study, there is a collective shudder of apprehension as well as genuine excitement about the educational opportunities available.

What **concurrent stresses** might Laurel experience? She has a dear great-grandmother who has always been the most special person in her life. Grandmother's health is generally fine, but she is at an age where ongoing good health cannot be taken for granted. In terms of overall assessment, Laurel is making an informed decision. She could have attended the local tribal college where her mother teaches, but Laurel feels ready for the challenge of the more distant campus.

Self

This category includes personal and demographic characteristics as well as psychological resources (Evans et al., 1998, p. 113). Laurel is from a somewhat economically challenged family, yet she and several members of her extended family (extended family *is* family to her) are readily identified as tribal and community leaders. All who know her describe Laurel as a high-functioning individual. Her personal psychological resources include intelligence, resourcefulness, a healthy and creative sense of humor, and a very positive outlook on the world and her own abilities. Laurel also has excellent physical health, wide interests, and strong ties to the traditions of her culture. She has a clear "sense of self," as Chickering would put it, and approaches her transition to college with a manageable degree of trepidation as well as a high level of self-confidence.

Support

Laurel has many sources of support. Her family, friends, school, and community are proud of her. While she fears being geographically distant from these treasured relationships, she is already constantly calling, texting, Facebooking, and Tweeting her friends; she suspects she would not be looking at moving so far away without these means of instant communication with those she loves. Another source of support is Laurel's strong belief in the traditional Lakota values of generosity, kinship, fortitude, and wisdom (kalloch.org/Lakota_four_values. htm). She is an enrolled member of a Lakota tribe. Perhaps this should be considered a psychological resource (as briefly mentioned earlier), but for Laurel it is a cultural and spiritual framework that shapes all aspects of her life. She is already thinking about how to keep these values central to her new existence away from home, as she believes with all her heart that they will sustain her. Laurel has a cousin who will be a senior at the college she is entering. When she visited the campus last year, her cousin introduced her to several Native students from many tribal communities across the nation. She also met the Native student organization advisor, who is originally from Laurel's home state and seemed to understand the challenges she is facing.

Strategies

Laurel is prepared with strategies that will help her cope with moving to a distant city and going into an academically demanding program of study. She intends to stay physically active by working out at the college wellness center and maybe even trying out for the women's basketball team. Collegiate athletics offer far more than regular physical activity to students; they offer a strong sense of belonging and transition support services from day one, in most cases. The Native student group is a must for Laurel to join. She knows her cousin will drag her there even if she feels shy, which she admits is unlikely. Laurel is social and looks forward to meeting other new students and making friends in the residence hall. One of her many strengths is her sheer determination. Also, she is not afraid to ask questions. She has already scoped out many interesting classes, activities, and events on the college website. She dreads saying goodbye to her family but is ready for the adventure of college.

Schlossberg and colleagues (1995) viewed transitions in terms of "moving in, moving through, and moving out" (Evans et al., 1998, p. 112). Laurel is clearly in the "moving in" phase of her transition. As she proceeds with her education, selects a major, finds friends, and comes into her own identity on campus, new challenges and strengths will emerge. Supportive, intentional student affairs responses and interventions will evolve as well, depending on where she is in this process.

Schlossberg (1989) also introduced the concepts of *marginality* and *mattering* on campus—the importance of looking for and creating ways for all students to fit in and feel a sense of being appreciated rather than experiencing alienation. It will be important to Laurel's success that her resident advisor, academic advisor, organization advisor, and other key personnel welcome her to campus and offer strategic support and acknowledgement. In other words, Laurel's successful transition is not entirely up to her; many people on campus will need to reach out and offer a variety of affirmation and reinforcement.

Multicultural/LGBT Theoretical Perspectives

"Cultural issues are central to most of the important conversations on our campuses, such as admissions policies, core curricula, campus violence, and how diverse student groups relate to one another" (Reynolds, 2009, p. 111). These issues are central not only in administrative and programmatic ways; understanding of student diversity, in its multiplicity of manifestations, has become a core competency for student affairs administrators across the board (e.g., Blimling, 2001; Pope, Reynolds, & Cheatham, 1997; Pope et al., 2004; Talbot, 2003).

As Amy Reynolds (2009, p. 113) points out, multicultural understanding and competence is a shared area of emphasis among student affairs and counseling professionals. Traditional theories of racial and ethnic identity development often studied in student affairs professional preparation programs (e.g., William Cross, 1995; Janet Helms, 1995) have direct parallels in the counseling-related work of Sue & Sue (2007) and Ivey, D'Andrea, Bradford Ivey, and Simek-Morgan (2007), to name just two. All these models follow a general pattern that can be loosely described as moving from a pre-encounter status, in which the impact of racism and racial identity is unknown or unexplored, through stages of encounter and realization that alter one's way of seeing the world (Cross, 1995). This movement can lead to psychological disintegration (Helms, 1995), followed by a reintegration period of forming new understandings of self and the world. The final stage (usually an ongoing effort) is one of autonomy or identity achievement, in which the person actively combats injustice and seeks positive connections with diverse communities.

Gay, lesbian, bisexual, transgender, questioning or queer/questioning (GLBTQ) studies have attained considerable breadth and received deserved attention in recent years. Many student affairs professionals consider Vivienne Cass (1979) and her work in Australia to be the foundational piece in this area. In creating a new developmental model, Cass saw the roles of intra- and interpersonal dissonance as catalysts for growth as a same-sex-attracted person. Her model describes the stages of identity confusion ("What's wrong with me? I have feelings and attractions I don't understand"); identity comparison ("I think I might be gay, but I have no idea what that really means in my life"); identity tolerance ("I'm figuring out that it's fine to be gay"); identity acceptance ("Look at me with all my gay friends!"); identity pride ("Gosh, how did you ever tell your parents that you're straight?"); and identity synthesis ("Being gay is just a part—an important part, but just a part—of who I am, at home, at work, and at school.")

Nancy Evans and Vernon Wall (1991) have written and edited work about GLBTQ identity development that contributed greatly to inclusive new ways of looking at student development. The many stages of the coming-out process can be seen as intensely personal yet also political and ideological at times (Pascarella & Terenzini, 2005, p. 30). The existence and role of the gay community, both on and off campus, can be an important asset. Its absence can be a painful void.

Raechele Pope, Amy Reynolds, and John Mueller (2004) make an extremely compelling case for multicultural competence in student affairs. In their critical look at student development theories, they state, "We believe it is important to acknowledge that all of our social identities (race, class, religion, gender, sexual orientation, age, and abilities) influence who we are and how we view the world" (p. xiv). They remind student affairs practitioners that theories describe rather than prescribe and are best used with an unwavering focus on the individual student (p. 34).

Cognitive Development Theories

In 1999, Patrick Love and Victoria Guthrie produced an exceptionally useful monograph that describes and synthesizes the major theories of college student intellectual development (Baxter Magolda, 1995; Belenky, Clinchy, Goldberger, & Tarule, 1986; Kegan, 1982; King & Kitchener, 1994; Perry, 1981). Most of these theories are at least somewhat familiar to student affairs professionals, particularly since the advent well over a decade ago of *The Student Learning Imperative* (ACPA,1996) and the *Principles of Good Practice for Student Affairs* (ACPA & NASPA, 1997). These works underscore the "educator" roles that nonfaculty college personnel play in supporting and enhancing student learning in a variety of venues, both within and beyond the classroom. In working with students, sometimes the most exciting developmental changes occur in the broad area of intellectual growth, and it is often student affairs professionals who provide key support and who co-create conditions that facilitate this growth.

William Perry (1981) interviewed students at Harvard and Radcliffe (almost all traditional-aged males) in the 1950s and 1960s to try to identify themes in how these students made personal sense of their experiences in college. Extending earlier research by Piaget, Perry found that a cognitive developmental process was at work among these students. Perry sought to document this process by identifying nine positions of cognitive growth, from basic dualism (black/white thinking in which authorities are the source of defined truths) to commitments in relativism (in which students accept the complexity of reality and take responsibility for making decisions based on their own thoughts, values, and critical judgments).

Perry's ideas were largely based on work with males. Mary Belenky, Blythe Clinchy, Nancy Goldberger, and Jill Tarule turned their attention to how women's cognitive development might be affected by powerful aspects of contemporary culture. Their book *Women's Ways of Knowing* (1986) called attention to the crucial concept of voice, that is, the idea that many people (primarily women) are ignored or even silenced by the world in which they live. The self-concepts of such people are, almost by definition, fragile and self-doubting.

It is always worth considering which students are without voice on a particular campus—and then addressing the reasons for that silence. At some colleges, gay and lesbian students are virtually invisible; on others, non-Christians are mute, their comments unwelcome. In other words, the concept can be extended to students who are not women or are not only women. Education, according to Belenky and colleagues, can be a means of moving beyond a position of silence to that of informed, confident voice.

Belenky and colleagues also made the distinction between connected and separate knowing. In connected knowing, the student relates personally in some way to what is being studied; in separate knowing, the student maintains a certain level of remove from the object of study. For instance, poverty and homelessness can be studied through off-campus service learning (connected knowing) or by reading and viewing films (separate knowing).

Love and Guthrie (1999, p. 27) provide rich, highly relevant implications for student affairs professionals. From informal individual conversations to student organization advising to formal teaching situations, student affairs staff members are in key positions to enhance student learning and provide valuable means of connected knowing. For instance, the *Seven Principles for Good Practice in Undergraduate Education* (Chickering & Gamson, 1987), adapted for work with a Millennial generation of students, can guide student affairs professionals to many creative efforts that support intellectual development (Wilson, 2004).

Building on the work of Perry—as well as that of Marcia and of Belenky and colleagues—Baxter Magolda (1995) conducted a longitudinal study that involved both male and female college students. Baxter Magolda focused on the ways in which individual students make meaning. To examine, for example, the worldview, individual experiences, reasoning patterns, and, to some extent, gender of a student is to begin to understand his or her model of epistemological reflection (Baxter Magolda, 1995). She identified four stages of cognitive development: (1) absolute knowing (passive learning of certain truths); (2) transitional knowing (truth is not always clear and peers can help discern what to value); (3) independent knowing (much is uncertain, all are entitled to opinions); and (4) contextual knowing (complex, critical analysis is needed to know).

Self-authorship involves the ability to think critically and to make and own considered, reflective judgments. A student who is at first terrified when a professor cannot supply the right answer to a complex question about, say, universal health care might eventually welcome the confidence that the professor places in her to read, think, talk with others (ideally, diverse-thinking others), and determine for herself what to believe. Rather than needing to "know," the student will seek to understand and will be able to compare her understanding with that of her peers as well as with what she is reading on the subject. And she may have learned quite a bit about how to do this by participating in Model United Nations or the residence hall council.

Patricia King and Karen Kitchener (1994) conducted hundreds of interviews with people to examine how they respond to "ill-structured" problems, that is, challenges with no obvious right or wrong answers. These interviews yielded evidence of a linear sequence of seven stages of cognitive development. The stages range from belief only in what one has actually witnessed and about which one is certain to a state of ongoing open inquiry in which "knowing" is a temporary status that will continue to be affected by new facts as evidence changes (Love & Guthrie, 1999, pp. 44–50).

This model of reflective judgment (not fully spelled out here) is highly useful to student affairs administrators, in that much of student affairs work can intentionally involve students in situations that facilitate cognitive development. Many college students begin their postsecondary education at the most basic level of thinking, that is, centered on personal experience and opinion. While this intellectual modus operandi will certainly be confronted in the classroom, it can also be challenged in student organization meetings, in residence hall conversations, in the student union, and on intramural playing fields.

For example, a student at King and Kitchener's (1994) level 1 or 2 might say, "I'm really uncomfortable with that gay guy on my soccer team. I mean, what's up with that? Why do I even have to know? But he's, like, all about 'I'm queer, I'm here' and stuff. My dad would freak out if he even knew there was a gay guy in my locker room, and it kind of freaks me out, too. I'll tell you, nobody was gay at my high school." At levels 4 and 5, in the same situation, a student might think, "Ray is kind of cool, and he makes it obvious that he's gay. I'm not into that gay thing, but man, the guy is an awesome soccer player. The coach seems to like him and the seniors actually hug the guy when he makes a goal. They slap him on the butt and everything. I guess it must be okay. And there was a program last night in my residence hall where the speaker said that being gay is biological, not some kind of choice. I actually read the article the hall director posted on our dorm's Facebook page and now I think I may have been told a lot of lies back home about gay people."

Parallel but not identical to research in cognitive development is the work of Lawrence Kohlberg (1969), and later, Carol Gilligan (1982) on moral development. Focused more narrowly in the area of how people (mostly young males) make principled judgments, Kohlberg found that the notion of justice is central to these decisions. In a three-level model, with two stages at each level, Kohlberg mapped a pattern of thinking that ranges from most naïve (merely staying out of trouble, meeting one's personal needs) to most sophisticated (behavior based on logical, even universal, rules and consciously chosen principles).

Gilligan (1982) studied the moral development of both women and men and discovered that women make moral judgments based more on relationship and care for others than on externally derived principles of ethics. Women, Gilligan found, are very contextual in their thinking, giving great importance to the welfare of others. In Gilligan's conceptualization of moral development, the three levels are (1) orientation to individual survival; (2) goodness as self-sacrifice; and (3) the morality of nonviolence (Gilligan, 1977, in Pascarella & Terenzini, 2005, p. 44). What Gilligan calls *the feminine voice* is grounded in being connected to and attending to the well-being of others.

Although these theories are tremendously condensed here, an example may help to illustrate contrasts among them. In 2007, President Ahmadinejad of Iran was invited to speak at Columbia University. Informed, thoughtful men and women on that campus might either support or disparage this controversial speaker's presence. Kohlberg's work says that a male is likely to determine his stance on this issue on the basis of, say, the rules that govern requests to all campus speakers or on principled consideration of Ahmadinejad's positions on the Holocaust, nuclear weapons in Iran, the provision of weapons to insurgents in Iraq—any number of issues. Gilligan's research, on the other hand, posits that a female would probably favor other factors in framing her reaction. A woman might support the United States building a civil relationship with the leader of Iran in the interests of better mutual understanding that could help avoid war. Alternatively, she might reason, "I have a cousin in the U.S. military in Iraq, and this man is arming people who might hurt him. I cannot tolerate Ahmadinejad on my campus and the implied approval this offers him." These theories, then, look at how men and women make moral decisions, not necessarily at *what* those decisions are.

With regard to moral development, students with certain disabilities, such as autism spectrum disorders, may undeservedly be considered "less than" other students because of the unique ways they think and interact with the world. Even the concept of *moral development* could be considered loaded and potentially unfair. If a student doesn't know or understand the rules, for example, how can he or she be held accountable? Very clear communication and the student's ability to understand and make choices are imperative. Some of these issues are explored in the case study about Ellie.

Student Involvement

In considering how most students learn, make critical judgments, and connect with the world, student involvement is an important factor. Alexander Astin has worked for many years to develop a theory that can be boiled down to this simple assertion: "Students learn by becoming involved" (1985, p. 133, in Pascarella & Terenzini, 2005, p. 53). This statement is considered by some to be the *raison d'etre* of student affairs work. It is focused on learning and claims (with much to back it up) that learning is enhanced by engaging students—with each other, with faculty and staff, with ideas, with service, with the greater (even global) community. These are the kinds of opportunities and activities student affairs professionals intentionally provide.

Astin's first three postulates say that involvement: (1) is the investment of physical or psychological energy; (2) exists on a continuum; and (3) has both quantitative and qualitative aspects. The other two postulates say that (4) the quantity and quality of learning relate directly to the quantity and quality of involvement; and (5) the value of any educational program or event can be gauged by the extent to which it involves students (Astin, 1984). In this conceptualization, both students and college professionals have crucial roles. According to Astin, an active student who seeks out every opportunity to learn, discuss, serve, evaluate, reflect, and travel in an environment that regularly generates and promotes such "occasions" is the ideal student in the ideal postsecondary setting.

Student affairs professionals encourage student involvement, particularly among less active students. From intramural sports to student organizations, residence hall programs, and community/campus events—lectures, dances, poetry slams, hypnotists, fundraisers—students can be invited, accompanied, or sometimes cajoled into participating, even into assuming leadership roles. This is more challenging in scenarios in which the majority of students are commuters, or where, say, students of color do not see themselves when they look at those in leadership roles.

Emerging Theories of Student Development

In an indirect sense, newer models of student development build on the identity development paradigm described by Chickering & Reisser (1993). However, more distinctive dimensions of gender, ethnicity, sexual orientation, social class, disability, religion/faith, and sometimes even geographic region are factored into contemporary studies of identity. "The importance of contextual influences to the development of identity" adds much-needed complexity and nuance to looking at how college students grow and become whole adult selves, according to Susan Jones and Marylu McEwen (2000, p. 412).

These writers acknowledge the vital contributions of Amy Reynolds and Raechele Pope (1991, in Jones & McEwen, 2000), who proposed *multiple oppressions* as a way of examining the lives of students. Four options are described in their Multidimensional Identity Model: (1) identifying with only one personal characteristic, such as ethnicity or sexual orientation, that is externally imposed (e.g., the student is perceived by others as, say, an Asian American male); (2) still identifying with only one characteristic, but that characteristic is self-selected (e.g., appearing and behaving as a traditional Muslim woman); (3) being aware of multiple dimensions of self but relating to others in terms of the context (e.g., being out as a lesbian on campus but not at home); and (4) integrating and embracing all aspects of a complex self and being that self in the world (e.g., a gay, White, Christian man who chooses to be his full self in all arenas of life) (Reynolds & Pope, 1991, in Jones & McEwen, 2000, p. 406). This theory is illustrated in the case study of Victoria later in this book.

Further expanding these ideas is a conceptualization of identity development that deals with how students with multiple aspects of identity (thus, all students) interact with their environments to learn to thrive in the college milieu (Abes et al., 2007). A qualitative study of lesbian students led to the creation of a model that takes into account multiple dimensions and interconnected aspects of the complex identities of today's students.

Drawing on the work of both Kegan (1994) and Baxter Magolda (2001), this reconceptualization of identity development stresses the central task of young adulthood, that is, moving toward self-authorship. Self-authorship refers to self-definition in balance with external and social aspects of life. For example, a heterosexual White female student who wishes to be an active ally to others on campus seeks to understand her points of privilege and to comprehend elements of social oppression that operate in the world. She does not hide her true self; neither does she operate from an inappropriate "pity" perspective. Rather, she uses her cognitive ability to gain knowledge; her introspective, reflective (intrapersonal) dimension to review and monitor her own attitudes and choices; and her interpersonal skills to relate intentionally and respectfully to those whose orientations, values, or behaviors might differ from hers.

Meaning-Making Filter

In the model created by Elisa Abes, Susan Jones, and Marilu McEwen (2007), self-perceptions such as race, social class, sexual orientation, gender, and religion are juxtaposed with environmental and contextual elements such as peer group, family, social norms and stereotypes, and sociopolitical conditions (p. 7). Extending earlier work by Abes and Jones (2004), this model incorporates a meaning-making filter "through which contextual factors are interpreted prior to influencing self-perceptions" (Abes et al., 2007, p. 6). They posit that the complexity (depth/thickness and permeability) of this meaning-making filter affects the degree to which contextual influences affect self-perceptions. Baxter Magolda's (1999) notions of making meaning at either formulaic, transitional, or foundational levels are integrated into the model, allowing a means for assessing where a student is in terms of ability to make meaning of self in the world. For example, the Asian American male mentioned earlier might be highly artistic; he may also be gay and from a wealthy family. As a first-year student, he might already be tired of the expectation that he is especially talented in math or the assumption that he is an immigrant. However, it might be much more comfortable for him to be openly gay at school than at home.

This model offers a powerfully comprehensive method for examining college student development in a more holistic, less fragmented manner. "Contemporary perspectives of fluidity, performativity, and salience in theory development and use, particularly related to multiple social identities" are possible in this way of thinking (Abes et al., 2007, p. 16). To intentionally consider not only a student's characteristics but also the influence of, say, heterosexual norms on the student's self-concept—and, further, how that influence is mitigated (or not) by staff or peer support, or active membership in a student organization—is extremely useful. The meaning-making filter "provides a lens to understand more clearly how students see themselves" (p. 19) and can also be used to examine the impact of campus culture. The sociopolitical system of higher education itself contains visible and invisible barriers to certain students—barriers that affect academic success and even mental health (Reynolds, 209, p. 116).

Consider, for example, Raina, who grew up in New York City. Her parents are from Puerto Rico, and she was born in the United States. Raina has a very high IQ and a moderate learning disability in the area of reading; her skills in mathematics are extraordinary. Raina's goal is medical school, as she is committed to helping people in her cultural community who lack access to quality medical care.

Although Raina is a first-generation college student, she and her parents worked hard with the high school counselor to make the best college selection. After a lengthy research process, Raina enrolled at a residential suburban community college in Connecticut that offers significant support to students with learning disabilities, a solid science program, and a strong record of successful transfers to New York University, where Raina would love to complete her bachelor's degree and enter medical school. Because of her excellent high school grades, she is offered a "full ride" financial aid package.

Raina moves into the residence hall with great enthusiasm but is soon calling home in tears. "I've never felt so Puerto Rican in all my life," she says. "It's one thing to be part of the old neighborhood where I know everyone, but it's so weird being the only Puerto Rican here with all these rich White kids. They seem to wonder how I got here, and I'm starting to wonder about that, too. I knew it would be hard, but not this hard. The students on my floor think I'm a scholarship student because I'm brown, not because I'm smart! The professors either act like I'm invisible or make a point of talking to me about all the 'help' they're sure I need. I do need *some* help—that's why I picked this school—but I'm not stupid! I hate it here!"

Raina's meaning-making filter in this setting is much different than it was back in her high school. Her ethnicity, which was just "part of the landscape" at home, has somehow become her most prominent characteristic on campus, something she feels she needs to justify. And her invisible learning disability now feels like part of a heavy overall "at-risk student" package that she must carry around and explain.

Student affairs professionals will find it useful to explore and consider the unique qualities, attributes, orientations, and characteristics that make up each student—and how those characteristics ease or challenge a student's development. A one-size-fits-all approach to college programs and services is no longer appropriate or even ethical—if it ever was.

Millennial Students

As the dates of many of the sources cited here reveal, much of the work of creating a body of theoretical knowledge about college student development was done decades ago. Ernest Pascarella & Patrick Terenzini (2005) have done a splendid job of updating the research and explicating its many direct and implied outcomes for student affairs professionals. In addition, Carney Strange took a reflective look at relating several of these theories to 21st century students (in Coomes & DeBard, 2004, pp. 44–57). While the early theories sought common ground among students, their characteristics, and their ways of developing, Strange notes, the current generation of students (and, therefore, theories) focuses on what is unique about each person. Strange says, "Notions of normalcy [are now] exposed as extensions of power and privilege that supported a dominant culture that favored the young, Caucasian, male, and heterosexual " (2004, p. 48).

As we can see even in the brief glimpse into contemporary student development theory in this chapter, factors such as age, gender, social class, sexual orientation, ethnicity, and level of acculturation need to be deliberately taken into account when working with students. In fact, these characteristics—whatever they may be in the individual student—are important, valued parts of a healthy identity. In his look at today's students, Strange challenges student affairs practitioners to "question certain models and strategies we have come to rely on . . . and look carefully at [the] present inventory of campus opportunities for engagement of these students" (2004, p. 55).

This stance is strongly underscored by Pope and colleagues (2004). They believe that student development theories "often illuminate evolving and complicated phenomena, and professionals must always strive to see an individual or organization from as many vantage points as possible to honor that complexity" (p. 35). These writers urge student affairs professionals to deconstruct not only existing theories but also their own "assumptions of universality" (p. 36) with regard to how college students grow and change.

In the area of cognitive development, for example, current research is exploring the massive impact of technology on student learning. Not only does technology offer obvious new venues for learning, but some people believe it is changing how students think and write in significant ways. For example, the Stanford Study of Writing is examining the impact of writing for online media, noting that a positive effect may be that students "are forced to be acutely aware of issues like audience, tone, and voice" (Keller, 2009, p. 3). As a result of the popularity of social networks, students write more than ever, and in ways that are increasingly self-directed and goal-oriented. There is much to explore simply with regard to the use of emerging technologies in all areas of student learning and development (Junco & Timm, 2008).

Conclusion

As Love and Guthrie remark at the close of their monograph, "For a more in-depth understanding, we recommend that student affairs professionals read the original works" (1999, p. 87). This comment is emphatically true for each and every theory and source mentioned in this chapter, particularly those identified as emerging theories. As an overview, these pages may provide a useful refresher or basic orientation to the theories that inform student affairs practice. In the case studies that make up most of this volume, these theories offer a backdrop of some of the best thinking that grounds, frames, and leads the student affairs profession.

References

Abes, E. A. & Jones, S. R. (2004). Meaning-making capacity and the dynamics of lesbian college students multiple dimensions of identity. *Journal of College Student Development, 45*, 612–632.

Abes, E. S., Jones, S. R., & McEwen, M. K. (2007). Reconceptualizing the model of multiple dimensions of identity: The role of meaning-making capacity in the construction of multiple identities. *Journal of College Student Development, 48*, 1–22.

American College Health Association (ACHA). (2009). *American College Health Association-National College Health Assessment II: Reference group executive summary, fall 2008.* Baltimore: Author.

American College Personnel Association. (1996). *The student learning imperative: Implications for student affairs.* Alexandria, VA: author.

American College Personnel Association / National Association for Student Personnel Administrators. (1997). *Principles of good practice for student affairs.* Retrieved October 26, 2008, from *www.acpa.nche.edu/pgp/princip8.htm*

Astin, A. (1984). Student involvement: A developmental theory for higher education. *Journal of College Student Development, 25*, 297–308.

Baxter Magolda, M. B. (1995). The integration of relational and impersonal knowing in young adults' epistemological development. *Journal of College Student Development, 36*, 205–216.

Baxter Magolda, M. B. (1999). The evolution of epistemology: Refining contextual knowing at twentysomething. *Journal of College Student Development, 40*, 333–344.

Baxter Magolda, M. B. (2001). *Making their own way: Narratives for transforming higher education to promote self-development.* Sterling, VA: Stylus.

Belenky, M. F., Clinchy, B. M., Goldberger, N. R., & Tarule, J. M. (1986). *Women's ways of knowing: The development of self, voice, and mind*. New York: Basic Books.

Blackhurst, A. (2008). Moving away from generalizing a generation: The triumph of the individual. *About Campus, 13*(1), 4–6.

Blimling, G. S. (2001). Diversity makes you smarter. *Journal of College Student Development, 42*, 517–519.

Cass, V. (1979). Homosexual identity: A concept in need of definition. *Journal of Homosexuality, 9*, 105–126.

Chickering, A. W. (1969). *Education and identity*. San Francisco: Jossey-Bass.

Chickering, A. W., & Gamson, Z. F. (1987). Seven principles for good practice in undergraduate education. *AAHE Bulletin, 39*(7), 3–7.

Chickering, A. W., & Reisser, L. (1993). *Education and identity* (2nd ed.). San Francisco: Jossey-Bass.

Coomes, M. D., & DeBard, R. (Eds.). (2004). *Serving the millennial generation.* New Directions for Student Services,106. San Francisco: Jossey-Bass.

Cross, W. E. (1995). The psychology of Nigrescence: Revising the Cross model. In J. G. Ponterotto, J. M. Casa, L. A. Suzuki, & C. M. Alexander (Eds.), *Handbook of multicultural counseling* (pp. 93–122). Thousand Oaks, CA: Sage.

Duys, D. K., Ward, J. E., Maxwell, J. A., & Eaton-Comerford, L. (2008). Career counseling in a volatile job market: Tiedeman's perspective revisited. *Career Development Quarterly, 56*(3), 232–241.

Evans, N. J., Forney, D. S., & Guido-DiBrito, F. (1998). *Student development in college: Theory, research, and practice*. San Francisco: Jossey-Bass.

Evans, N. J., & Wall, V. (Eds.). (1991). *Beyond tolerance: Gays, lesbians, and bisexuals on campus*. Alexandria, VA: American College Personnel Association.

Gilligan, C. (1982). *In a different voice: Psychological theory and women's development*. Cambridge, MA: Harvard University Press.

Heiberger, G., & Harper, R. (2008). Have you Facebooked Astin lately? Using technology to increase student involvement. In R. Junco & D. Timm (Eds.), *Using emerging technologies to enhance student engagement*. (New Directions for Student Services, No. 124, pp. 19–35). San Francisco: Jossey-Bass.

Helms, J. E. (1995). An update of Helms's white and people of color racial identity models. In J. G. Ponterotto, J. M. Casa, L. A. Suzuki, & C. M. Alexander (Eds.), *Handbook of multicultural counseling* (pp. 93–122). Thousand Oaks, CA: Sage.

Ivey, A. E., D'Andrea, M., Bradford Ivey, M., & Simek-Morgan, L. (2007). *Theories of counseling and psychotherapy: A multicultural perspective* (6th ed.). Boston: Allyn & Bacon.

Jones, S. R., & McEwen, M. K. (2000). A conceptual model of multiple dimensions of identity. *Journal of College Student Development, 41*, 405–413.

Josselson, R. (1987). *Finding herself: Pathways to identity development in women*. San Francisco: Jossey-Bass.

Junco, R., & Timm, D. M. (Eds.). (2008, Winter). Using emerging technologies to enhance student development. *New Directions for Student Services, 124*. San Francisco: Jossey-Bass.

Just the facts: University of Phoenix's Background. (2009). Retrieved November 25, 2009, from http://www.phoenix.edu/about_us/media_relations/just-the-facts.html

Kadison, R., & DiGeronimo, T. F. (2004). *College of the overwhelmed: The campus mental health crisis and what to do about it*. San Francisco: Jossey-Bass.

Kegan, R. (1982). *The evolving self: Problem and process in human development*. Cambridge, MA: Harvard University Press.

Kegan, R. (1994). *In over our heads: The mental demands of modern life.* Cambridge, MA: Harvard University Press.

Keller, J. (2009). Studies explore whether the Internet makes students better writers. Retrieved June 27, 2009, from http://chronicle.com/free/v55/i39/39writing.htm

King, P. M. & Kitchener, K. S. (1994). *Developing reflective judgment: Understanding and promoting intellectual growth and critical thinking in adolescents and adults.* San Francisco: Jossey-Bass.

Kohlberg, L. (1969). Stages and sequence: The cognitive-developmental approach to socialization. In D. A. Goslin (Ed.), *Handbook of Socialization Theory and Research.* Skokie, IL: Rand McNally.

Kohlberg, L. (1976). Moral stages and moralization: The cognitive-developmental approach. In T. Lickona (Ed.)., *Moral development and behavior: Theory research, and social issues* (pp. 31–53). New York: Holt, Rinehart, & Winston.

Komives, S. R., Woodard, D. B., Jr., and associates. (1996). *Student services: A handbook for the profession* (3rd ed.). San Francisco: Jossey-Bass.

Love, P. G. & Guthrie, V. L. (1999). *Understanding and applying cognitive development theory.* New Directions for Student Services, 88. San Francisco: Jossey-Bass.

Marcia, J. E. (1966). Development and validation of ego-identity status. *Journal of Personality and Social Psychology, 3,* 551–559.

Moore, L. V. (Ed.). (1992). *Evolving theoretical perspectives on students.* New Directions for Student Services, 51. San Francisco: Jossey-Bass.

NASPA Parent and family relations knowledge community. (2009). Retrieved March 28, 2009, from www.naspa.org/kc/pfr/default.cfm

National Alliance on Mental Illness. Retrieved June 27, 2009, from www.nami.org/Content/ContentGroups/Advocate/Spring_2003/CounselingStudy

Palmer, P. J. (2004). *A hidden wholeness: The journey toward an undivided life*. San Francisco: Jossey-Bass.

Pascarella, E. T., & Terenzini, P. T. (2005). *How college affects students: A third decade of research* (Vol. 2). San Francisco: Jossey-Bass.

Perry, W. G. (1981). Cognitive and ethical growth: The making of meaning. In A. W. Chickering & Assoc. (Eds.), *The modern American college* (pp. 76-116). San Francisco: Jossey-Bass.

Pope, R. L., Reynolds, A. L., & Mueller, J. A. (2004). *Multicultural competence in student affairs*. San Francisco: Jossey-Bass.

Pope, R. L., Reynolds, A. L., & Cheatham, H. E. (1997). American College Personnel Association (ACPA) strategic initiative on multiculturalism. *Journal of College Student Development, 38*, 62–76.

Reynolds, A. L. (2009). *Helping college students: Developing essential support skills for student affairs practice*. San Francisco: Jossey-Bass.

Sanford, N. (1967). *Where colleges fail: A study of the student as a person*. San Francisco: Jossey-Bass.

Schlossberg, N. K. (1981). A model for analyzing human adaptation to transition. *Counseling Psychologist, 9*(2), 2–18.

Schlossberg, N. K. (1984). *Counseling adults in transition*. New York: Springer.

Schlossberg, N. K., Waters, E. B., & Goodman, J. (1995). *Counseling adults in transition* (2nd ed.). New York: Springer.

Schlossberg, N. K. (1989). Marginality and mattering: Key issues in building community. In D. C. Roberts (Ed.), *Designing campus activities to foster a sense of community* (New Directions for Student Services, 48, pp. 5–15). San Francisco: Jossey-Bass.

Strange, C. C. (2004). Constructions of student development across the generations. In M. D. Coomes & R. DeBard (Eds.), *Serving the millennial generation* (New Directions for Student Services, 106, pp. 47–57). San Francisco: Jossey-Bass.

Sue, D. W. & Sue, D. (2007). *Counseling the culturally diverse: Theory and practice* (5th ed.). New York: Wiley.

Talbot, D. M. (2003). Multiculturalism. In S. R. Komives & D. B. Woodard (Eds.), *Student services: A handbook for the profession* (4th ed., pp. 423–446). San Francisco: Jossey-Bass. *The four values of the Lakota.* (n.d.). Retrieved March 29, 2009, from http://kalloch.org/lakota_four_values.htm

Wilson, M. E. (2004). Teaching, learning, and millennial students. In M. D. Coomes & R. DeBard (Eds.), *Serving the millennial generation* (New Directions for Student Services, 106, pp. 59–71). San Francisco: Jossey-Bass.

CHAPTER 2

Counseling Theories
for Student Affairs
Professionals

Nona L. Wilson

Tracing the historical and philosophical origins of counseling, Sweeney (2001) quotes Arthur J. Jones, a secondary education professor and an early advocate for "guidance" in schools:

> Guidance is based upon the fact that human beings need help. To a greater or lesser degree, we all need the assistance of others. The possibility of education, as well as the necessity for it, is founded upon the essential dependence of people upon one another. Young people, especially, are not capable of solving life's problems successfully without aid. Many critical situations occur in our lives, situations in which important and far-reaching decisions must be made, and it is very necessary that some adequate help be provided in order that decisions may be made wisely. (Jones, 1934, p. 3, as cited in Locke, Myers, & Herr, 2001, p. 6)

Although Jones was writing about young students, and much has changed in the 75 years since his appeal for "adequate help," the essential truth of his message still holds. There are critical events that challenge us, that have long-lasting significance for the course of our lives, and with which we need help. It is unlikely that Jones was envisioning today's highly trained, specialized, credentialed, and regulated mental health clinicians. While there is unquestionably a need for such professionals on campus, Jones's simple but eloquent plea reminds us that the origins of counseling ("guidance" in its early form) are rooted in a much broader, more developmental concept of helping. And while it might seem counter intuitive to invoke this earlier conceptualization of guidance at a time when mental health issues on campus are more widespread and more severe than ever before, it is exactly that reality that makes a broader notion of helping relevant. More than ever, our campuses need "adequate help," and student affairs professionals are well situated to meaningfully connect with and help students.

In fact, most student affairs professionals find themselves in helping roles on a daily basis: advising undecided students about choosing a major, supporting first-year students in adjusting to campus, comforting students when they experience personal loss or academic disappointment, helping students connect with services on campus, collaborating with them in planning events, and supervising them as work-study employees or residence hall, admissions, or orientation staff members. To perform their role well, student affairs professionals need strong communication and facilitation skills, yet they may have to piece together those skills from graduate training that does not provide enough emphasis on helping skills (Burkard, Cole, Ott, & Stotlet, 2005) or that is far too clinical in nature and may blur the important boundary between helping and offering therapy (Reynolds, 2009). Student affairs professionals are in a unique position with students: bridging the gap (often substantial) between the support that family and friends offer and the clinical services that licensed mental health professionals provide. Student affairs professionals can greatly benefit from learning certain counseling concepts and skills, but they will use them in an adapted form that makes sense for student affairs practice.

This chapter presents three well-established counseling theories—Person-Centered, Solution-Focused, and Cognitive-Behavioral—and a brief overview of mindfulness. The intention of the chapter is to help you use the theories and selected techniques to organize your thinking about the helping process and to guide your helping behaviors. Because student affairs professionals come into the field with such disparate backgrounds and skills, the intended audience for this chapter is, most likely, quite diverse. Because of this diversity, the level of explanation and depth of discussion offered here are intended to appeal to as many readers as possible, but primarily to those who are relatively new to counseling theories or those who need help in applying the theories to their work.

The discussion of each model is organized into two major sections: conceptual framework and skills/techniques. Each theory advances its own system for making sense of personal challenges: which factors play a role in the development and maintenance of those issues, which elements of a person's experience to attend to when seeking to understand and help, and which strategies help people resolve their problems. The skills and techniques that arise from or are closely associated with the theoretical models are the tools for putting into practice the values and priorities of each theory.

Because this chapter is designed to help you understand how to use the theories and skills, the text (in this chapter and in the case studies that follow) speaks directly to "you," the reader. Envision yourself in the helping role, using these ideas and strategies.

Person-Centered Helping

Conceptual Framework

Many people in the counseling field consider Person-Centered counseling the bedrock for helping professionals. Carl Rogers developed Person-Centered theory over a lifetime of helping people; it is deeply rooted in a profound respect for individual autonomy and self-determination (Murdock, 2009). At its core, the theory maintains that students are experts on their own experiences. They are not only capable of resolving life's difficulties but can best do so when unimpeded by guidance and direction—however well-intended—from others. This is not to say that Person-Centered theory suggests that "all we have to do is listen," as some believe. Such a characterization of Person-Centered theory is misleading in two important ways. First, it implies that effective listening is easy. Second, it suggests that the helper can assume a passive role, merely lending an ear as the student resolves his or her concerns independently. Avoiding giving advice is far from doing nothing but listening. Together, those errors create the false impression that the helper, working from this model, needs neither skill nor discipline. The truth is the helper must have both.

In the Person-Centered framework, the helper is actively attuned to creating what Rogers considered the "necessary and sufficient conditions" for effective facilitation, whether in counseling or education (Prochaska & Norcross, 2010, p. 135). Those conditions, frequently referred to as the "core conditions," can effectively form the foundation for caring conversations in student affairs practice as well. The conditions include genuineness, unconditional positive regard, and empathy. They are the core of the relationship, and from a Person-Centered perspective, the relationship is central. It is the quality of the relationship that determines how the student will respond—whether or not the student will trust the helper, value the interaction, and benefit from it.

The first core condition, **genuineness,** speaks to the need for the helper to be authentic. That is, the helper must not be playing a role or assuming a part when interacting with the student. The helper must genuinely care about the student, and the student must sense that the helper is being honest in the interaction. Genuineness is also referred to as **congruence.** In plain language, this means that the helper's messages—verbal and nonverbal—must match; they must work together to convey the same intention to the student. If you intend to convey openness to hearing a student's perspective, then you would direct your full attention to the student: orient your body toward the student, maintain regular eye contact without staring, and use a welcoming tone of voice. While this process might sound obvious and easy, Tolan (2003) describes the aim as creating a "distortion-free zone" (p. 43), and that can be harder than you might imagine.

Remaining congruent also means staying focused and attentive even when the student is incongruent, for example, joking or laughing about an experience that is actually troubling. Being congruent means staying true to your intention to help the student talk through an experience and, therefore, not following an invitation to make light of a concern. Similarly, if you intend to create a learning opportunity for a student who struggles with social skills, remaining congruent requires not allowing yourself to be distracted by competing impulses to take personal offense or to criticize the student during challenging interactions. Congruency requires helpers to be clear in their own heads and hearts about what their primary intentions are, to stay aware of those intentions while working with students, and to use those intentions to guide their actions. It is extremely easy to get distracted from primary intentions. Slipping away from them happens in a flash in a conversation, and it is easy to not notice that you have done so—that does not mean, however, that the student you are talking to will not notice. Learning to stay with your intentions requires practice over time.

The second core condition involves cultivating **unconditional positive regard** for students. This element of the Person-Centered framework means that the helper must strive to fully accept students—value and care for them—just as they are (Prochaska & Norcross, 2010). Students do not have to adhere to any terms or conditions to be deemed worthy of respect and care. The Person-Centered helper subscribes to the belief that everyone, regardless of flaws or challenges, is fully acceptable and worthy of positive regard. This kind of regard is **nonpossessive**; it is caring without attempting to own or take over others' problems or their choices about managing those problems. Like other elements of the Person-Centered framework, this simple concept is easy to understand and yet extremely difficult to consistently practice.

The nonpossessive aspect of unconditional positive regard requires that you stay mindful that the student's experience belongs fully, exclusively to him or her. Helpers do not get to annex or co-own a student's experience, no matter how much they have helped or how much they care. While that might seem obvious, helpers can stake a claim to a certain outcome in numerous and often subtle ways. It can be easy to want a student to make a certain choice, to stop engaging in behaviors that are clearly destructive, or even to value what you value. Being possessive in these ways is not reserved to unskilled helpers.

Every time a helper makes a meaningful connection with a student, the door is opened to becoming overly invested in a particular outcome. The trouble is that when helpers do that, even in subtle ways, they "crowd" the students they are trying to help by imposing their own values, aspirations, or beliefs. For example, you might believe that a student you are working with is truly capable and would benefit from staying enrolled. You might even believe that the student should make completing a degree a priority; you might feel committed to your institution's retention goals.

If a student tells you that his family needs him at home, that he cannot afford the tuition, or that he believes the campus is not the right fit for him, you can explore those ideas with him and even invite him to question his beliefs before making a final decision. Ultimately, however, you must not only permit the student to make his own choices—free from pressure or a sense of failure—but you must actively support him in doing so.

In the Person-Centered framework, the ultimate goal is to open up space for students to discover their own paths, to guide their own journeys, not to follow a helper's lead. Nonpossessive caring is not attempting to control. Taking control includes trying to get students to see something you see, hoping that your vision might speed their process along somehow. Tolan (2003) says that some people might consider such action as "appropriate challenge" from the helper, "but in person-centered work it is known as *pushing the river*" (p. 121). Her point is that trying to control or hurry someone else's experience is futile; it simply does not work. Nonpossessiveness is not just about resisting the urge to tell students what to do; it is about not having the urge. This is an important distinction and can be a real challenge.

For some helpers, caring and controlling are closely knit. One triggers the other, and it can take ongoing effort to tease them apart. But if helpers get attached to their own agendas rather than being curious about and interested in a student's experiences, they can leave the student feeling pressured and unheard, or sensing that future support is conditional. Unconditional positive regard and its nonpossessive quality encourage helpers to let go of judgments, to resist pursuing their own agendas, and to prize students for who they are.

The third core condition is **empathic understanding,** or simply **empathy.** Most people are familiar with the concept of empathy, but Rogers's use of the word is somewhat different, or at least more specific, than the way it is used in common parlance. Sometimes people use the word to mean something more akin to sympathy, which is an expression of concern for another but from a position once removed. That is, if you have a friend who has just lost her home to a hurricane, you might feel sympathy for her. Only if you try to close the experiential gap between you—to step into her world as *she* experiences it—can you approach her experience with empathy. In Rogers's model, then, it is crucial that you stay clear about the difference between empathy and sympathy. Empathy is not about feeling sorry for someone but about trying to grasp what he or she might be experiencing.

Likewise, it is important not to confuse endorsement with empathy (Meier & Davis, 2011). You might hear someone say after listening to a student, "Oh, yes, I can empathize." What might be happening is that the listener can relate to the student's description and might be thinking, "Oh, yes, that's what I'd be feeling, too, if I were experiencing that." Rapid identification with a student is more likely based on drawing on one's own perspective and assuming it is the student's perspective rather than on a careful, cautious, and deliberate effort to fully apprehend the student's frame of reference. With empathy, the helper is not just endorsing his or her own worldview heard in another person's story but attempting to adopt, temporarily, another's point of view.

Empathy sounds like an easier concept to master than it is. For most people, it is extremely challenging to set aside personal views, values, and assumptions and see the world from another's perspective (Hazler, 2007). In fact, the greater the differences between the helper and the student, the harder it can be to achieve accurate empathy. This reality has important implications for culturally competent practice (Sue & Sue, 2008, pp. 140–154). You must always be careful about substituting your own experiences and perspectives for students' perspectives, especially if you are a member of a traditionally privileged group and are helping students who have experienced oppression or marginalization.

Person-Centered Skills

In some ways, discussing skills in the Person-Centered framework is a contradiction in terms. Rogers himself expressed concern that when his model was broken down into a set of skills so that it could be taught, the essence of the approach was distorted (Murdock, 2009; Wickman & Campbell, 2003). The core conditions require that the helper be genuine, so simply mimicking a set of responses or skills associated with Person-Centered facilitation will not suffice. You must pursue *a way of being* with students out of which the skills genuinely flow.

Fisher (2007) operationalizes Rogers's concepts in the process of reflective listening, which he describes as including one central guiding question and a set of three subsequent choices. He says, "The central question for the helper is not 'What can I do for this person?' or even 'How do I see this person?' but rather 'How does this person see himself or herself?'" (p. 430). After listening from the other's point of view, the helper "makes three more basic choices: (1) to respond to what is personal rather than what is impersonal; (2) to respond to rather than lead the other; and (3) to respond to feelings, not just to content" (p. 432). Your goal, then, is to attend to what is true for the student and offer a response that captures the meaning—not just the content—of his or her statements.

A common error that helpers new to reflective listening make is to simply parrot back what a person has just said. While occasionally this is a useful strategy to ensure that you have heard accurately, merely repeating statements does not deepen the other person's self-understanding, nor does it advance the conversation. The objective is to hear the significance of the content, the meaning of statements, and to tentatively offer back that essence. Finally, it is crucial to attend to *all* of what the other person is saying, not only to the parts that make sense to you. As Tolan (2003) has noted, "The fullest empathy does not censor or discriminate" (p. 18). Helpers can easily slip into overattending to aspects of another's experience that they agree with or can relate to; reflective listeners strive to hear the other's experience from that person's subjective point of view.

Wickman (1999) identifies conversational devices that Carl Rogers used during a 30-minute taped session he conducted in 1965, which is considered a classic demonstration of his approach. Excerpting Rogers's responses, Wickman and Campbell (2003) show how the devices (in three categories) helped Rogers—and can help you—create the core conditions.

Communicating Genuineness

From a Person-Centered helping perspective, you are not the expert; the student is. Use **nonexpert language** to reflect that. Statements such as *"We have half an hour together an' I really don't know what we'll be able to make of it, but, uh, I hope we can make something of it. I'd be glad to know whatever concerns you . . ."* or *" I guess . . . this is the kind of very private thing that I couldn't possibly answer for you"* underscore the idea that you do not see yourself as the expert (Wickman & Campbell, 2003, p. 180).

Meta-statements involve adopting a narrator's voice and making comments about the interaction as it is occurring. Wickman and Campbell (2003) note that such statements allow the helper to introduce slightly risky ideas by softening them. Examples include: *"I guess I'd like to say . . ."* or *"what I wanna ask now is"* (p. 180). You might tell a student, *"I guess I want to ask about how the conversation with your roommate went, but I also don't want to push you to talk about it."*

Communicating Empathy

Affiliative negative assessments allow you to demonstrate a shared perspective with the student when things seem bleak. Such comments communicate that you "get it": *"It's damn hard"* or *"Sounds like a tough assignment"* or *"Life is risky"* (Wickman & Campbell, p. 180). These sorts of comments allow you to come alongside students and join them for a moment in recognizing their hardship.

First-person quotes involve saying out loud what you believe the other person is thinking, using "I" statements so that you have, for a moment, truly adopted their perspective. For example, Rogers said, *"But something in you says, 'But I don't like it that way . . .'"* and also, *"You sort of feel, 'I want them to have just as nice a picture of me as they have of their dad'"* (Wickman & Campbell, p. 181). You might notice that when you use person-first quotes accurately, students will begin to collaborate with you, adding *"Yes, and . . ."* to capture details you may have missed but that they now feel allowed to voice.

Invitations for repair are direct and indirect ways of communicating to students the idea "correct me if I'm wrong." Such invitations not only build trust, but also increase the likelihood of accurate understanding. Comments such as *"Is that right?"* or

"Maybe that's not exactly right" or *"Is that what you meant?"* convey your interest in truly knowing the student's perspectives and a willingness to adjust your own.

Communicating Unconditional Positive Regard

Withholding direct responses to requests for advice is a way of honoring students' own expertise and demonstrating unconditional positive regard. Withholding advice, especially when students directly ask for it, can be challenging. From the Person-Centered perspective, however, withholding advice arises logically from the deep conviction that students are not only capable of finding their own way, but ultimately must do so. Rogers captured the sentiment beautifully: *"But you see, one thing that concerns me is it's no damn good your doing something that you haven't really chosen to do. That's why I'm trying to help you find out what your own inner choices are"* (Wickman & Campbell, 2003, p. 182).

Reformulating the problem is a common counseling strategy, sometimes referred to as "reframing" (Murdock, 2009, p. 477). It is a technique used to describe concerns so they can be seen in new, typically more manageable, ways. When students are upset, for example, they might present their concerns in dramatic terms that contribute to their sense that the problems are insurmountable. Reformulating problems in more moderate language can have a marked calming effect. You must be careful, however, to do this in ways that do not deviate so far from students' original disclosures that they feel misunderstood or that you have minimized their concerns. For example, a student might describe a situation in dire terms: "I'm a terrible student. I'm failing everything, and there's no way I'm going to get through this semester." After talking with her for a short while, you might hear details in her description that allow you to offer the following reformulation: *"I can hear that things seem really terrible for you right now and you aren't sure how you're going to make it through. And yet, you seem also to be saying that you're not really failing everything—it's a couple of tough courses, but even so there are still opportunities for extra credit or an extension if you can just figure out how to make time."*

Solution-Focused Helping

Conceptual Framework

Like the Person-Centered approach, Solution-Focused thinking posits that the answers to personal dilemmas usually lie within rather than outside the individual. Solution-Focused helping maintains that there is not necessarily a connection between problems and solutions. To help students move toward solutions, helpers need not spend time uncovering the origins of problems or exploring how those problems have developed. In fact, from a Solution-Focused point of view, doing so represents "problem talk" and only sharpens students' focus on their concerns. The goal, instead, is to encourage a shift of attention away from problems and toward solutions by actively encouraging discussions of strengths and future goals—even when a student's focus seems stuck on the problem.

Solution-Focused work is grounded in constructivism, a school of thought that maintains that people create their realities through culture, perception, and language (Prochaska & Norcross, 2010). The inner scripts that people construct and rehearse—both through internal self-talk and in the larger social and historical context of their lives—largely determine their experience (Prochaska & Norcross, 2010). If a student is having conflicts with a friend, rehashing the ways in which the friend is disappointing or annoying strengthens that storyline, keeps attention riveted on the problem, and increases the likelihood that the student will notice future examples of the friend's shortcomings. In the simplest terms, rehashing unsatisfying circumstances only gets people more of what they do not want, because the complaining focuses their attention on the problem and limits the amount of attention they can give to solutions.

The Solution-Focused perspective maintains that even while the problem is occurring, so are its solutions. Regrettably, many people become so consumed with tracking problems that they fail to recognize or acknowledge solutions that are already available to them. Thus, people need not undergo extended analysis of concerns as a first step to problem solving, nor must they undertake major changes to experience improvement. They simply need to shift—at times pry—their attention from the problem, focus on the things they are already doing that work, and then do those things more. Much like the Person-Centered framework, Solution-Focused work is rooted in deceptively simply concepts. A shift in attention sounds like an easy task, as does doing more of what works; in practice, this approach can represent a radical and profoundly life-altering change. Luckily, dramatic changes can be achieved through the cumulative effect of small steps.

Solution-Focused Skills

Like the Person-Centered framework, the Solution-Focused approach attends to who and what are important to the student; unlike the former, this model is more directive in purposefully guiding the conversation toward solutions. De Jong (2001) has provided a clear and user-friendly guide to four central elements of solution-building conversations: (1) listening, (2) co-constructing goals, (3) co-constructing competence, and (4) measuring progress. Although the elements and their attendant skills were developed for counselors, they are well suited to the kinds of assistance student affairs practitioners routinely provide. In fact, solution-building conversations can be especially useful in helping student affairs staff establish and maintain clear boundaries in their work.

Listening is, obviously, a crucial element in all helping models. What is somewhat different about listening in Solution-Focused conversations is that the listener is particularly attuned to two kinds of information: (1) who and what are important to the student, and (2) what the student wants. While listening for these two things might sound easy, ferreting out these elements from a laundry list of complaints can be challenging. If a student is describing what he does not want, you will want to briefly acknowledge the complaint, then shift attention to what the complaint implies about what he *does* want. For example, if Anthony is distressed that his boyfriend Barry does not seem to have time for him anymore and is distracted when he does manage to spend time with Anthony, you might offer the following reflection: *"So, it's important to you to spend time with Barry, and you want to feel more connected in your relationship"* instead of simply repeating what Anthony is upset about. By doing this, you attend to the embedded message.

Solution-Focused listening is targeted. It takes discipline to resist being drawn into the details of problems. Unfortunately, there is much in the culture at large that fosters attention to problems, especially dramatic problems, and it is easy to get caught up in that. In fact, some students think they have to provide details about their problems to get help with them. They might have been rewarded for "problem talk" in the past, garnering attention and concern, and may be confused by a Solution-Focused approach that de-centers the problem. You must be persistent in listening "through" descriptions of problems to hear what those problems suggest about what matters to students.

Co-constructing goals. The Solution-Focused helper establishes a collaborative tone very early in the relationship. After listening to a student's concern, you might begin the process of co-constructing goals by asking, *"What would you like to have be different as a result of our meeting today in order for you to say that our talking was worthwhile?"* (De Jong & Berg, 2002). This single question accomplishes several important tasks: It conveys to students that you are not going to provide a prepackaged set of services but rather will tailor your response to their unique interests; it asks students to take responsibility for identifying what they want; it sets a purposeful, goal-oriented tone to meetings right away (both you and the students you work with will know very quickly where to focus your efforts); and finally, it provides a measure by which to evaluate meetings.

The hallmark of Solution-Focused interviews, and a key technique for co-constructing goals, is the "miracle question" (Murdock, 2009, p. 478). The miracle question directs students to describe in significant detail what they would be experiencing if their problems were solved. The following is the classic formulation of the miracle question:

> *Suppose that while you are sleeping tonight, and the entire house is quiet, a miracle happens. The miracle is that the problem that brought you here is solved. However, because you are sleeping, you don't know that the miracle has happened. So, when you wake up tomorrow morning, what will be different that will tell you that a miracle has happened and the problem which brought you here is solved?"* (de Shazer, 1988, quoted in De Jong & Berg, 1998, p. 77–78)

Most helpers develop their own versions of the miracle question. For example, an academic advisor might ask a troubled, undecided student, *"If you could major in anything at all—something that truly grabs your attention and makes you excited about going to class—what would that be?"* A residence hall director who is meeting with a student who is upset about hall policies could say, *"I know you are upset about the visitation policies. I can't wave a wand and change the rules overnight, but I am willing to listen to your ideas about what an ideal policy would look like."* In both cases, the conversation goes from problem-focused to solution-focused, and the student is invited to think about and share positive possibilities.

The miracle question invites students to begin envisioning (constructing) solutions to their concerns. Your challenge is to engage students in painting as detailed a picture as possible. When people are troubled by something, they often ruminate on it—polishing the details of what is wrong until they gleam brilliantly in the mind's eye. To supplant that shiny portrait of the problem, the picture of the solution must likewise be vivid and detailed enough to capture the imagination and inspire hope. You will need be to ready with follow-up questions that prompt students to come up with more details.

The miracle question must be worded in a way that does not place responsibility for the solution on someone else. In Anthony's case, you would frame the questions so that Anthony does not start envisioning major changes on Barry's part. Rather, the change must originate with Anthony. For example, *"Suppose that, miraculously, your relationship with Barry is just what you want. You're no longer upset with him and things between you are going well. What is the first change you experience in yourself? What is happening for you?"*

The question invites Anthony to get out of the rut of thinking about the problem, living the problem, and anticipating the problem; instead, he can imagine being free of it. Anthony could respond in a wide variety of ways, but he might indicate that he would be in a better mood, feel happier, more secure, or less needy. You would encourage Anthony to stay with that image by asking any of the following: *"What will you be doing when you're in a better mood? What will other people, for example Barry, notice about you that will indicate you're in a better mood? How will you act with Barry when you are feeling good about the relationship? When*

Barry notices that change in you, what might he do? Regardless of how Barry might respond, how will acting in this way have a positive effect on you?"

Encouraging Anthony to notice changes that the "miracle" produces in his thinking, his emotions, and his behavior, as well as in major life domains (work, school, relationships, hobbies), can elicit rich detail that will build his investment in the solution he is generating as he speaks. The more he describes it, the more depth and dimension he gives it, the better he can "see" it, and the more likely it becomes. When students trace over the details of grievances, they are often reminded of other grievances. So, too, when they spend time envisioning solutions and positive interactions, their memories are stirred about other pleasing interactions, and their imaginations are activated for positive possibilities.

Solution-Focused helping is fundamentally a "glass half-full" approach, so the notion of **co-constructing competence** is not about determining what students lack and then correcting the deficit by teaching them new skills. Rather, it is about noticing the ways in which students are already competent and addressing their concerns in small ways they might not fully appreciate otherwise. Solution-Focused helpers assume that students can solve their problems; that, in fact, they are doing many things effectively every day. Thus, these helpers approach the process with a genuine curiosity about students' existing strategies.

Much like what happens in the expression of unconditional positive regard, when Solution-Focused helpers notice and appreciate students' day-to-day abilities, the students themselves begin to develop an enhanced sense of competence. Berg and her colleagues at the Brief Family Therapy Center developed the acronym EARS to describe the process of co-constructing competence through a set of four skills: (1) eliciting exceptions, (2) amplifying, (3) reinforcing success, and (4) starting again (De Jong & Berg, 2002, p. 143).

Eliciting exceptions is essential to loosening the grip that problems may have on students. This technique entails encouraging students to develop a keen eye for times when their circumstances are better, even if only slightly or briefly. Eliciting exceptions is a bit like looking at one of the *Where's Waldo?* books. It is challenging, even frustrating, but ultimately rewarding to search. Helping students find exceptions hiding inside the details of a concern is gratifying for the helper and useful for the student, and practice sharpens one's skill. Once students have identified exceptions, the Solution-Focused helper encourages them to notice when and how those exceptions occur—and to take credit for creating them. You might say to Anthony, for example, *"Tell me about a time when things were great in this relationship. What was happening then?"* or *"Has there been a time recently when you and Barry really got along and had fun? How did that happen?"*

If students cannot find any exceptions, you can shift the discussion to coping (rather than back to the problem). *"How are you managing all this?"* and *"What are you doing to make it so things are not getting worse?"* are helpful prompts to keep the conversation away from problem talk and remind students that coping is a strength they can build on.

Amplifying in solution-building conversations refers to the helper's efforts to strengthen, magnify, or increase attention to any aspect of a student's experiences that build solutions. Attending to small changes, helping students specify what they would be doing if a miracle happened, and focusing closely on the first small step of a bigger desired change are all ways of doing this. Amplifying is a kind of conversational spotlight; it highlights the topic at hand and conveys to the student that a particular detail is worth attending to. Amplifying is rooted in the idea that what we pay attention to grows; the more we attend to something—a feeling, a behavior, an interaction—the more it is going to happen. A Solution-Focused helper never encourages detailed discussion of the problem, because that would amplify it. Rather, the helper directs the discussion to what is working and what might be done more often. For example, a student might confide in you that she is feeling lonely and sad. Acknowledge her concern (*"Oh, I'm sorry to hear that, and I'm glad you came to talk with me"*), then ask, *"What has helped you feel better in the past when you felt this way?"* This might prompt her to talk about coping strategies she has successfully used in the past: joining a student organization, playing tennis, or keeping a journal. You can support these and other strategies as options in the current situation, and can follow up in a few days to ask whether she has acted on any of them.

In solution-building conversations, the helper should ***reinforce success*** at every opportunity, because doing so strengthens the student's sense of competence. Genuinely appreciating students' successes not only helps them feel good in the moment, it helps them develop a sense of themselves as capable and successful. Amplifying is a useful technique for reinforcing success. Spending time talking through the details of successes—how and when they happen, what students do to make them happen, and their positive effects—draws students' attention to their accomplishments and helps them do more of what works.

The S in EARS reminds helpers that repetition—***starting again***—helps changes become permanent. Solution-Focused helping builds big changes out of small successes; thus, the process cycles through many iterations: elicit exceptions, amplify them, reinforce successes, and start again. Changing behavior—especially long-standing, unhelpful habits—requires practice. "Start again" emphasizes the need to repeat the new ways of thinking and acting.

Measuring progress is integral and central to Solution-Focused helping; in fact, the process revolves around this concept. The EARS sequence depends on noticing and tracking progress. Improvements, exemplified as exceptions to the problem, however slight, are significant. The goal is to find, amplify, and reinforce what students do to make them happen, then start the process again. Often, when people want big changes, they expect them to occur in dramatic fashion. Likewise, when people are facing big challenges, they may focus on all that must happen and feel overwhelmed, wanting to be at the finish line rather than the starting gate. Solution-Focused helping seeks to break those changes and challenges into smaller, more manageable components or steps. Those components offer ongoing opportunities to notice and reinforce progress.

Students are encouraged when they realize that they can experience some (even if small) degree of relief or improvement fairly quickly and are more likely to continue to work toward a goal. For example, the student who confides in you that she is lonely and sad might decide to take a 15-minute walk every morning and to contact friends through Facebook at least once a week. These are both low-intensity, low-risk actions that might result in surprising improvements in her mood, as well as an increased sense of social connection.

Scaling questions are an extremely versatile and user-friendly tool for measuring progress. The same question renders a baseline measure and an indication of progress, depending on when it is used. For example, asking, *"On a scale of 1* *to 10—with 1 being not motivated at all and 10 being the most motivated you've ever been—how motivated are you to solve this problem?"* during the first meeting with a student provides a quick, easily understood measure of the starting point. Asking that same question in subsequent meetings allows you (and the student) to track progress. By inviting students to scale their experiences, you can reduce the chance of all-or-none thinking and help students recognize the importance of small changes.

The following are some sample scaling and follow-up questions that can be helpful in talking with students.

- *"On a scale of 1 to 10—with 1 being unwilling to take action to improve your grade and 10 being willing to do whatever it takes—what number would you give yourself right now?"* . . . *"What number would your instructor give you?"* . . . *"Okay, you've said she'd give you a 5; what would she need to see change in you for her to think you are at a 6?"*

- *"On a scale of 1 to 10—with 1 being not sad at all and 10 being as sad as you've ever been—how sad are you right now?"* . . . *"Okay, you're at a 7, that sounds significant, and yet it's impressive that you're not any higher than that. What's helping you stay at a 7 instead of an 8? . . . What could you do to get to a 6?"*

- *"Last time we talked, you said your confusion about your major was at a 9; you were almost completely confused and were even considering dropping out. You had a great idea about talking to a couple of juniors you know about how they finally chose their majors. Did you get the chance to do that? Terrific! So where would you rate your indecision this week?"* . . . *"Eight? That's great—you came down a whole point. That's tremendous progress for one week. What might help you move even further toward choosing a major or being okay with not choosing right now?"*

Scaling questions are extremely useful and flexible. They can be used from the first meeting to the last and can be constructed around virtually any issue. They help maintain perspective and offer opportunities to celebrate even small changes.

Cognitive-Behavioral Helping

Cognitive-Behavioral Therapy (CBT) is well known and well respected in the counseling field for generating effective and empirically supported treatments for a wide range of mental health concerns. For readers who are familiar with cognitive-behavioral protocols, the idea of student affairs professionals incorporating CBT principles into their practice might seem over-reaching—that is, far too "therapeutic." Attempting cognitive-behavioral *therapy* would be dangerous and unethical, but there are aspects of the conceptual model and quite a number of cognitive-behavioral *techniques* that can be readily adapted for the kinds of helping student affairs professionals provide. In other words, you do not have to be a cognitive-behavioral therapist to use or and benefit from these principles.

Conceptual Framework

The conceptual model is straightforward and can be captured in plain language. The model maintains that there are reciprocal relationships among our thoughts, feelings, behaviors, physiology, and interpersonal/environmental contexts (Beck, 1995; Padesky & Greenberger, 1995). Together, these elements create, enhance, and maintain our experiences. One element does not "cause" another (as in thoughts causing feelings); rather, these five elements operate together, influencing and encouraging one another. The elements tend to cluster, with certain kinds of thoughts encouraging certain kinds of behaviors, which foster certain kinds of emotions, which support certain physiological responses, and all of which influence and are influenced by the interpersonal/environmental context.

For example, a student who is feeling down is more likely to think negatively about herself, others, and her future (Beck, Rush, Shaw, & Emery, 1979). Her negative feelings and critical, pessimistic thinking in turn may reduce her motivation to do much. Lacking a sense of motivation, she might decline to go out with her friends or attend a student organization meeting. Bypassing those activities diminishes her opportunity for positive social interaction and creates more uninterrupted time for negative thinking and unsatisfying feelings to take hold. Moreover, if she lies around in her residence hall most of the day (thinking negatively and feeling bad), she may have trouble sleeping. Without enough sleep, she may feel even less motivated the next day to engage in coursework or connect with friends. She may then use her lack of motivation as justification for more self-criticism—and to feel bad, stay home, avoid her friends, and stare down another sleepless night.

In our day-to-day lives, we tend not to distinguish among these individual elements; they become so tightly knit that we experience their combined effect without truly appreciating how each element contributes to an overall experience. (A wave is composed of droplets of water, but when a wave is rushing over us, it is not really the droplets we notice.) Although the example here is a distressing one, the model itself is optimistic in that it posits that a change in one element (usually most easily achieved by altering behaviors or thoughts) will prompt changes, in a similar direction, in the other elements. If the student in the example chose not to stay in but, rather, to meet her friends for dinner and a movie, her experience might be quite different. She might confide in one of the friends that she has been down. The friend might comfort her and remind her of some of her positive qualities. Experiencing a sense of connection with her friend and thinking more positively about herself, the student might return to her room, tired from a full day's activity and primed for a reasonable night's sleep. The next morning, she might feel better able to face her responsibilities and opportunities. The model does not suggest that a single, important factor (thoughts or behavior) determines our experience; rather, it is the compounding influence of the five elements interacting with one another.

Given the important role that thoughts and behaviors can play in activating change, strategies for modifying thoughts and behavior are prominent in the model. A number of those strategies are described in the skills section that follows, but first we will consider two important aspects of the conceptual model: collaboration and guided discovery. Both pertain to the mind-set that helpers should adopt to facilitate the change process.

Collaboration is a fundamental principle in Cognitive-Behavioral Therapy and is the centerpiece of the helping relationship (Beck, 1995). Collaboration typically conjures up images of a good-spirited partnership, cooperation, and teamwork, and that is exactly what it means here. Helping, in this framework, is an active process that requires you to seek a balanced alliance with students in which you neither dominate nor fail to fully engage. It involves "mutual problem solving rather one-sided decision making" (Padesky & Greenberger, 1995, p. 9). You must be present and active but not overpowering. Collaboration is a dynamic process, continuously negotiated between the helper and those helped. To maintain a true collaboration, you will have to ask students their opinions (not only about their concerns but also about how you can help them), seek feedback about how the process is going, and be willing to adjust your impressions or actions on the basis of what students tell you. Collaboration increases the likelihood that you are working on shared goals, decreases the potential for misunderstandings, and fosters a sense of agency and self-direction in the students you help.

Guided discovery is a process in which counselors act as guides, encouraging clients to engage in personal discovery, to explore their own experiences to better understand the ways in which the five elements of their experiences are interconnected. Guided discovery can be a useful frame for student affairs practice as well. Being an effective guide is not about telling others what to think or what to do; rather, it is about skillfully drawing their attention to details so they can consider and more fully appreciate the significance of those details.

Socratic dialogue is a key tool in guided discovery. Sometimes Socratic dialogue is characterized as using questions to change another person's mind. That description is close but inaccurate in two ways. First, questions are only one part of the process. Socratic dialogue is not interrogation; it is conversation. Second, the goal is not to force change but to invite exploration. Used in this collaborative way, Socratic dialogue facilitates guided discovery. Padesky and Greenberger (1995) outline four steps in Socratic dialogue:

1. **Ask informational questions** that clarify the details of students' concerns. This helps make the concerns concrete and understandable for both you and the student. Sometimes

students present their concerns in broad strokes: "My relationship is terrible." "I'm depressed." "I'm freaking out." To effectively address their concerns, you must get the specifics.

2. **Listen** carefully and empathically. Refrain from drawing speedy conclusions by staying curious and open to hearing something unexpected. Your role here is not to evaluate the circumstances of students' lives but to impartially invite them to do so.

3. **Summarize** what you are hearing. Reflect and clarify what students tell you. Summarizing allows you to check that you are accurately understanding what you are hearing, and it brings together the details in ways that allow students to hear them all together and perhaps make new connections.

4. **Ask synthesizing or analytical questions.** This step sounds more complicated than it is. Synthesizing and analytical questions are questions such as *"What do you make of all this?"* and *"When you put those pieces together, what do you think?"* and *"How does all this fit with your idea that . . . ?"* Synthesizing and analytical questions invite students to reconsider what they know and put together information they already have in new ways that might open up new possibilities.

Cognitive-Behavioral Skills

CBT uses a wide range of strategies to help clients make positive changes. The five strategies below are straightforward, easily understandable, and broadly applicable. You can incorporate them into your helping conversations with students or recommend them to students as self-help strategies.

Monitoring self-talk—invite students to pay attention to how they talk to themselves, to track their self-talk. Each of us has an ongoing inner monologue, and noticing its tone and content can be instructive. In times of distress, inner monologues can become both more negative and more active. When a student is struggling with low self-esteem, he is probably reminding himself more often about his flaws, and exaggerating their number and magnitude. If you can help him notice that he has a harsh critic as his constant companion (hurling insults and anticipating negative outcomes), he may be able to see a connection between his self-talk and his low self-esteem. If he can see the connection, invite him to question the validity of what he tells himself.

Assessing risk-to-resource ratio—Freeman, Simon, Beutler, and Arkowitz (1989) note that when we enter new or potentially threatening situations, we ask ourselves two questions: What are my risks? What are my resources? How we answer those questions strongly influences our experience. If a student overfocuses on risks—or inflates the threat they represent or their likelihood of occurring—she needlessly increases her anxiety. She might, however, accurately assess her risks but underestimate her resources—both the internal and external supports available to her, as well as their capacity to neutralize the threats she perceives. Conversely, a student might fail to notice risks (or might dismiss their significance) and overestimate resources (or their effectiveness), and thus pursue imprudent behaviors. Inviting students to realistically appraise the balance of risk and resource can effectively moderate both extremes.

Activity scheduling—When students are distressed, especially when they are feeling overwhelmed or unmotivated, variations on CBT's activity scheduling can be very useful (Friedberg & McClure, 2002). Most students are well acquainted with schedule books or daily planners (print or electronic), and rely on them to organize their busy lives, so the strategy is easy to introduce. You might simply say to a student, *"As you talk about how overwhelmed you're feeling, I'm wondering if we could look at your daily schedule and get a good look at what all you've got going on."* If the student has a schedule book, review what is in it and inquire about other obligations and activities that are not written down. This process provides useful information, but probably nothing new to you or the student. What might be novel, and helpful, is to consider the balance of mastery and pleasure in the student's day-to-day experience. A sense of mastery or accomplishment derives from meeting obligations, completing tasks, and developing skills. Such activities may or may not be pleasant, but they are rewarding. They include doing homework, practicing a new language, cross-training at the gym, paying bills, and so forth. Sources of pleasure are usually much more readily identifiable—friends, food, romance, hobbies—but they vary from person to person. The notion here is that a balance between mastery and pleasure produces a sense of both satisfaction and motivation.

When students are struggling, consider inviting them to evaluate the balance between mastery and pleasure in their lives. You can simply explain the concept and ask the students to label each activity in their schedule with an M or a P. Students may want to rate the extent of mastery and pleasure derived from the activities. A 10-point scale is an easy way to do this. A student might appear to have a good balance of Ms and Ps, but after rating the activities, he might realize that his "pleasure" activities are not really very pleasing to him. With such data in hand, students can decide if they want to adjust the balance by deliberately scheduling more (or fewer) M or P activities.

Distraction is an underrated coping strategy. Students will encounter problems that are not quickly solved; they will also find themselves, at times, stymied by relatively manageable problems. In both cases, you should make sure they do not overlook the value of a bit of respite. Getting away from a problem—physically or psychologically—can make a world of difference. Not only can intentional distraction provide temporary relief from painful situations, it can also improve subsequent problem-solving efforts. In the midst of distressing situations, students can overfocus on the source of their concerns (a threat, loss, or transgression) and its consequences, both real and anticipated. Such a mind-set does not engender the flexibility needed for good problem solving. In fact, the more intense our emotions, the more constricted our focus—this is the phenomenon commonly called "tunnel vision."

Intentional distraction can be an effective antidote. Useful options include "physical activity, social contact, work, play or visual imagery" (Young & Beck, 1980, p. 20). Note that intentional distraction is not the same as denying a problem. And it is usually not a viable long-term strategy for substantial concerns. It is most useful as one piece of a larger, purposeful response.

Coping cards—Some students may benefit from composing self-instructions that will remind them of coping strategies and encourage them to use them (Beck, 1995, p. 213). You can collaborate with students to tailor coping cards to their unique needs and strategies, but the following list provides a model for developing the cards (Friedberg & McClure, 2002):

1. Acknowledge/accept the feelings.

2. Recognize that the situation is temporary.

3. Look at resources.

4. Initiate constructive action.

5. Think of what I would tell a friend.

A student who is very anxious about an upcoming speech she has to give in a communications course might create a coping card by writing the following on a card she can slip into her purse or a pocket and keep with her:

When I panic about my big speech, I can remember that:

1. I am really nervous and that is okay. Everybody gets nervous sometimes.

2. I won't always feel this way; I really do think it will get easier (eventually).

3. I am preparing and practicing, and that helps. I've delivered speeches before and done okay. I have friends in the class I can look at during the speech. My teacher is supportive.

4. Right this minute, I can either practice some more or—if that isn't possible or isn't going well—I should take a break. I can go exercise, call my mom, work on my history project.

5. If Jason were worried like this, I'd remind him that it's only one speech, only 6 minutes. I'd tell him he is probably going to do better than he imagines. I'd tell him it isn't going to kill him.

Cognitive-behavioral strategies provide a structure for engaging students in guided discovery. These strategies offer a means, often direct and relatively simple, by which students can examine their experiences or take constructive action. When paired with Socratic dialogue in the context of a collaborative relationship, the strategies can be effectively integrated into your work as a student affairs professional.

Mindfulness-Based Strategies

In addition to the counseling theories, student affairs staff may want to consider incorporating two relatively simple and related concepts into their practice: mindfulness and acceptance. Both are gaining increasing attention in a wide range of helping professions and may be especially well suited to supporting college students. Kabat-Zinn (2003, p. 145) defines *mindfulness* as an "awareness that emerges through paying attention on purpose, in the present moment, and nonjudgmentally to the unfolding of experience moment to moment." It is a state of mind that is the opposite of being distracted, preoccupied, "zoned out," or "on overload." It draws on the capacity almost all of us have to be more fully present in the moment. Most people can identify experiences that were totally absorbing: events or interactions during which their minds did not wander, their attention did not drift, and, as a positive consequence, their worries disappeared—even if only momentarily. Mindfulness can be a simple, widely available, and life-altering resource.

The word *mindfulness* is the English translation of one of the core teachings of Buddhist psychology that emerged approximately 2,500 years ago (Germer, Siegel, & Fulton, 2005). Thus, while mindfulness might seem tailor-made for the modern generation of overstressed multitaskers, the healing properties of being fully awake to the present moment have long been recognized. Deliberately focusing awareness on being present might seem like a bad idea during times of distress. If someone feels sad, angry, or fearful, why direct attention to those feelings?

It is reasonable to wonder about the benefit of being more fully aware of our pain, especially when so much of our culture encourages avoidance and distraction and thus, directly or indirectly, teaches us to be frightened by uncomfortable or painful thoughts and feelings. From the Buddhist perspective, however,

> Feelings like disappointment, embarrassment, irritation, resentment, anger, jealousy, and fear, instead of being bad news, are actually very clear moments that teach us where it is that we are holding back. They teach us to perk up and lean in when we feel we'd rather collapse and back away. They're like messengers that show us, with terrifying clarity, exactly where we're stuck. This very moment is the perfect teacher, and, lucky for us, it's with us wherever we are. (Chodron, 1997, p. 12)

Such ideas, though drawn here from Buddhist teachings, are compatible with the common practice in Western counseling of "leaning in" or moving toward painful experiences in order to work through them (Germer et al., 2005). Counselors recognize that, although it might seem daunting, exploring problems often helps resolve them. To lean in, however, we must allow ourselves to fully experience our reality in the moment. That is, we must stop denying, judging, or resisting our experiences long enough to fully apprehend them.

For most people, experience and judgment are tightly bound. In fact, judgment can seem inherent to experience, as if it arises almost simultaneously. If we are not practicing mindfulness, it is rare to experience *anything* without judging it. Our days may be an unending series of judgments—about other people, our circumstances, and ourselves.

As a result, our minds may routinely "dismiss the present moment in order to get somewhere else, become someone else" (Kornfield, 2000, p. 34) and, in doing so, create a gap "between how things are and how we desire them to be." This is the source of suffering (Germer et al., 2005, p. 13). It is common to speak of our thoughts "running away with" or "from" us, and Hanh (1998) conveys this all-too-common relationship: "There is a story in Zen circles about a man and a horse. The horse is galloping quickly, and it appears that the man on the horse is going somewhere important. Another man, standing alongside the road, shouts: 'Where are you going?' and the first man replies, 'I don't know! Ask the horse!'" (p. 24).

Nonjudgment is a crucial partner of mindfulness. It involves "realizing that whatever occurs is neither the beginning nor the end. It is just the same kind of normal human experience that's been happening to everyday people from the beginning of time" (Chodron, 1997, p. 27) If we continue judging and criticizing, turning our attention inward can intensify our suffering. That is, if a student leans into her sadness about a recent break-up but does so filled with self-criticism or recriminations of herself or the former partner, she is not likely to benefit. Neither is she likely to truly "see" her experience; she will simply solidify her judgments and increase her pain. Alternatively, if she experiences her sadness as simply that and embraces it, she can be "with" her emotions and, over time, realize that "feelings are creations of (her) mind's view of things, and that maybe that view is not complete" (Kabat-Zinn, 1994, p. 245). If the student is patient and forgiving with herself and others, she might eventually know herself in new and meaningful ways as a result of the break-up.

In partnership, then, mindfulness and nonjudgment reduce suffering and can lead to peace. If we are fully present, we cannot be lost in our thoughts; consequently, we are freed from the suffering our judgments cause. Likewise, if we are not judging (others, our circumstances, or ourselves), we are not as agitated and therefore less inclined to escape the present moment through reverie (pleasant or unpleasant). Freeing ourselves of judgment is not about permitting reckless or destructive behavior, or setting aside values and commitments. Mindfulness and nonjudgment are rooted in self-discipline. When practiced in ways that honor their true intention, these ways of being reduce harm to self and others.

Acceptance modifies nonjudgment slightly by adding "a measure of kindness or friendliness" (Germer et al., 2005, p. 7). Hanh (1998) explains that "embracing" is an important element in the calming effect of mindfulness practice. He describes the process this way, using anger as an example: "We hold our anger in our two arms like a mother holding her crying baby. Our mindfulness embraces our emotion, and this alone can calm our anger and ourselves" (p. 26).

Hayes has developed an entire approach to helping (ACT, or Acceptance and Commitment Therapy) built on the notion of acceptance as an antidote to suffering. He cautions, however, that because most people are unfamiliar with "active forms" of acceptance, the concept can be easily misunderstood (Hayes & Smith, 2005, p. 7). It is not a kind of "nihilistic self-defeat" (Hayes & Smith, 2005, p. 7) in which we give up, but rather a loving choice to stop struggling with our experiences, to stop judging them harshly and fighting with them.

Through active acceptance, "we can learn to meet whatever arises with curiosity and not make it such a big deal. Instead of struggling against the force of confusion, we could meet it and relax" (Chodron, 1997, p. 27). Hayes and Smith pair acceptance with commitment to personal values (2005). Their approach encourages us to stop postponing our dreams, to stop avoiding our lives, and to pursue what is most meaningful to us even as we embrace what is true right now with considerable compassion.

Consider, for example, an undecided sophomore, Andy. He is thinking about dropping out of college because he cannot answer with any certainty the recurring questions "What are you majoring in? What are you going to do after college?" However, Andy loves being at college, is involved in a variety of service learning activities that bring him joy, and is maintaining a B average. The frustration and embarrassment he feels about being undeclared may be coming from his belief that he "should" know by now where he is headed. If Andy could accept that is he engaged in the process of deciding, without generating judgments about how long that process should take or what its outcome should be, he would be better able to embrace what is true for him and thus reduce or even eliminate his suffering. Acceptance does not mean that he would not take action to move forward in the process of deciding. In fact, Andy might be more motivated to explore his options if he felt less pressured to determine the outcome.

Mindfulness, nonjudgment, and acceptance are simultaneously simple and deeply complex concepts. They are intertwined with other Buddhist principles and practices such as compassion, loving-kindness, gratitude, and living peacefully in the world. Understanding these ideas can take a lifetime of study and practice. But you don't have to become a Buddhist or devote a considerable amount of your life to these concepts to reap their benefits. Germer and colleagues (2005) identify three levels at which therapists have integrated mindfulness into their practice: (1) personally practicing mindfulness; (2) using a theoretical framework informed by mindfulness principles; and (3) explicitly teaching mindfulness. These three approaches offer a model for student affairs practitioners. The following are practical suggestions within each level for integrating mindfulness, nonjudgment, and acceptance into your work.

Practicing Mindfulness

To understand mindfulness, you must practice it. You could use both informal and formal mindfulness practices in your personal life. Informal practice involves a range of measures to help you become more mindful in day-to-day life, from simply practicing bringing your awareness fully into the moment, to limiting the amount of time spent multitasking, to setting a timer that alerts you to bring your attention back to the present moment. It can be as simple as turning your attention to your breath whenever you hear the campus carillon or every time you stop at a red light. What is important is interrupting the chatter in your mind that distracts you from the present moment.

Formal mindfulness practice can entail establishing a routine in which you set aside a designated time, several times a week or every day, to do nothing but attempt to stay in the present moment. You could practice a daily meditation or reflection, mindful eating, mindful walking, even mindful dishwashing—the avenues are endless. Numerous useful books and CDs are available. Formal practice might also involve finding a teacher and joining a group that meditates or does other mindfulness-based work together. You might bring such practice into your professional development or supervision process to enhance your awareness of, and compassion for, yourself as a professional and the challenging work you do.

As Bien (2006, p. 133) writes, "To embody love and compassion, it is first of all important to exercise these capacities toward ourselves." The more compassion you have for yourself, the more capable you will be of extending it to your students. Imagine how you might feel if at the end of a particularly demanding day, you said to yourself, *"I did the best I could; I am fortunate to work every day with college students. Even when it is difficult, I am lucky to have a role in helping students find meaning in life, learn important skills and concepts, have fun, and build lifetime friendships. Tomorrow I will begin again."*

Campus wellness centers are often in tune with the benefits of mindfulness. Many offer yoga, tai chi, qigong, and other such classes to students and staff. Mini-versions or introductions to these practices can be scheduled in residence halls or incorporated into staff meetings or student leadership retreats.

Using a Theoretical Framework Informed by Mindfulness Principles

While there are no specific mindfulness-based models of student development, you can incorporate mindfulness into the way you conceptualize students and their experiences. Bien (2006, p. 63) writes, "Mindfulness is entering fully into each experience, knowing that this experience is precisely what it is and neither more nor less, knowing that it is impermanent, and knowing that you are more and larger for the experience." Using this idea as a touchstone in your work could have a considerable calming effect on you, which your colleagues and students might notice and value. Grounding your professional practice in mindfulness would likely help you convey your "true presence" to others and enable you to offer them deep listening (Bien, 2006, p. xv), which they might not easily find elsewhere in our overly busy and highly distracted world.

Teaching Mindfulness

You could also consider bringing mindfulness concepts into your conversations with students, incorporating them into your helping process, or even setting up workshops and study groups for students on this topic. Talking with students about what they experience when they are caught up in judging themselves or others is a fairly easy and natural way to bring in mindfulness. Encouraging students to consider how often they are just going through the motions or operating on autopilot is something they can easily understand. You might also want to try bolder, more creative approaches. For example, consider sharing this story with students:

> What if I told you that you had at your disposal wondrous, magical, mystical powers? In fact, you do have such powers. Only, they are powers that you may tend to overlook or underestimate. You overlook them because you are like the king's son in the Lotus Sutra, who wandered the world as a beggar, not knowing that precious gems, capable of meeting all of his needs easily and abundantly, had been sewn into the lining of his own clothes. You have within you all that you need to be happy, to

find your way out of suffering and become a free, joyful, enlightened human being. (Bien, 2006, pp. 109–110)

In the counseling and psychological communities, mindfulness practice is increasing at such a rate—and amassing enough empirical support—to suggest the professions may be on the brink of a new model for psychotherapy (Germer et al., 2005). It makes sense that student affairs professionals should be in the forefront of supporting and encouraging full engagement with life and the self-awareness it fosters. Chodron (1997) writes that "the way to dissolve our resistance to life is to meet it face to face" (p. 30). The very business of student affairs is helping students meet life face to face—fully and optimistically. Mindfulness, acceptance, and nonjudgment are tools that can support that task.

Setting and Maintaining Boundaries

This chapter began with the dual recognition that college students, like everyone else, need help navigating life's demands, and that student affairs professionals occupy a unique place on a continuum of available help—somewhere between the support of family and friends and the clinical services of licensed mental health professionals. To effectively fulfill that role, the student affairs professional needs strong communication and facilitation skills. This chapter described how three well-established counseling theories and mindfulness can help you build those skills. The purpose of the chapter is to help you draw on this information and integrate counseling theories and skills into your work. The chapter closes with a word of caution.

Because your professional life is situated somewhere between social supports and clinical services, the boundaries for "helping" can be murky. You are not a professional counselor; that is clear and easy enough to understand, at least on a conceptual level. On a day-to-day basis (in the moment with a student), however, what distinguishes effective student support from counseling is often a lot less clear. Much as a definitive answer or formula for distinguishing between the two would be comforting, one does not exist. NASPA and ACPA's *Principles of Good Practice for Student Affairs* (1997) and ACPA's *Statement of Ethical Principles and Standards* (2006) can guide your work. In particular, the ethical principles that form the foundation of ACPA's standards—beneficence, justice, autonomy, fidelity, and avoidance of harm—must be paramount in your decision making. But questions about how much and what kinds of help you can and should offer will be recurring concerns in your professional practice. The more you engage those questions—in supervision, in discussions with peers and mentors, and in your ongoing professional development—the more clarity you will gain, not necessarily about the ultimate answers but about a process for answering.

The first step is to identify the end points of the continuum of helping that you must navigate: What is too little? What is too much? You must develop a way of recognizing when the help you are offering is insufficient support and when it crosses into counseling services you are not qualified or authorized to provide. The following list offers some indicators. You will need to adapt the list to your position in conjunction with your role and supervisor.

Offering Insufficient Help

The risk here is that you prematurely close off conversations with students, quickly referring them to someone else on campus when they tell you about their concerns. While this strategy guards against the possibility that you might overstep your role, it may have unintended negative consequences. Not only will instant referral sometimes cause you to fail to sufficiently help students or build your skills, it also may decrease the likelihood that the students you refer will accept the referrals or ask again for your help. If students perceive that you are not interested in talking to them, their unsatisfying experiences with you could lead them to spread the word—particularly among smaller, marginalized populations on your campus who may already feel vulnerable and cautious about seeking help. Pay attention to the following potential indicators:

1. The student seems to shut down in conversation with you. His or her voice tone and eye contact change.

2. The student retracts a concern or apologizes for bringing it up.

3. The student leaves the meeting early or fails to return.

Students can exhibit the same indicators if you are overstepping your role and they perceive you as intrusive. While this can be confusing, it is true, and you may need help from your supervisor to sort it out. Pairing these indicators with an examination of your actions can help you determine if you are providing insufficient help to students.

Overstepping Your Role

The danger here is that you might go beyond good student affairs practice and attempt to help students in ways that, ethically, should be done only by licensed mental health professionals. What constitutes overstepping can be difficult to discern; however, the following indicators can alert you that you are at risk of crossing a boundary or have already done so:

1. You feel flattered by the idea of being the only one the student trusts or can talk to.

2. You are tempted to bend rules, break policies, or keep information from your supervisor to go on helping the student.

3. You are providing atypical levels of support and contact (e.g., private phone calls, e-mails, or meetings that are not normally part of the services you offer) or in times, places, or venues that are not available to all students (e.g., by private cell phone or instant messaging).

4. You feel overwhelmed, personally invested, or important to the student in ways that other professionals (your peers or supervisor) would probably find troubling.

5. You are attempting to help the student come to some deep insight or explore personal concerns in depth.

6. You believe you know the right answers for the student.

While helping students is not always an easy task, it is a rich and rewarding one.

As a student affairs professional, you are in a unique position to help students every day. Negotiating your role requires strong communication and facilitation skills, and an ongoing effort to work fully within the boundaries of your profession. To provide the best services within those boundaries, you will need ongoing supervision, consultation, and professional development. Be sure to seek guidance from your immediate supervisor, and establish a good relationship with your campus counseling center staff.

References

American College Personnel Association. (2006). Statement of ethical principles and standards. Retrieved September 28, 2009, from www2.myacpa.org/ethics/statement.php

American College Personnel Association / National Association for Student Personnel Administrators. (1997). *Principles of good practice for student affairs*. Retrieved September 28, 2009, from *www.acpa.nche.edu/pgp/princip8.htm*

Beck, A. T., Rush, A. J., Shaw, B. F., & Emery, G. (1979). *Cognitive therapy of depression*. New York: Guilford.

Beck, J. (1995). *Cognitive therapy: Basics and beyond*. New York: Guilford.

Bien, T. (2006). *Mindful therapy: A guide for therapists and helping professionals*. Somerville, MA: Wisdom Publications.

Burkard, A., Cole, D. C., Ott, M., & Stoflet, T. (2005). Entry-level competencies of new student affairs professionals: A Delphi Study. *NASPA Journal, 42,* 283–309.

Chodron, P. (1997). *When things fall apart: Heart advice for difficult times*. Boston: Shambhala.

De Jong, P. (2001, February). *How to build solutions with clients*. Paper presented at South Dakota State University, Brookings, SD.

De Jong, P., & Berg, I. K. (1998). *Interviewing for solutions*. Pacific Grove, CA: Brooks/Cole.

De Jong, P., & Berg, I. K. (2002). *Interviewing for solutions*. (3rd ed.) Pacific Grove, CA: Brooks/Cole.

Fisher, D. (2007). *Communication in organizations*. (2nd ed.). Mumbai: Jaico.

Freeman, A., Simon, K. M., Beutler, L. E., & Arkowitz, H. (1989). *Comprehensive handbook of cognitive therapy*. New York: Springer.

Friedberg, R., & McClure, J. M. (2002). *Clinical practice of cognitive therapy with children and adolescents*. New York: Guilford.

Germer, C. K., Siegel, R. D., & Fulton, P. R. (2005). *Mindfulness and psychotherapy*. New York: Guilford.

Hanh, T. N. (1998). *The heart of the Buddha's teaching: Transforming suffering into peace, joy, and liberation*. New York: Broadway Books.

Hayes, S. C., & Smith, S. (2005). *Get out of your mind and into your life: The new acceptance and commitment therapy*. Oakland, CA: Harbinger.

Hazler, R. J. (2007). Person-centered therapy. In D. Capuzzi & D. R. Cross (Eds.), *Counseling and psychotherapy: Theories and interventions* (4th ed) (pp. 18–215). Columbus, OH: Pearson.

Kabat-Zinn, J. (1994). *Wherever you go, there you are: Mindfulness meditation in everyday life*. New York: Hyperion.

Kabat-Zinn, J. (2003). Mindfulness-based interventions in context: Past, present, and future. *Clinical Psychology: Science and Practice, 10*(2), 144–156.

Kornfield, J. (2000). *After the ecstasy, the laundry: How the heart grows wise on the spiritual path*. New York: Bantam Books.

Locke, D. C., Meyers, J. C., & Herr, E. L. (Eds.). (2001). *The handbook of counseling*. Los Angeles: Sage.

Meier, S.T. & Davis, S.R. (2011). *The elements of counseling* (7ᵗʰ ed). Belmont, CA: Brooks/Cole.

Murdock, N.L. (2009). *Theories of counseling and psychotherapy: A case approach.* (2ⁿᵈ ed.). Upper Saddle River, New Jersey: Pearson/Merrill.

Padesky, C., & Greenberger, D. (1995). *Clinician's guide to mind over mood.* New York: Guilford.

Prochaska, J. O., & Norcross, J. C. (2010). *Systems of psychotherapy: A transtheoretical analysis* (7ᵗʰ ed.). Belmont, CA: Brooks/Cole.

Reynolds, A. L. (2009). *Helping college students: Developing essential support skills for student affairs practice.* San Francisco: Jossey-Bass.

Sue, D. W., & Sue, D. (2008). *Counseling the culturally diverse: Theory and practice* (5ᵗʰ ed.). Hoboken, NJ: Wiley & Sons.

Sweeney, T. J. (2001). Counseling: Historical origins and philosophical roots. In D. C. Locke, J. C. Meyers, & E. L. Herr (Eds.), *The handbook of counseling.* Los Angeles: Sage.

Tolan, J. (2003). *Skills in person-centered counseling and psychotherapy.* Los Angeles: Sage.

Wickman, S. A. (1999). "Making something of it": An analysis of the conversation and language of Carl Rogers and Gloria. Unpublished doctoral dissertation, Southern Illinois University, Carbondale.

Wickman, S., & Campbell, C. (2003, Spring). An analysis of how Carl Rogers enacted client-centered conversation with Gloria. *Journal of Counseling and Development, 81,* 178–184.

Young, J. E., & Beck, A. T. (1980). *Cognitive therapy scale manual.* Retrieved September 28, 2009, from www.academyofct.org/upload/documents/CTRS_Manual.pdf

CHAPTER 3

Multiple Marginalized Identity Development and Depression
Victoria

Chris Linder, Nona L. Wilson, and Ruth Harper

As director of the Women's Resource Center, you do a lot of presentations on campus—in classrooms, for student organizations, and in the residence halls. Victoria Gonzales has attended several of these presentations and has begun to visit your office on a regular basis. She appreciates the way you listen, validate, and support all aspects of her identity, and she shares with you her difficulty finding places in her life that allow her to be her whole self. She describes her experience this way: "I feel like I have all these borders inside me where I don't understand certain parts, and I always feel like I'm fighting to emerge." Victoria identifies as a bisexual Latina from a working-class family with some White and Jewish ancestry. Every aspect of her identity is extremely important to her, and she has trouble finding people and organizations that support all her identities together. When Victoria visits the Latino Cultural Center on campus, she does not feel supported as a multiracial person; when she visits the GLBT Resource Center, she feels marginalized as bisexual because people want her to "pick a side."

Victoria experiences similar invalidation and marginalization within her own family. "Being multiethnic, I've had identity issues my whole life. The step side of the family is racist against Jews. I'm Jewish. My dad's side of the family is racist against White people. I'm White. My mother's side of the family is racist against Mexicans. I'm Mexican. When I was younger I yelled at my grandfather because he used the word 'spic'—I was like, 'What the hell do you think I am?'"

Victoria deals with racism and homophobia on a regular basis, both on and off campus. She describes growing up in northern Colorado as extremely challenging because of her multiple marginalized identities and people's misperceptions about her. "When I was little, I didn't feel accepted at school. Chicano children made fun of me for being too White. They're like, 'You're not Mexican, look at your skin.' I'd be like, 'Okay, well, you want to meet my father?' And so I'd have to introduce them to my father to prove that I was, in fact, Mexican." After her experiences at predominantly Latino schools, Victoria moved to another part of town where she went to school with more White kids—there she was made fun of for being poor. She describes the experience, saying, "For half of my childhood, I grew up on the north side of town, and they made fun of me for being White, but when I transferred to a White school, they made fun of me for being Mexican and poor. So, I was just like, 'I want to go back to school with the Mexicans, because at least they didn't make fun of me for being poor, too.'"

With regard to her experiences on campus, Victoria says that the community is "just so White. All my teachers are White, all my bosses are White," leading her to feel somewhat frustrated and alone. She feels validated in her Ethnic Studies classes and as a member of a student organization that focuses on multiracial identities. "Everyone else thinks I'm, like, crazy because I always talk about all these social justice issues, and people just don't get it, so I feel kind of like an outcast because of it."

However, Victoria says, "sometimes people in Ethnic Studies are bothered by my sexuality." She tells about trying to come out as bisexual while in junior and senior high school: "I tried to come out about my sexuality two times. In junior high, I lost all of my friends, who were, like, 'I'm bi, too,' and then after awhile, they were saying, 'You're still bi?' and it just wasn't cool anymore to be bi, so they weren't cool with me. I guess they felt sexually threatened by me. Then in high school, I tried to come out, and my best friend just acted weird around me all the time, so I pretended it was a phase. But I finally came out to everyone here on campus—except for my family—last October, and I'm actually coming out to my father in two weeks when I go home for break."

Through your visits with Victoria, you are aware that these identity struggles have taken a toll on her emotional well-being. She feels exhausted and burned out by constantly shifting identities, depending on the context. "When I'm around White people, I need to act White; when I'm around Mexican people, I try to act Mexican. If I'm around gay people, I feel more gay." Recently, Victoria shared that she feels she's going crazy because so few people validate and understand her experience. When she talks about things that concern her, people tell her she's too sensitive or that she exaggerates things. When you encourage Victoria to visit the counseling center, she says that she does not feel safe there. Because so few people on campus seem to understand her experiences, she feels alone and wonders if, in fact, she *is* too sensitive. "What would a counselor do? Validate that I am crazy and being way too touchy?"

Victoria describes the mental exhaustion and depression she often suffers: "When I leave my house feeling prepared to deal with things that day, I can challenge others' perceptions and ignorance. When I'm in a bad mood or I'm feeling depressed, or when I haven't really had time to focus in the morning, I'm not prepared to respond to what happens. This is exhausting and makes me just want to stay home by myself and sleep."

Student Development Response

Victoria's experience is not uncommon. Many women of color and queer women experience similar marginalization in organizations across the country, both on college campuses and in the community at large. In fact, even the feminist movement has a long history of racism and White privilege (Smith, 1980). As a result, women of color often feel alienated from offices such as yours unless specific efforts are made to reach out to their communities. Additionally, identity development theories generally focus on one marginalized identity at a time, making it difficult to accurately discuss situations like Victoria's, where she is experiencing marginalization regarding multiple important aspects of her identity.

The complexity of multiple identities and the contexts in which individuals operate cannot be described in the linear structure offered by early identity development theories in student affairs (Abes & Kasch, 2007). Jones (1997) led student affairs scholarship in understanding the complexity of multiple dimensions of identity by exploring identity development in female college students through a constructivist grounded theory approach. By looking into the ways college women understand their experiences—as opposed to the identities that are imposed on them from outside—Jones proposes ten key influences on the construction of identity (1997, p. 379):

1. Relative salience of identity dimensions in relation to difference

2. Multiple ways in which race matters

3. Multiple layers of identity

4. Gender braiding with other dimensions

5. Importance of cultural identifications and cultural values

6. Influence of family and background experiences

7. Current experiences and situational factors

8. Relational, inclusive values and guiding personal beliefs

9. Career decisions and future planning

10. Search for identity

Building on Jones's grounded theory study, Jones and McEwen (2000) created a model of multiple dimensions of identity development to help scholar-practitioners understand and explain identity development in more nuanced, accurate ways. This model highlights the way core identities and contextual influences intersect with outside identities to reveal a more fluid model of identity development. Women in this study described their core identity as being their "inner identity" or "inside self" as opposed to their "outside self" (p. 408). The women described core identity as having multiple intersections, with the salience of each identity dependent on the context in which it was experienced. The model's strength lies in its description of both dominant and marginalized identities as they connect with the salience of identity dimensions (Jones & McEwen, 2000).

Abes, Jones, and McEwen (2007) explored students' meaning-making capacity related to the identity development of lesbian college students. They described a "meaning-making filter" (p. 7) of varying complexities that allows contextual influences to pass through, providing an understanding of the way students make meaning of their layered identities. Borrowing from Baxter Magolda's (2001) self-authorship model, three participants' stories illustrated formulaic, transitional, and foundational meaning-making capacities integrated with identity perceptions. The student who displayed the formulaic meaning-making capacity allowed stereotypes or beliefs about identities to pass through her filter without making meaning of them. The transitional student saw contradictions between what she believed and the stereotypes, and filtered some information to make her own meaning before integrating ideas into her identities. The student associated with the foundational meaning-making capacity filtered stereotypes and presented her identities in the same manner in every environment (Abes et al., 2007).

Abes and Kasch (2007) reanalyzed the data from the meaning-making study using queer theory and suggested that scholars explore student development theory as a fluid process and analyze it from critical perspectives, focusing on how the development of marginalized identities leads to resistance toward the dominant power structures. Students are forced to understand their marginalized identities more quickly than their dominant identities because they must make meaning of those marginalized aspects of self in order to counter the negative messages they receive about marginalized identities being abnormal and undesirable.

Each of these explorations of multiple identity development encourages student affairs practitioners and scholars to think about the ways students develop differently depending on context, intersections of identities, and cognitive development. The models imply that development is an individual and unique process; helping students develop wholly is a complex task that cannot be understood by merely layering linear identity models on top of one another.

Counseling Response

Victoria says that she is skeptical about a counselor's ability to help her, adding that she does not believe it is "safe" for her to go to the counseling center. Given what she tells you about feeling exhausted, overwhelmed, and depressed, however, you will need to help her revisit the idea of counseling. You can build credibility with her, and increase the likelihood that she will accept the referral, by striving to be as skilled a helper (listening, supporting, encouraging) as you can be at your skill level and within your professional boundaries. Solution-Focused helping is grounded in the idea that people "have what it takes to resolve their difficulties," and it offers an ideal framework for your conversations with Victoria (Sklare, 1997, p. 11).

Although some people around Victoria are not aware of or do not value all aspects of her identity, her unique ethnic, sexual, and socioeconomic characteristics are sources of strength, increased empathy, and diverse, rich perspective. Moreover, Victoria is intelligent, motivated, resourceful, and involved. She is self-reflective, competent, courageous, and willing to extend and test herself academically and socially. In other words, although Victoria is struggling, she has a wealth of assets. By noticing and valuing her strengths—while you attend to her concerns—you can convey to Victoria that you are interested in her as whole person.

Helping Victoria look for exceptions and solutions should never be used as a means to excuse the social injustices and inequalities that plague our society and that are manifesting themselves in Victoria's life. She is dealing with issues that *could* fragment, exhaust, and overwhelm her. Your use of the Solution-Focused helping model to highlight her strengths is not intended to question the truth of her concerns. Rather, because the issues she is contending with are, in fact, overwhelming a times, it is all the more important that she stay in touch with her strengths. Clarifying her goals, supporting her sense of competence, helping her savor moments of respite or success, and encouraging her to seek out positive experiences and affirmations—hallmarks of Solution-Focused helping—can empower Victoria without trivializing her circumstances.

Listening

Listening in a Solution-Focused manner means "hearing [the student's] story without filtering it through your own frame of reference" (De Jong & Berg, 2008, p. 21). This means that as Victoria tells you what is happening with her, you do not, for example, react defensively to her criticisms of the university or the student affairs division. Neither do you share a similar experience another student had. You maintain an open and nonjudgmental attitude and refrain from problem solving. You listen.

Victoria has a lot going on in her life that is causing her distress. She is also an energetic and insightful woman, so she might have a lot to say when she comes to see you. You will want to demonstrate concern for and interest in her through careful and caring attention. Be especially attentive to what she reveals about who and what are important to her (De Jong & Berg, 2008, p. 21). Her interests, values, and aspirations might be embedded in her complaints and concerns; strive to listen through the descriptions of what is missing or what is not happening to hear what she wants, what matters to her. In fact, she has already conveyed some important things about herself. Being authentic matters to her; she wants to be accepted and have a sense of belonging; and she cares about social justice. Those are admirable qualities. Let Victoria know that you can hear them in her stories as she talks with you.

Eliciting Exceptions and Co-constructing Goals

Finding a break in the problem is a central strategy of Solution-Focused helping. Even the tiniest sliver of an opening will do, because then Victoria can begin to wedge her way into a better place, and, over time, carve out more and more space for her solutions. As you gain a clearer understanding of what she experiences at your college, you can explore with her times when things have not gone so badly, or even when things have gone well. In fact, Victoria might like the opportunity to talk about instances when she has felt not quite so alienated, or when she felt she connected with others in meaningful ways. Use Solution-Focused questions such as these: *"Tell me about just one day when things were a little better. What happened that day? When things are going well, what are you doing differently? What would your professor notice, perhaps? What would your girlfriend or boyfriend or best friend notice? What would your mother or father notice?"*

Eliciting exceptions to the problem (Guterman, 2006, p. 36) and identifying times when the problem could have occurred but didn't encourage optimism and help to identify directions for future action. When, for example, during a typical day on campus, does Victoria feel *least* marginalized, alone, or frustrated? What is happening at those times? Whom is she with? What are the settings that allow her to be most comfortable and open? When does she feel most herself? Can she describe events or occurrences when she felt affirmed as an entire person, rather than in just one aspect of her identity? Victoria is reflective and self-aware and will be able to provide detailed examples of positive situations. These occasions are most likely to contain the seeds of her success.

Without overstepping your role as director of the Women's Resource Center, you can ask Victoria a version of the miracle question (De Jong & Berg, 2008, p. 85): *"If a miracle happened, and you were able to be your whole self with your friends, family, and people on this campus—in both classes and co-curricular settings—what would be different?"* As Victoria envisions the possibility of better circumstances, she will begin to experience the power of change in her life. Elicit as many details as possible in this discussion; they can eventually become goals to work toward. This kind of discussion with students who are as discouraged as Victoria is can engender hope and feelings of self-efficacy.

Co-constructing Competence

In the Solution-Focused framework, you want to help Victoria see herself as competent to solve the problems she faces. (She won't single-handedly solve the larger systemic causes of her struggles, but she can significantly reduce the day-to-day toll they take on her.) A primary strategy for building students' competence is to adopt a "not knowing" stance (De Jong & Berg, 2008, p. 20). This doesn't mean pretending not to know things but rather not advocating your own assessments, advice, or ideas, and instead inviting Victoria to tell you more about any given situation and what it means to her, what it's like to be her on your campus. The fact is that no one else—including you—knows what it is like to be in her position. Her ability to make meaning of her experiences can be further explored in this way, as you "communicate an abundant, genuine curiosity" and are "informed by" the student (De Jong & Berg, 2008, p. 20).

As Victoria tells you about her experiences, you can recognize her insights and be curious about how she knows what she knows and how she has figured out the strategies she is currently using to cope. While her strategies are not perfect—she is, after all, distressed—she is still enrolled, active, and invested in succeeding in college. Those elements of her story are just as important, as well as ultimately more inspiring for her. Inviting Victoria to share what she knows and how she knows it will foster her sense of competence, demonstrate your trust in her perceptions, and remind her of her strengths.

Ideally, Victoria's sense of competence will grow and she may arrive at the point where she is willing to address the campus environment and its shortcomings for students like herself who are not White, middle-class, or heterosexual. Moving from the transitional to the foundational perspective in a meaning-making way (Abes et al., 2007), she could, for example, become a student leader in the Women's Resource Center (WRC). When you sense that such a level of engagement would not overwhelm her, you could contribute to her emerging sense of competence by letting her know that you see this leadership potential in her. This would truly affirm her full identity, benefit her in multiple ways, and offer the additional advantage of putting Victoria in a position to influence the college environment that marginalizes so many. A first step for Victoria may be to attend more WRC programs and join an event planning committee. Taking such a step can become part of her "miracle" (Guterman, 2006, p. 51).

Amplifying

Amplifying supports the forward momentum generated by discovering exceptions and occurs in at least two important ways in Solution-Focused helping.

First, Victoria can amplify her successes not only by noticing them but also by repeating them. Once she identifies an element of her solution, encourage her to do more of it. In doing so you help her transform a problem into an opportunity—which is the central motif of most great success stories. Perhaps Victoria enjoys eating breakfast in her room with her roommate, lunch in the Union with her Latina/o friends, and dinner off campus with a small group of students in the GLBT student organization she is getting to know well. These are aspects of "a really good day" by her account, but in the past she has rarely been intentional about securing them for herself. As she begins to see elements of her schedule that she can influence regularly (not necessarily control completely), Victoria can prioritize positive interactions in her day.

"Small changes have a ripple effect that expands into larger changes" (Sklare, 1997, p. 11). Suppose Victoria identifies her Ethnic Studies professor as one person with whom she can relax, a person who seems to accept, affirm, and encourage her. Can she plan to take additional courses with this professor? Can she ask him or her to be her academic advisor? Does the professor advise a student organization in which Victoria can become more involved? The idea is not to create dependency on this faculty member but to create more opportunities for Victoria to be her fully engaged self, to learn what that feels like and how to replicate that experience in other situations.

Amplifying is also a conversational strategy. You can notice and highlight Victoria's competencies as well as the exceptions to her concerns. Take a genuine interest in the exceptions she identifies and invite her to describe in detail how she helps create them.

Giving compliments is another way to amplify. You might say, *"You are remarkably adaptable, given your multiple school experiences."* By offering sincere compliments, you can potentially reframe problematic situations. Ideally, your compliments will emphasize how Victoria is already solving her problem (De Jong & Berg, 2008). The more sincere and specific you can be with Victoria in affirming what she wants to do and how she intends to do it, the more reinforcing your efforts will be.

Compliments are also a good way to close Solution-Focused conversations.

With Victoria, it will not be difficult to come up with options: *"You have amazing insights on very complicated interactions here on campus and how they affect you"* or *"I hear true dedication in your voice about doing the work you need to do to become a tremendous woman."*

Reframing allows students to see themselves "through a different (more positive) lens" (Young, 2009, p. 367). For example, in her conversation with you, Victoria shares that she feels frustrated, alone, and invalidated. Do not deny the reality of those feelings, but notice as well the positive qualities they suggest: high expectations for herself and others, and a unique identity that she is just beginning to explore. When she describes being "exhausted and burned out," you can reframe that experience to underscore her determination and dedication to the cause of equality on campus. When Victoria says that others claim that she is "too sensitive," you can explore with her the positive connotations of sensitivity, such as compassion and commitment.

Measuring Progress

Scaling questions (De Jong & Berg, 2008, pp. 106–107) will be very useful in talking with Victoria. Because she has mentioned mental exhaustion and depression, you will need to refer her to a mental health professional. As you talk with her, look for a natural opening to introduce the idea. You can say, *"I'm concerned that you mention the word depression. Do you mind if I take a moment to find out a little more about what you mean by that? On a scale of 1 to 10—with 1 being no depression at all and 10 being depression so severe that you don't want to do anything, can't enjoy what you used to, and just want to give up—what number represents where you usually are?"* You are not trying to treat depression, but you are trying to discover what she meant and how urgent the need is for referral. Be sure to talk with Victoria about what the number she selects means to her (it might mean something quite different than what you assume); then talk about the counseling center's services. Remember that Victoria has mentioned feeling "unsafe" about going to the college counseling center; by establishing credibility with her, you may be able to help her reconsider seeing a counselor. When you do refer Victoria to the counseling center, honor her trust in you by making sure that the referral is to someone you know is sensitive to and knowledgeable about the issues with which she is grappling.

Scaling questions can be used to gain perspective on many of the issues Victoria has presented; for example, with her concerns around identity: *"You say you've had identity issues all your life—with your friends, your schools, even within your family. These experiences have made you feel fragmented and misunderstood, very alone at times. I hear you say that your overall goal is to emerge as a whole person, to find more places in your life where that is possible. Just to help me understand the scope of this issue for you, would you allow me to ask a scaling question? On a scale of 1 to 10—where one is personal unity and wholeness in all areas of your life and 10 is utter chaos and complete lack of validation for your identity—which number best represents how you see yourself and your life right now?"* While this is a complex question, it can help put Victoria's situation into a context that may seem more manageable for her. She might choose to respond by scaling her experiences in each context, such as family, friends, classes, and specific student organizations. This could provide both of you with a much better understanding of her concerns and possibilities for solutions. Her response could also alert you to an urgent need for referral to a professional counselor.

For example, if Victoria, says that she is "at a 6" with regard to feeling alienated and alone at college but says that 6 is a manageable number or level, you could explore with her what that means. Why did she select 6? What is she already doing that puts her at 6 instead of at 10? What would it take for her to go from a 6 to a 5—or even a 5.5—with regard to this issue? How committed is Victoria to working on some changes? What number is her goal?

These amplifying questions can help Victoria see how she can "get good things to happen" and further increase her "sense of self-efficacy" (Guterman, 2006, p. 52). She is not going to be able to transform the university, but it is quite possible for Victoria to experience greater self-confidence and comfort. It is possible for her to learn to be her "whole self" happily and more often. And, over time, she might even contribute to change at the college itself.

Discussion Questions

1. What reactions arise in you when you talk with students who voice their sense of being marginalized and misunderstood?

2. What experiences in your life and learning help you empathize with Victoria?

3. What is the primary value in adopting a "not knowing" stance with Victoria? What will be challenging for you in maintaining that stance?

4. What will you do as you make the referral to the counseling center to minimize the possibility that Victoria might think you are just handing her off to someone else and to maximize the possibility that she feels understood and supported?

References

Abes, E. A., Jones, S. R., & McEwen, M. K. (2007). Reconceptualizing the model of multiple dimensions of identity: The role of meaning-making capacity in the construction of multiple identities. *Journal of College Student Development, 48*(1), 1–22.

Abes, E. A., & Kasch, D. (2007). Using queer theory to explore lesbian college students' multiple dimensions of identity. *Journal of College Student Development, 48*(6), 619–636.

Baxter Magolda, M. B. (2001). A constructivist revision of the measure of epistemological reflection. *Journal of College Student Development, 42*(8), 520–534.

De Jong, P., & Berg, I. K. (2008). *Interviewing for solutions* (3rd ed.). Belmont, CA: Thomson Brooks/Cole.

Guterman, J. T. (2006). *Mastering the art of solution-focused counseling*. Alexandria, VA: American Counseling Association.

Jones, S. R. (1997). Voices of identity and difference: A qualitative exploration of the multiple dimensions of identity development in women college students. *Journal of College Student Development, 38*(4), 376–386.

Jones, S. R., & McEwen, M. K. (2000). A conceptual model of multiple dimensions of identity. *Journal of College Student Development, 41*(4), 405–414.

Sklare, G. B. (1997). *Brief counseling that works: A solution-focused approach for school counselors*. Thousand Oaks, CA: Corwin Press.

Smith, B. (1980). Racism and women's studies. *Frontiers: A Journal of Women Studies, 5*(1), 48–49.

Young, M. E. (2009). *Learning the art of helping: Building blocks and techniques* (3rd ed.). Upper Saddle River, NJ: Pearson.

CHAPTER 4

Finding Herself, Finding Her Voice
Justyna

Jason A. Laker, Nona L. Wilson, and Ruth Harper

Justyna is a second-year student majoring in biomedical sciences, one of the most rigorous areas of study at your private university. She is 19 years old and Caucasian, and was born in Lithuania. Her parents brought her to the United States as an infant, and she is now a U.S. citizen. She is reserved and slow to warm up in conversation but projects an air of confidence and intensity. Justyna was raised in the Roman Catholic faith and attended parochial schools. Her grandparents emigrated from Lithuania to the United States and moved in with the family when Justyna was ten. Her grandfather died of a heart attack in August, just before Justyna began at the university; her grandmother is relatively healthy.

Both grandparents were very religious and insisted that the family attend Mass each Sunday. However, her grandfather doted on Justyna, and they enjoyed an affectionate relationship that included occasionally colluding to skip church in favor of a day at the mall, museum, or park. She felt a tremendous loss when he died. Justyna's father is generally supportive but emotionally distant. Her mother expresses loving support, often coupled with well-intended but irritating judgments about Justyna's clothing or circle of friends. Both parents want Justyna to enjoy, in their words, "a prosperous and full American life"—ideally, working as a physician and having a family. During high school, Justyna achieved a near perfect grade point average, was a National Merit Scholar, did well in several AP courses, and was involved in a full range of clubs and volunteer activities. She received several merit-based scholarships, including the prestigious Chancellor's Fellowship, which provides full tuition for four years. This fellowship requires her to maintain a 3.5 GPA (on a 4.0 scale), complete an approved summer internship, and present a portfolio at the conclusion of her degree. Justyna also won a scholarship from her local parish; it covers the costs of books and a summer service-learning trip. Despite this generous support, Justyna has become increasingly stressed about money, as her family's financial situation has deteriorated in the wake of her grandfather's death. She took a private room in her residence hall because of the intense academic demands of her studies and her desire for privacy but now is worried that she cannot afford to keep it.

Justyna has not discussed her level of stress or her sense of being overwhelmed with anyone; she has no close friends at the university. She hasn't found the social scene at college very attractive because of the prevalence of drinking and drunkenness. During high school, she had a circle of friends with whom she enjoyed shared activities that did not include alcohol. Because of her concentration on school and her parents' strict views, Justyna has virtually no experience with dating or amorous relationships. She has been quite successful in her studies, so much so that one of her professors, Dr. Marja Ergma-Alvarez (herself of Lithuanian descent) invited Justyna to participate as a research assistant on a grant-funded study in her laboratory. Justyna is thrilled to be the only undergraduate student to be asked and is extremely excited about the opportunity. She can envision being just like Dr. Ergma-Alvarez, whom she holds in very high esteem as a mentor. Dr. Ergma-Alvarez, (or Mimi, as her research assistants and colleagues call her) enjoys the youthful energy Justyna brings to the project; she sees a bit of herself in this precocious student.

Over the course of the past semester, Justyna developed a romantic fascination with one of the female graduate laboratory assistants, Cameron. However, Cameron does not seem to notice Justyna any more than anyone else in the lab.

Justyna seeks every opportunity to interact with Cameron and works hard to elicit attention by asking questions and seeking advice. Cameron is always polite, neither familiar nor cold, in response to Justyna's consultations. One evening, Justyna and Cameron are the last remaining students at work. They finish their respective tasks around 9:30 and leave together, locking up the laboratory. Cameron asks Justyna if she can get back to her residence okay, or if she would like to be walked home. Justyna is electrified by this show of concern and accepts the escort. Along the way, the two share a friendly chat, laughing about a movie they both enjoyed. Cameron leaves Justyna at her residence hall lobby, remarking, "Hey, I think you're great, 'J.'" Justyna stammers back, "You, too!" She impulsively hugs Cameron—to their mutual surprise. Cameron hugs back, hurriedly says, "See you tomorrow," and leaves. Justyna is embarrassed but can barely contain her excitement at this interchange as she returns to her single room.

Over the next two weeks, the two see each other in the laboratory and interact as politely as before, but Cameron does not initiate any conversation unrelated to the experiments. Justyna is too intimidated to be as familiar as they were during that brief exchange. She is privately mortified at the possibility that she put Cameron off by initiating a hug, but she doesn't know what to do. Intensely preoccupied with Cameron, Justyna is so self-conscious about their private interaction that she is unable to concentrate on her studies.

Justyna grows more uncomfortable with her sexuality in general. Although she has questioned her orientation for years—unable to identify as straight, gay, or bisexual—this is her first experience with intense romantic feelings. Her feelings for Cameron make her anxious about how her religion, family, professors, coworkers, peers, and even deceased grandfather would view her if she were not straight. The more pressure Justyna feels about her sexuality, the more nervous she becomes around Cameron, and the more anxiety she feels.

Unfortunately, this all-consuming self-reflection takes place during midterms; consequently, Justyna does not complete one of her essays and gets a "C" on a major exam. She is so unnerved by these circumstances that she does not attend classes for a week. She also misses a meeting with the research team and, since this is unusual, Mimi sends her an e-mail asking if she is all right. When Justyna doesn't reply, Mimi asks the other research assistants if they've seen her. Cameron says she knows which residence hall Justyna lives in, so Mimi asks her to check on Justyna.

Cameron calls Justyna's room from the front desk (they don't disclose room numbers). Justyna sounds out of sorts, so Cameron asks her to come to the lobby (an escort is required to enter the residence wing). Justyna has her hair in a messy ponytail and is wearing pajamas; despite her appearance, she rushes downstairs to greet Cameron. Given her disheveled look, Justyna is horrified to see that the reception area is quite busy. Even worse, some of the students in the lobby are part of a small social clique that Justyna is convinced has been judging her harshly for her studious lifestyle. A couple of the young women glance at her and giggle, rolling their eyes and whispering to each other. Justyna apologizes to Cameron for her appearance, doing so just loudly enough to be overheard by the clique. Cameron laughs and puts her arm around Justyna, saying, "Don't be silly, you look adorable. I was worried about you!" Unable to speak, Justyna takes Cameron back to her room. There, Justyna sits on her bed and begins to cry. Cameron looks startled and concerned; she sits down next to Justyna and puts her hand on Justyna's shoulder, asking what's wrong.

Justyna says she is "so sorry for flaking out," and proceeds to tell Cameron how she missed classes and her grades are ruined; she's going to lose her scholarship and her parents will pull her out of school; how she let Mimi down and will never be trusted again; and how "everything is falling apart." Cameron is overwhelmed by the extent of Justyna's emotional upheaval. Since she does not feel equipped to counsel Justyna, she says that she's sure this can all be sorted out and perhaps Justyna should talk to someone—maybe a counselor or advisor. Cameron says she will ask Mimi to let Justyna take a couple of weeks off the project until she is able to catch up with her studies. Justyna is appreciative, but also feels a bit hurt by Cameron's rational and level response. Justyna tells Cameron that she hasn't been able to sleep, so Cameron offers to make her some tea. Cameron sits in Justyna's beanbag chair, and the two talk until they both end up falling asleep.

Cameron wakes with a start at 6:00 a.m., and quickly realizes that she didn't do any of the work she had planned for last evening. Justyna is still sleeping in her bed, so Cameron leaves quietly and passes two of the young women who reside on that wing. The two notice Cameron, recalling her from the lobby the previous evening, and note that she is wearing the same outfit and her hair is mussed. They giggle and whisper, but Cameron doesn't notice (and wouldn't care) and heads off to the library. When Justyna wakes up around 8:30, she heads down the hall to the communal bathroom to shower. The two young women who had seen Cameron are now leaving for class. When they see Justyna, they giggle and, as they exit the bathroom, one remarks, "Busy night with the girlfriend, huh?!" Justyna doesn't understand at first, but then realizes what they are implying. She is so upset by the weight of everything going on that she returns to her room and remains there for the next week, leaving only to use the restroom or to get food. She doesn't go to class, check her e-mail, or do any work.

The next Monday, a teaching assistant tells Dr. Ergma-Alvarez that Justyna has not turned in a major paper, and that her otherwise perfect average in the course is now severely jeopardized. The TA notes that Justyna has been a very engaged student up to this point. He is worried because she has missed several class sessions and has not responded to several e-mails he sent expressing concern. Dr. Ergma-Alvarez considers the situation and agrees that someone in Student Services should look into this matter. She decides to contact you, the university's scholarship coordinator, to intervene, since Justyna is at risk of losing her Chancellor's Fellowship. Dr. Ergma-Alvarez says, "I have a straight-A student here who is stumbling badly, not attending class, not coming to work on our research. I think there's more than just academics going on with her. I have no way of knowing whether it is true or not, but I heard from a graduate student that Justyna might be infatuated with another girl over here in the lab; perhaps that is confusing for her."

You promptly call Justyna and schedule a time to meet with her the next day. Justyna arrives 15 minutes late for the appointment, looking haggard.

Student Development Response

Like many of her peers, Justyna is trying to find her way—in college specifically and in life more generally. She has always been a hardworking student, achieving a great deal of success. Academic disruption is unfamiliar to her, and experiencing it now is quite frightening. In common parlance, responses to threat include "fight, flight, or freeze," and Justyna appears to be frozen. Faithfulness to her family's values has been a strong theme for her, even as she explores some of the new feelings, influences, and opportunities associated with a more independent life at college. Her grandfather's death is a source of grief, and may increase her vulnerability to guilty feelings associated with distance (geographic and philosophical) from her family.

As noted in chapter 1, theories of college student development are intended to be descriptive rather than prescriptive. That is, when student affairs practitioners use such theories to inform their work with individual students or groups of students, they must not attempt to "diagnose" students in terms of which category, stage, dimension, and so on they might possibly "be in." Rather, the theories and models provide conceptual guidance, helping professionals name elements of students' developmental journeys. Theory can start the process but ought to remain humbly inquisitive. Moreover, no single theory or conceptual model can fully address the multiple aspects of identity or the wide variety of lived experiences represented among college students. Even with such limitations, however, theory is the foundation, the starting point, of professional practice. Thus, your task is to find conceptual frameworks that do not so much summarize Justyna's experience but rather generate useful questions for you to ponder.

As you seek to understand Justyna's concerns and how best to assist her, you might begin by acknowledging her as a woman and wondering how gender and its social construction frame her experience. Feminist scholars assert that all experience is gendered, and Wharton (2005) posits, "Gender remains a central organizing principle of modern life" (p. 6). This is not merely a Western phenomenon; Harding (1986) notes that "In virtually every culture, gender difference is a pivotal way in which humans identify themselves as persons, organize social relations, and symbolize meaningful natural and social events and processes" (p. 18). In graduate school, you may or may not have been encouraged to critically examine students' identities and developmental tasks as gendered or to consider the extent to which many of the early—and most widely influential—theoretical models used in student affairs were developed using male subjects. You may already be aware that, as Meth and Pasick (1990) explain, although psychological writing has been androcentric, it has also been gender blind and it has assumed a male perspective but has not really explored what it means to be a man any more than what it means to be a woman. (p. vii)

Male subjects were not sought to examine masculinity and its influence on experience; rather, male (often White, middle and upper class) subjects served as the standard, as a proxy for all people.

Eventually, researchers acknowledged the distortion that such practices can produce and began in earnest to study specific social identities, including gender. Over the past 25 years, this research has yielded significant contributions to the literature. Gilligan (1993) and Belenky, Clinchy, Goldberger, and Tarule (1986), for example, have not only critiqued male-centered identity theories; they have proposed new, gender-informed models based on research with women participants. Similarly, Josselson (1987) sought to "view identity in women in women's own terms" (p. 27). As summarized in chapter 1, Josselson's research considers how a developmental "crisis" might lead to a particular "commitment" in four areas that are particularly salient in women's lives: occupation, politics, religion, and sexual values and standards. In other words, a woman may encounter critical moments during her life that challenge her belief systems, requiring or at least inviting her to decide on a path that affirms or departs from the views into which she has been socialized. Critical moments can involve peers, new or unfamiliar situations, media, and a host of other encounters or exposures to information—the hallmarks of a college experience.

The descriptions associated with Moratoriums and Identity Achievers (Josselson, 1987) seem to capture the essence of Justyna's crisis: She is conscious of the myriad choices available to her, and becomes immobilized and overwhelmed. Despite the fact that Justyna is quite upset about her circumstances, Josselson's framework suggests that this time is also ripe with potential. Thus, although Justyna is experiencing a developmental crisis, with support she can turn her experiences into powerful and positive opportunities for personal growth.

Josselson notes that crises in relationships, more than any other area, lead to developmental progress for women. However, Justyna is away from family and her high school friends, and has yet to form deep and meaningful relationships in college. If relationships are indeed the anchor for women's identity development, Justyna will need substantial support to become more involved socially (Komives & Woodard, 1996, p. 167). Justyna also may be renegotiating her childhood system of beliefs in light of her recent adult experiences, a process that parallels the tasks of Identity Achievers. Such renegotiation often entails some level of conflict, such as guilt feelings over departing from family or community beliefs. If Justyna can accommodate these changes and their attendant guilt, she can continue to develop her own identity.

Justyna might be encouraged if you explained this model to her. You could tell her that you know she is having a very hard time, perhaps feeling very much alone, and you want her to know that many of her peers are facing similar issues. Be sure to clarify that you are not suggesting that the specifics are identical; rather, that her reactions are common during periods of personal growth. In other words, she is on the right track. Pointing out this paradox (e.g., being upset can mean that you are healthy) can liberate students. Justyna may be feeling shame for having allowed herself to get sidetracked. If so, her negative self-talk will limit her ability to be present, reflective, and self-forgiving.

The first part of an effective developmental response is to provide validation. From there, you can summarize the components of the problem (e.g., running afoul of scholarship grade requirements, being behind in her classes, letting Dr. Ergma-Alvarez down, feeling awkward around Cameron—if you know about her) to acknowledge that the list is challenging. At the same time, however, you will want to convey that Justyna's concerns are surmountable. Explain the resources (programs, services, offices) and policies that can help her, and ask her how she would like you to help. You will want to strike a balance between conveying confidence in her and contributing to the pressure she already feels. Likewise, you must offer support without in any way shaming her by implying that she is incompetent. One way to seek that balance is to explain that you know she has the necessary intelligence and drive, but since college is still somewhat unfamiliar territory, you can help her apply her strengths in the right directions.

After deescalating the immediate problem, it might be helpful to invite

Justyna to participate in programs or organizations on campus that appreciate the unique characteristics she possesses. For instance, a Women's Center meeting or event, or a women's club or organization, might expose Justyna to a supportive peer group and provide new social contacts for her. Interacting with other women who are experiencing similar developmental themes, or have in the past, could help Justyna to strengthen herself as a person and as a woman.

Further consideration of Justyna's experience at college through the lens of gender can be useful. Two women figure prominently in Justyna's concerns. Dr. Ergma-Alvarez, her mentor and role model, placed considerable trust in her. Justyna admires and respects Mimi and felt honored, initially, to take on additional responsibilities. Cameron, a female graduate student, captured Justyna's attention in compelling, yet ambiguous, ways. A variety of reasonable interpretations suggest themselves regarding Justyna's feelings toward Cameron, but you will want to avoid making overly simplistic assumptions about their present and future implications. To do this, you will need to consider the gendered nature of your own assumptions. For instance, if you assumed that Justyna is lesbian, how has your own gender conditioning and education encouraged you to label her in that way, when she herself has not?

Seeing gender as a way to frame your thinking about Justyna can generate many important questions. Other aspects of her identity, however, must be taken into account as well. The ways in which her religious beliefs, for example, intersect with her emerging sexuality may be especially significant. Although Justyna has questioned her sexual orientation for some time, she has had almost no opportunity to explore her feelings or discover what it is like to act on those feelings. The sudden freedom and privacy of college life might be both exciting and intimidating. Justyna is especially vulnerable to compounding guilt if she reconsiders—and ultimately rejects—the religious traditions of her family. She might benefit from connecting with people on your campus who can help her integrate the sexual and spiritual dimensions of her identity, people of whom she can safely ask questions.

Also, Justyna is grieving the death of her grandfather, the most supportive male in her life. That loss may be affecting her in ways she has yet to recognize but that likely intensify her need for meaningful, supportive connections. Finally, her status as a member of an immigrant family may complicate her transition to the university. She may feel responsible to excel academically to make her family proud of her. Her efforts to meet that obligation might eclipse other equally important aspects of her growth and development.

The norms evident in her residence hall as well as her family and church may make it difficult for Justyna to honestly explore her sexuality. Additionally, her situation exemplifies the ways in which Chickering & Reisser's (1993) vectors of student development can intersect. Justyna is capable and well prepared academically; however, her interpersonal competence is underdeveloped, so much so that interpersonal challenges are affecting her academic standing. Moreover, Justyna's current social difficulties likely come as a surprise to her—in high school, she had friends, assumed leadership roles, and was involved in her community. Justyna's identity comprises multiple dimensions. As you consider how best to help her, you must take into account all those dimensions and how the campus environment supports—or fails to support—each one (Abes, Jones, & McEwen, 2007).

Counseling Response

As the student development response makes clear, Justyna is experiencing a number of challenges typical for students her age: developing a sense of competence, managing emotions, and establishing mature relationships. Additionally, she is grappling with questions about her sexuality and attempting to handle all of this during a significant transitional period.

Justyna is moving from the safety and predictability of her immigrant family home—with its strong Catholic influence, extended family network, and close parental involvement in decision making—to a much more independent, liberal, and somewhat isolating campus environment. Her primary responses to the new opportunities and new relationships she has encountered have been largely positive and optimistic. She moves toward possibilities as they present themselves (working in the lab, reaching out to Cameron) in a healthy, growth-seeking manner. She continues to show strength of character by resisting social pressure to drink.

With so many new challenges and prospects, Justyna understandably feels a bit precarious, a common sensation during periods of growth. Then, when she begins to question the significance of her feelings toward Cameron, her coping strategies are simply overwhelmed. Justyna's circumstances provide a good example of how a crisis can arise at the intersection of challenges that on their own are relatively common—and manageable—developmental tasks but that in combination can overcome a student.

Because she is in crisis, you clearly must refer her to the campus counseling center. That referral is best offered in the context of a caring conversation in which you have conveyed a genuine interest in and concern about her. You are part of a network of campus services that can support her. Your conversations with Justyna should help her see how the pieces of that network come together, and you should clarify the roles that each campus service plays. Ideally, you will use good helping skills to set the boundaries around what you can and cannot do, and then offer the best support you can within those boundaries. You will not assume the primary role in helping Justyna through her crisis—the counseling center should do that—but you can play an important supporting role.

There are two fairly obvious possibilities regarding how Justyna might respond to being referred to you, the scholarship coordinator. Given her interpersonal style, you could reasonably expect that she might be reserved in the meeting, keeping most of the details to herself and downplaying the significance of anything you have been told. Justyna is a highly responsible person; she also likely feels a sense of obligation to her family. In keeping with that, she might assure you that she will redouble her efforts and get back on track—although she may have no clear idea of how to do that. Such an approach makes sense as a form of self-protection, even if it might limit the kinds of support you and others can offer her. The second possibility is that Justyna might attempt the first strategy but be unable to maintain it. She's extremely stressed and seriously distraught and, although she might prefer to not reveal her emotions, it is possible that her confusion and fears might surface, forcefully, during your meeting. Although that would create an opening for you to offer a greater range of support, Justyna would feel less in control, so you would want to be careful to respect her fragility.

Regardless of how she presents herself, your role as scholarship coordinator is not to attempt to explore and resolve the layers of challenges with which Justyna is contending. Those challenges are, however, contributors to and context for the academic difficulties that triggered her appointment with you—and they will continue to press upon her as she interacts with you. You will have to figure out how to support her if she is either reserved and somewhat closed or overcome with emotion during your meeting. You will need a framework for considering the impact Justyna's struggles are having on her and a set of communication skills to help you convey sensitivity. What follows is an explication of how concepts and skills from the Person-Centered model can be helpful with Justyna. It is not intended to cover every aspect of a Person-Centered approach that could be useful in your work with her; rather, it provides an introduction to how these counseling concepts can support and enhance your student services work with a student in crisis.

Person-Centered Helping

Bringing the Person-Centered model into a caring conversation with Justyna begins with your orientation to the kind of relationship you will foster with her. Your focus shifts from yourself and what you might want to do *for* her and turns instead to learning to understand how she experiences herself. Your goal is to create an open, accepting space in which Justyna can really listen to herself. You trust that as you value and accept her, she will be encouraged to do the same. As she is given space to listen more closely and compassionately to herself, you hope that Justyna will more fully connect with her ability to know what she needs to do and will pursue those things. Advice giving, correcting, and directing are not part of your intentions with Justyna.

Genuineness

Being authentic in your interactions is crucial to the Person-Centered approach. You will need to have real concern for Justyna—not pity for her situation or a caretaking stance rooted in the idea that she is unable to manage, but a desire for her well-being and trust in her ability to make good choices. You're interested in her as a person and her success as a student, and you seek to convey that without trying to impress her or achieve something for yourself in the meeting. If Justyna is reserved and hesitant in the meeting, you want to respect her signals; yet her reserve does not put a cap on your concern. The content of your conversation will likely be constrained, but your interest in her well-being does not lessen. If you stay grounded in a genuine interest and caring for Justyna, your intentions will come through in your interactions.

You might say, *"I can see that it is uncomfortable for you to talk about the things that are making it hard for you to stay focused on your studies. You don't have to talk about them with me. I want you to know, though, that I recognize that it's a difficult time for you and I want to help—within the limits of my ability and your comfort."* Offering such a statement is an invitation that doesn't have any pressure behind it. Justyna is fully free to decline. That freedom opens up space for her to decide what she wants to tell you.

If Justyna is more emotional in the meeting, you might say something like this: *"I appreciate that you did not plan for these emotions to come up. Part of you might feel some relief in letting your feelings out, and I also see that part of you doesn't want to show me how hard it is for you. I want you to know that whatever you want to do right now, I'll respect your choice."*

Congruence

One aspect of being congruent involves ensuring that what you say and how you say it match; that is, your tone of voice should support the content of your statements. A second, and perhaps more important, aspect of being congruent in your work with Justyna entails what is going on inside you. This aspect of congruence requires you to be clear about your intentions and stay true to them as you interact with Justyna. In the abstract, it can be easy to endorse the Person-Centered stance of trusting students to know what is right for them, of resisting giving advice, and of unconditional positive regard. In reality, it is hard not to doubt a student's ability to manage, not to attempt to take charge or direct at least a little bit, and not to judge.

Many people who are drawn to helping and to student affairs are problem solvers—they're able to assess situations quickly and generate multiple options almost instantly. But evaluating Justyna's circumstances from your own perspective and urging her to act in certain ways is not consistent with the Person-Centered approach to helping, and it is not congruent. That might seem obvious, but incongruence creeps into caring conversations in subtle ways. If Justyna were very quiet or expressed a sense of helplessness, it could be easy to begin—gently, kindly—to make a plan for her, to lead her in the direction you think she ought to move.

More congruent with an intention to listen carefully, you might say, *"It's hard right now to figure this out on your own. You're really not sure what to do. It's also hard to let people know you're struggling."* You're simply acknowledging what is true for her and encouraging her to do the same. If she were more emotional, it might be tempting to offer reassurances that "everything is going to be okay"—an assessment that clearly is not her own at the moment and that, although well intended, actually negates her experience. Instead, you could say, *"It all seems really overwhelming at the moment. And I can see that you're worried that you won't be able to figure it out. I imagine that feels pretty scary."*

Having acknowledged her perspective, you might ask if it would be okay to share some information you have—about her options, about the time frame in which decisions need to be made about course work, and about other support services on campus. Stay attuned to any urges that arise in you to take over for Justyna, or any "if she would only..." kind of thinking. Those things happen in a flash and can easily get you off course. The art of Person-Centered helping is learning how to concentrate your attention on her and her perspective while also staying aware of yourself and your intentions. It's a balancing act and, just as with physical balancing, it is an active, fluid process that takes practice.

Tips for Person-Centered Helping

Those who are new to Person-Centered helping sometimes doubt that they are "doing" anything. The temptation can be strong to be nondirective and accepting throughout most of the meeting and then, near the end, slip in some advice. Sometimes the advice is disguised as a question, but the question has an agenda—its real function is to suggest something. If you find yourself struggling with this approach, spend some time considering what it is YOU are worried about. Do you fear that you're not being helpful? If so, what is your definition of helping? Do you basically think you know what is best for the student? Do you prefer your assessment to the student's assessment? Being honest with yourself—not harsh or judgmental, just honest—can help you sort through some of the challenges inherent in Person-Centered helping.

Using Person-Centered methods does not mean that you cannot share information. You can tell Justyna about many different options and services available to her. The keys to doing so effectively from a Person-Centered point of view are timing and intention. If you listen carefully, with an attitude of accepting what is true for Justyna at the moment, you will notice when she is open to information and able to hear it. Ask yourself, "Am I offering resources right now because she seems receptive or because I would feel better doing so?" Consider what your intentions are in offering information. Are you trying to persuade or convince the student that she ought to think, feel, or act in a certain way? If she doesn't, will you be annoyed or disappointed? If the answer to either of those questions is yes, then you've strayed from the Person-Centered model. If the answers are no, you are providing options and information in a nonpossessive way in keeping with Person-Centered principles.

Discussion Questions

1. How often and in what ways do you consider the role and impact of gender in your work with students?

2. Which additional ways of thinking about student development are useful to you as you reflect on Justyna and her current circumstances?

3. What aspects of Justyna's situation and her reactions to it might make it challenging for you to maintain empathy? What in your own life experience and interpersonal style makes you different from her and creates a different perspective? How could you work on closing that gap?

4. What would help you maintain a nonpossessive stance when working with Justyna?

5. What resources are available on your campus to support Justyna? What are the best ways to connect students with those resources?

References

Abes, E. A., Jones, S. R., & McEwen, M. K. (2007). Reconceptualizing the model of multiple dimensions of identity: The role of meaning-making capacity in the construction of multiple identities. *Journal of College Student Development, 48*(1), 1–22.

Belenky, M., Clinchy, B., Goldberger, N., & Tarule, J. (1986). *Women's ways of knowing: The development of self, voice, and mind.* New York: Basic Books.

Chickering, A. W., & Reisser, L. (1993). *Education and identity* (2nd ed.). San Francisco: Jossey-Bass.

Gilligan, C. (1993). *In a different voice: Psychological theory and women's development.* Cambridge, MA: Harvard University Press.

Harding, S. (1986). *The science question in feminism.* Ithaca, NY: Cornell University Press.

Josselson, R. (1987). *Finding herself: Pathways to identity development in women.* San Francisco: Jossey-Bass Publishers.

Komives, S. R., & Woodard, D. B., Jr. (1996). *Student services: A handbook for the profession.* San Francisco: Jossey-Bass.

Meth, R. L., & Pasick, R. S. (1990). *Men in therapy: The challenge of change.* New York: Guilford Press.

Wharton, A. (2005). *The sociology of gender: An introduction to theory and research.* Malden, MA: Blackwell Publishing.

CHAPTER 5

Sexual Assault
Kiah

Rebecca Caldwell, Nona L. Wilson, and Ruth Harper

Kiah is a 20-year-old African American woman. She is a junior at your mid-sized, predominantly White, Southern state university and an emerging student leader in the student government association you advise. So far in her college career, she has been an active member of several multicultural student organizations. She joined the student government association because she was eager to become involved in broader leadership experiences and build up her co-curricular résumé for graduate school. She is a hard worker and is well liked by her student leader peers. You've heard through the grapevine that Kiah recently started to date Mark, a 22-year-old White male who is also a leader in student government. You got to know Kiah better on a recent organization retreat and are working closely with her on a major upcoming event.

Kiah is a second-generation college student; her mother graduated from college before Kiah was born. Kiah grew up in the predominantly African American rural community where her mother was born and raised, and where her extended family lives. To send Kiah to a private, mostly White high school, Kiah's mother worked two jobs. Kiah has great respect for her mother and a very close relationship with her.

One afternoon, you have a meeting scheduled with Kiah and she is uncharacteristically late. As you look out your office window, you see Kiah and Mark in what appears to be a heated argument. She sees you, ends the discussion, and arrives in your office moments later, clearly very upset. You ask if she is okay and how you can help.

Kiah tells you that she has chosen to avoid getting into any serious relationships, both in high school and thus far at college. She has not dated a White man before, although she says that she has always thought that she was open to dating men of any ethnicity. Although her extended family is predominantly African American, her cousins and other relatives have, over the years, introduced people from other races into the family with a fair amount of ease. Her mother, newly single, recently went out on a date with a White man.

Kiah got to know Mark through the student organization and found him to be extremely sweet, thoughtful, and open-minded. Kiah and Mark both place a high priority on religion in their lives, and that is also part of what drew her to him. Although they usually attend their own religious services, lately Kiah has attended a few services at Mark's contemporary, multiracial mega-church; she thought it was "different, but pretty good."

Kiah has told you that in high school she often felt caught between two worlds and was very lonely, finding genuine acceptance neither in her private school nor among her childhood friends and acquaintances. When she arrived on campus, she was thrilled to find a small but strong African American student community. She felt as though she made the first "real friends" she had ever had and spent most of her time with them in formal and informal interactions. She enjoyed learning about empowerment and political action through the campus NAACP chapter. Kiah decided to get involved in student government this year to bring a more multicultural perspective to the group and to make sure that the voices of African American students were heard.

Student government has taken up more time than Kiah expected and, as a result, she and her friends have not been hanging out as much. Part of the reason for the new distance, however, is that many of her friends are immersed in studying, internships, and other organizations this year. When Kiah started to date

Mark, a few of her African American female friends made comments to the effect that dating a White guy was typical once you got involved in more "White" student organizations. Generally, though, she has not received strong reactions one way or the other from most of her friends.

Kiah was excited to be dating Mark at first, but lately things have been "coming up." Recently, Kiah has found herself pushing Mark away or picking fights with him. She blames her inability to trust him on "bad experiences" with guys in high school. Lately, one experience in particular keeps coming up for her. During the summer between her sophomore and junior years of high school, Kiah was hanging out with a group of girls from her neighborhood. She had grown up with them but didn't see them much during the year because she attended a different school. They were going to parties where people were drinking and smoking pot. Kiah was enjoying the chance to shed her "good girl" image a bit and was joining in.

One night, when Kiah had had quite a bit to drink, an older male who was a casual friend offered to walk her back to her house. She agreed, but instead of walking her home, he took her to his apartment. There, in Kiah's words, he "took advantage" of her sexually. She was very upset at the time but told herself that she was drunk and never should have let him take her to his apartment. She also thought about how he was known as a decent guy—one of the young men in her neighborhood who was going to make it. In fact, later that summer, he left to go to a prestigious university in the state. She's heard that next year he will begin law school. He and Kiah attended the same church, and their names are often mentioned together by people in their hometown as successes. When she is home, Kiah tries to avoid this man and his family, but inevitably they run into each other on occasion. He has never spoken to her in private since the incident, and he acts cool and detached when they are in the same room. Kiah says that when high school started again that fall, she threw herself into classes and getting ready for college as a way to keep what happened out of her thoughts.

Kiah says that since that summer, more than three years ago now, she has kept her distance from guys and initially found her relationship with Mark to be a welcome surprise. She was nervous about introducing him to her mother and friends, but when she did, they were very accepting of him. Despite all the positive aspects she can cite about Mark and their relationship, she finds herself unable to trust him. Kiah describes herself as feeling anxious and nervous lately. Uncharacteristically, she loses her temper easily. She finds herself fighting with Mark and is troubled by her thoughts. Two nights ago, she told a close female friend from high school about her experience; her friend identified Kiah as a sexual assault survivor. Kiah dismisses the idea that what happened to her was rape but says she would like the memory to be less intrusive and troubling. Kiah thinks that things were a lot easier when she avoided dating and wonders if she should simply end her relationship with Mark.

Student Development Response

You quickly recognize that Kiah is trusting you with a complex and multilayered concern. As an African American woman at a predominantly White university, Kiah experiences multiple oppressions. Thus, her experiences might be best understood through a Multidimensional Identity Model (Reynolds & Pope, 1991). She has been negotiating predominantly White academic environments since high school, but when she entered the university, she identified with—and immersed herself in—the non-White culture on campus. Her choices reflect the needs and coping strategies cited in the Immersion-Emersion status of Helms's Black Racial Identity Model (1995). Immersion for Kiah is positive; in college, she initially chose to associate mainly with other African American students, gain additional cultural information through the NAACP and other organizations, and consciously enlarge and affirm her identity as an African American woman. In terms of Emersion, Kiah's recent involvement in the prominent and predominantly White student government could signal a move to a more integrated identity and a commitment to move in majority circles as a proactive strategy against cultural oppression. (Helms does not suggest that one stage is "better" than another; the stages simply reflect different needs and priorities.)

In addition to the day-to-day challenges of being on a White campus and responding to developmentally expected challenges such as solidifying identity and negotiating intimacy, Kiah is grappling with a resurfacing personal trauma. Her primary coping strategies have focused on regaining control and minimizing the impact of the event: keeping it secret, describing it to herself in measured language, assuming much of the responsibility, and distracting herself with her studies. Those strategies worked until she began to date Mark. The closeness and attraction Kiah experiences with him are both welcome and unsettling, simultaneously stirring up the hope of a promising relationship and the memory of something very painful.

If you have been fortunate enough to complete training with a sexual assault advocacy group on your campus, you will likely recognize that Kiah's coping strategies are common early stage responses. Understanding the typical trajectory of recovery (from denial to awareness to healing and then recovery) will help you understand Kiah's struggle (UC Santa Barbara Women's Center, 2008). Kiah's avoidance of dating relationships is also consistent with many women's reactions to unwanted sexual experiences. Although there is a wide range of reactions—from avoiding sex to hypersexuality—it is common for women to report decreased sexual activity and diminished sexual enjoyment, as well as distrust and negative attitudes toward men. Additionally, some African American women who have experienced intraracial assaults report negative attitudes toward Black male-female relationships (Pierce-Baker, 1998; Wyatt, 1992, as cited in West, 2006; West & Rose, 2000).

However, each survivor's response is personal, shaped by an idiosyncratic mix of internal and environmental resources and challenges. Kiah's recovery will be influenced by the unique circumstances of her life and by who she is. You can understand which factors are significant for Kiah by talking with her. One issue you should be mindful of—especially if you are White—is the uneasy position Kiah is in as an African American woman, on a predominantly White campus, dealing with an intraracial assault. The United States has a particularly painful and shameful history related to sexual assault and the African American community. This legacy of injustice, born of both racism and sexism, is profound. One small piece of that complicated past that can be addressed here is that for some African American women, being assaulted by an African American man is not simply a personal trauma; it can be a social and political dilemma that recalls cultural trauma. As a result, recovery can be fraught with questions about loyalty and empowerment—for one's self and one's community.

These historical and cultural factors create a filter through which Kiah may be trying to make meaning of her experience (Abes, Jones, & McEwen, 2007). Her reluctance to label the incident as rape is consistent with many survivors' early reactions to trauma, and it parallels the historical reluctance of African American women to acknowledge and report rape within the African American community (West, 2006). Her assailant is a young man whose future success is a source of pride for his family, church, and community. Kiah knows that publicly accusing him of sexual assault would have significant ramifications for people she cares about and possibly for her relationships with them. What to call her experience and what to do about it may be very complex issues for her, but Kiah has the right to control when, how, and with whom she undertakes those tasks.

You may struggle with how to respect Kiah's right to maintain control while ensuring that you give her important information about support services. Keep these key points in mind. First, use her language. If she does not consider what happened to her rape, do not call it that. Kiah began her conversation with you by stating that she had been "taken advantage of." Use that phrase as you talk with her. Over time, if she talks with others—a counselor, her peers, her boyfriend—she will likely hear responses from them that will prompt her to question her view. Until then, however, it is her experience, and only she has the right to label it. Second, as you begin to talk with Kiah about how she is managing and what might be helpful, you will want to share information about services on your campus. You might say, *"Kiah, I care about you and I'm sad to hear you've gone through this, but I'm glad you're talking to me. I'm here and I want to help in whatever way I can. Part of what I want you to know is that you're not alone. There are people here who can help. I have cards with contact information for some support services on our campus. Can I tell you about them?"* If Kiah agrees, start with the counseling center, since you can discuss it as a place where students can go whenever something is troubling them, even when they are not sure what they are going to say. Be sure to tell her that all services there are confidential. If possible, make a direct referral to a counselor whom you know to be both knowledgeable about sexual assault and culturally competent.

If your campus has a women's center or sexual assault advocacy office, you can ease into telling Kiah about those offices by first reinforcing her autonomy. For example, you might say, *"I know your friend from high school labeled what you went through in a way that doesn't fit for you. I don't want to do that, and yet I do want you to know about the sexual assault advocacy center. They are here for anyone who has experienced something of a sexual nature that they did not want—something like what you went through. The center isn't just for rape survivors. Anytime students have questions about what has happened to them or just want to talk, they can go there. They have professional staff [name them] and students—volunteers and support groups. And it's all confidential."* Give Kiah this information in writing if she is interested in taking it. One final point to remember is to offer options; do not push specific ideas or actions. If Kiah is not interested in the information, do not pressure her to take it. Instead, respect her choice and let her know that if she changes her mind, she can get the information from you or the university website.

Talking—privately or in groups, with a counselor or with peers—is one pathway to recovery. West (2002), in addressing the needs of Black women who are sexual assault survivors, advocates several other avenues that are both culturally appropriate for Kiah and professionally appropriate for you as a student affairs professional. The following are four of West's suggestions:

1. **Encourage activism.** Kiah has already made use of action as a coping strategy. Immediately after the incident, she focused on her studies and preparing for college, and she has become actively involved on campus. Some might be tempted to dismiss her action as distraction, but it has been an adaptive response to a highly stressful experience. Her choices are consistent with her values and goals, and have led to a growing circle of meaningful relationships. Because Kiah is highly social and action-oriented, advocacy groups dedicated to women's rights, to reducing violence in the African American community, or to working against the exploitation of girls and women might be important options in her recovery process. Such groups provide opportunities for action focused on issues that are likely to register deeply with Kiah and would bring her into contact with other women who have had similar experiences.

2. **Improve social support.** Even if Kiah does not want to discuss the details of the incident or of her current struggles, you can ask her about the people in her life she considers supporters. Which people foster feelings of self-worth and competence? With whom does she feel safe? Who accepts and supports her? What events, roles, or rituals help renew her spirits? It is an error to assume that recovery comes only through focusing on the traumatic event. Helping Kiah strengthen and build her sense of self by engaging her social support system is also extremely important. If exploring these questions individually with Kiah seems to be overreaching—and it could, depending on your role and interpersonal style—consider discussing these questions in a group setting (such as a workshop on self-care for the student group to which Kiah belongs and that you advise) and framing the exercise in terms of wellness and good leadership.

3. **Draw on strengths.** Kiah has a wide range of strengths: social, emotional, physical, intellectual and academic, and spiritual. You can help her remember and use these skills as she moves forward. A word of caution is in order here, however. Although African American women are respected for their resilience (West, 1999), the concept of resilience can turn into a burden when it becomes a societal script or expectation (Washington, 2001). Be careful to balance praising Kiah's strengths with asking about what else she needs. She may believe that as "a strong Black woman" she should not need or ask for help. Inviting her to consider what she would tell a friend in similar circumstances can be an effective way to help her discover whether she holds a double standard—one for herself and one for others—when it comes to seeking support. The questions outlined in item 2 can also be useful here.

4. **Understand the importance of spirituality.** Recent publications such as *Encouraging Authenticity & Spirituality in Higher Education* (Chickering, Dalton, & Stamm, 2005) and *Sex and the Soul: Juggling Sexuality, Spirituality, Romance, and Religion on America's College Campuses* (Freitas & Winner, 2008) detail the ways in which campuses—and student affairs professionals—have failed to acknowledge or sufficiently respond to students' spiritual development. This omission has important implications for cultural competence, given the well-established significance that religion and spirituality have for many students, especially people of color (Sue & Sue, 2008, p. 226).

Kiah has told you that she places a high priority on religion in her life; her religious community and practices are likely to be significant sources of support for her in times of distress. Asking her if she has been able to draw on those resources is appropriate; failing to do so is insensitive. If Kiah feels unable to reach out to her church because her assailant is part of that church community or because she fears harsh judgment in some way, she is cut off from a valued source of meaning making, coping strategies, and social support. While it is not your role to advise her on spiritual matters, you can acknowledge the role the church plays in her life and validate the loss she probably feels if that source of support is somehow diminished. Make sure you are familiar with the resources on your campus that support students' spiritual and religious development—particularly those consistent with Kiah's traditions—and share those resources with her.

Counseling Response

Kiah was scheduled to meet with you to discuss a major event she has been helping to plan for the student government association. Because she knows you saw her arguing with Mark—and because she is still upset when she comes into your office—she discloses some very personal information to you. What she tells

125

you is not directly related to what you were scheduled to talk about. In fact, it's not what either of you was expecting.

Negotiating your role and figuring out how to support Kiah can be challenging in several ways. First, because her disclosures were unplanned, she has not thought through the choice to tell you. She may have felt "caught" in some way by her emotions and the situation; she's been on edge, fighting back upsetting memories, and confused by her relationship with Mark. Their argument in front of your office likely brought some of that to the surface, and the timing of your invitation to talk may have seemed impossible to resist. No one has done anything wrong here. In fact, this is often how student affairs professionals find themselves helping students with personal concerns. Unplanned disclosure is a common consequence of hidden burdens—eventually, the burden is expressed. Fortunately, your office is a safe place, but you will want to be mindful that Kiah is vulnerable not only because of what she is telling you, but also because of the circumstances under which she is doing so.

Second, even though she is telling you about what happened to her, she's ambivalent. An important piece of what she is saying is that she does not want to talk about the experience or even think about it—yet she keeps thinking about it. And even as she says she wants it all to just go away, you can hear her need to talk about it. Your task is to figure out the right balance of support and boundary, for her and for yourself. Kiah has shared something deeply personal, something she has entrusted to almost no one else. You must strive to convey to her a willingness to listen and a genuine interest in her well-being. Conversely, when the wave of emotion that prompted her disclosure subsides, she could feel overexposed and regret the conversation if she says too much, too quickly. Her need for a balance between support and boundary parallels your obligation to support her without overreaching your role as a student affairs professional. As discussed in chapter 2, there is no fail-safe formula for determining the right balance; however, the self-assessment questions in that chapter are especially relevant and helpful in this situation.

At some point in your conversation with Kiah, you must talk about seeing a professional counselor. Although she does not identify herself as a survivor of sexual assault—and it is not your job to persuade her to do so—you must validate that she has been hurt by what happened and encourage her to consider talking with a counselor. Creating a safe, nonthreatening, and supportive environment for Kiah will enhance your ability to refer her to a counselor. Person-Centered helping offers a very useful framework for this conversation.

Person-Centered Helping

Rogers's core conditions of genuineness, unconditional positive regard, and empathy are embedded in the student development response, and they provide a strong foundation for effectively responding to Kiah. Maintaining and conveying unconditional positive regard is important in all student support services; in your work with Kiah, it is essential. If you have been through training with your campus advocacy group or if you addressed trauma and recovery in your graduate program, you will know that many assault survivors blame themselves for what occurred. Kiah has told you that she believes she shares responsibility for what happened to her because she had been drinking and because she went to the man's apartment. She might be especially sensitive to indications that you, too, hold her responsible. Make sure that you do not, even in subtle ways, suggest that she is to blame for her experience. Because you are one of the first people she has told, your reactions can influence whether or not she continues to reach out to others for help. In addition, you will want to cultivate the nonpossessive aspect of unconditional positive regard as Kiah explores what she wants to do, including how she labels her experience and whether or not she seeks support. You will want to steadily support her in finding her own best ways of dealing with her situation, and she must be able to perceive that kind of support in you.

Solution-Focused Helping

Recovery is not achieved only by focusing on the traumatic event. West's (2002) suggestions to encourage activism, improve social support, draw on strengths, and understand the significance of spirituality underscore the importance of positive action. This is the kind of support that you can provide without overstepping your professional boundaries. And a Solution-Focused framework can help you.

As with any case that involves oppression, you must be careful in using this framework not to minimize what has happened to Kiah or in any way indicate that you are trying to gloss over the problem. The Solution-Focused framework can empower Kiah to see herself as essentially competent and encourage her to build on her many strengths. In this situation, you could use several basic Solution-Focused strategies.

Explore what Kiah is already doing that is helping her cope. For example, you can ask, "*Kiah, what are you doing right now that is allowing you to be such a successful, involved student?*" or "*What can you do today or tomorrow that will let you know that you are moving in the direction you want with this issue?*"

Encourage Kiah to create a list of resources, including her personal strengths, to call upon as necessary. When Kiah feels preoccupied or distracted during a student government meeting, for example, she may want to briefly step out of the meeting and review the list. You could pair this with the Cognitive-Behavioral coping card strategy.

Invite Kiah to envision herself in the future, doing well. You might ask her, "*When you are off in graduate school in a couple of years and you think back about what was most helpful to you here at this time, what do you think you might recall?*" Kiah might say that her academic success gave her confidence in her intellectual abilities and that her leadership roles in student organizations helped her know that she was respected and capable. Her close relationships and positive choices in the present can help validate her sense of self-efficacy, letting Kiah know that she can trust herself. Memberships and leadership positions in groups and organizations that she values can be especially useful in this regard. In addition to her campus involvement, Kiah might identify other choices—such as telling her mother, seeing a counselor, or just taking good care of herself—as important to her recovery.

Give meaningful compliments. Compliments "affirm what is important to the [student], . . . affirm [her] successes, and the strengths these successes suggest" (De Jong & Berg, 2008, p. 116). Kiah has demonstrated a multitude of strengths; acknowledging some of these strengths, as you see them, is important. You might tell her, "*What you are telling me today shows me things about you I never realized. You have been carrying a secret sorrow—yet you are on the dean's list and are an ac-*

tive leader on campus. I am amazed at your strength. And I am impressed that you have the insight to reach out at this point. I am honored that you shared your story with me. I will support you in any way I can."

You could integrate mindfulness-based strategies into your work with Kiah in a variety of ways. You might choose to draw your attention to your own experience of working with Kiah, either before, during, or after your conversation. If you are having strong reactions—such as anger at her offender, sadness for Kiah, or fear about whether you are doing the right thing—simply notice those reactions and offer yourself acceptance and kindness. Learning to be gentle with yourself in the moment can be surprisingly helpful in reducing your sense of urgency to act. You could also encourage a similar process for Kiah by inviting her to bring her attention back to the present moment. That is relatively easy to do through questions such as *"What do you notice right now about what you're feeling?"* Strive to balance such questions across your conversation so that you help her notice both pleasant and difficult feelings.

If you discuss the concept of acceptance with her, you will want to be especially careful to limit the conversation to Kiah's self-acceptance. While Kiah may ultimately benefit from working on forgiving or accepting her offender—as a person who hurt her deeply and exists in the world with his own pain and limitations—that sort of work is complicated and beyond your role as a student affairs professional. Finally, you could use mindfulness-based strategies as a bridge to refer Kiah to the counseling center. If she values the chance to turn her attention to her experience and notice her thoughts and feelings more closely, she is likely to become aware of strong indicators that she would find counseling very helpful.

Remember that the ultimate goal of any kind of helping, including much of student affairs work, is to create space and structure for students to more fully understand themselves and discover their own pathways. Doing that requires you to genuinely trust students to grow and develop in positive, productive ways when they are given the freedom and support to do so. When students have been hurt, as Kiah has, it can be tempting to adopt a caretaking role—to guide them, do for them, "educate" them—but such well-intended efforts can actually impede student development and learning. Trusting Kiah to know what is right for her and supporting her decisions (especially when those decisions are not the ones you might make) is the bedrock of developmental helping and will enhance your effectiveness.

Discussion Questions

1. How does the historical and cultural oppression of African American women affect Kiah's story? Consider your own background as you contemplate the historical, cultural, social, and political aspects of this scenario. Are there particular challenges for you as a student affairs professional?

2. What strategies would you use to work with a student who engages in self-blame?

3. How would you handle your own emotions, as well as possible urges to share those emotions with Kiah? How could being an assault survivor yourself or being close to a survivor affect your response?

4. What are your assumptions about students like Kiah, who are especially capable and strong? How might their poise and strength influence your response?

5. How would you maintain the right balance between support and boundary with Kiah? What kind of reminders would help you refrain from sharing too much or delving too deeply? How can you use supervision to help you?

References

Abes, E. S., Jones, S. R., & McEwen, M. K. (2007). Reconceptualizing the model of multiple dimensions of identity: The role of meaning-making capacity in the construction of multiple identities. *Journal of College Student Development, 48*(1), 1–22.

Chickering, A. W., Dalton, J.C., & Stamm, L. (2006). *Encouraging authencity & spirituality in higher education.* San Francisco, CA : Jossey-Bass.

De Jong, P. & Berg, I. K. (2008). *Interviewing for solutions.* (3rd ed.). Belmont, CA: Brooks/Cole.

Freitas, D., & Winner, L. (2008). *Sex and the soul: Juggling sexuality, spirituality, romance and religion on American's college campuses.* New York: Oxford University Press.

Helms, J. (1995). An update of Helms's White and people of color racial identity models. In J. Ponterotto, J. Casas, L. Suzuki, & C. Alexander (Eds.), *Handbook of multicultural counseling* (pp. 181–198). Thousand Oaks, CA: Sage.

Pierce-Baker, C. (1998). *Surviving the silence: Black women's stories of rape.* New York: W.W. Norton & Company.

Reynolds, A. L., & Pope, R. L. (1991). The complexities of diversity: Exploring multiple oppressions. *Journal of Counseling & Development, 70,* 174–180.

Sue, D. W., & Sue, D. (2008). *Counseling the culturally diverse: Theory and practice.* (5th ed.). Hoboken, NJ: John Wiley & Sons.

University of California-Santa Barbara Women's Center. (2008). Recovering from sexual assault. Retrieved September 19, 2009, from www.sa.ucsb.edu/women'scenter/ViolenceHarassment/recovering.aspx

Washington, P. A. (2001). Disclosure patterns of Black female sexual assault survivors. *Violence against Women, 7,* 1254–1283.

West, C. M. (2002). I find myself at therapy's doorstep: Summary and suggested readings on violence in the lives of Black women. *Women and Therapy, 25*(3/4), 193–201.

West, C. M. (2006, October). *Sexual violence in the lives of African American women.* Harrisburg, PA: VAWnet, a project of the National Resource Center on Domestic Violence/Pennsylvania Coalition Against Domestic Violence. Retrieved June 14, 2009, from www.vawnet.org

West, C. M., & Rose, S. (2000). Dating aggression among low income African American youth: An examination of gender differences and antagonistic beliefs. *Violence Against Women, 6,* 470–494.

West, T. C. (1999). *Wounds of the spirit: Black women, violence, and resistance ethics.* New York: New York University Press.

CHAPTER 6

Isolation and Traditional Native Identity
Hodekki

Heather Shotton, Stephanie J. Waterman,
Ruth Harper, and Nona L. Wilson

One of your Native American students, Seneca nation member Hodekki Henry, appears in the Student Services office without an appointment. In his usual way, he tells the secretary he will wait for you, then sits on the couch in the reception area reading a book. From your experience with Hodekki, you know that he will wait patiently—a long wait upsets you more than it appears to upset him. Luckily, you can see him immediately.

When you ask the purpose of his visit, Hodekki softly tells you that your previous suggestion that he introduce himself to faculty members during office hours has resulted in professors calling on him in class. As Hodekki speaks, he often looks at his hands or sometimes out the window behind you. He says that in class he feels that he must always answer, and answer well, when a faculty member says, "Mr. Henry, tell us how a traditional Native American would respond to this issue" or "Can you tell the class the Indian perspective on this, Hodekki?" These prompts create great pressure to represent not just himself but his family, tribe, and maybe even all indigenous peoples. He thinks he cannot say, "I don't know" or even "Speaking just for myself . . . ." Those options seem disrespectful to him. And once the professors started asking him questions, non-Native students began asking him questions, too, such as "Did you grow up in a teepee?" One male athlete has started patting him on the back every time he sees him, calling him "Chief."

Hodekki is dark-skinned, with wavy, dark brown hair that hangs well below his shoulders. He tells you, "It is a gift from the creator, so we should wear our hair long." Hodekki has a rather stocky build; other than playing club lacrosse, he shows no interest in sports on campus.

His resident assistant (RA) referred Hodekki to you because he worried that Hodekki always seemed to be alone: He walked in and out of the residence hall alone; he ate meals alone; and the RA sometimes saw him in the library studying alone. The RA asked whether he was in any student groups and Hodekki just shook his head—the RA couldn't recall whether he had even spoken, although there had been some brief interaction.

As assistant director of student services, your first suggestion to Hodekki was to get involved with the Native American student group—Native Americans at Ivy College. Hodekki later reported that he did go to several meetings, but he said the other Native students spoke very fast and all seemed to know each other. At the first meeting, he introduced himself in his Native language as he had been raised to do. No one responded, and the room was very quiet after he spoke. He talked with a few people after the meetings but told you he did not feel as though he fit in at all. The other Native students "acted White," he said, and he did not understand why they did not speak their tribal languages or act "more Native."

Today, as you talk about his experiences in class and more broadly on campus, he tells you that he was invited to a Native American campus ministry group. Hodekki follows traditional tribal spiritual practices and says he would feel uncomfortable there. His grandmother, a boarding school survivor, had warned him that they would try to convert him at college, so he is wary of people who invite him to any activity sponsored by campus ministries.

You are not a Native American person and are not familiar with boarding schools, so you ask Hodekki about them. Looking down again, he speaks quietly about the residential schools where Native American children were sent to remove all traces of their culture. Hodekki tells you about his grandmother being struck in the face for speaking her language in boarding school and having to recite Bible verses and sing hymns in English. Her long hair was cut short, and she was not allowed to have contact with her family for a year. Ivy is far from Hodekki's home; he says it was very difficult for him to accept the full scholarship he received, because it meant he would have to leave his home, his large family, and his dear grandmother. His grandmother cried when he told her he would be going to college in the East. Telling her that he was going away to college was the hardest thing he had ever done, Hodekki confides; telling his little sister that their dog had been hit by a car was easier.

In a moment you wish you could take back, you ask him if his grandmother does not understand what an honor it is to attend Ivy. Hodekki looks you directly in the face and says, "All that mattered was I was leaving and not being a part of home." He adds that being away from home means having no one to speak his language with, eating strange foods, not going to ceremonies, and being inside all the time instead of outdoors. He does not tear up, but his voice quivers a bit as he says, "It is not easy for me to be me here."

Hodekki has a few people he hangs out with: Roger and Cathy, and occasionally Andy. Andy is Puerto Rican and very quiet. Roger is Native, grew up on a reservation, and has the same last name, Henry, although he is from a different tribe. Easygoing and talkative, Roger jokes that he and Hodekki are relatives even though they are not. Cathy, who is White and from a small town in rural Pennsylvania, has a crush on Roger. When you ask about Roger and Cathy, Hodekki smiles sadly. Apparently, very late one night after studying, Roger started to sing a traditional song. After Roger finished, Hodekki started to cry. Cathy asked him why he was crying, but Hodekki had no answer. There was a very long, uncomfortable silence. Finally, Roger said he knew only a few songs.

Hodekki believes that Cathy told others, in the Native group and also her other friends, about the incident. Some students have started to tease Hodekki, patting their eyes when they say his name. Others avoid him altogether. Waneta, a very pretty Native student who dances at pow-wows during the summer, told

Hodekki that she thought he was just plain weird. Hodekki says he thought at least Waneta would understand, but although she knows songs and is a dancer, she grew up in a Christian home and has never lived on a reservation. She has very little idea of what he is experiencing and is openly unsympathetic.

The song incident has further isolated Hodekki, and he feels betrayed by Roger and Cathy. Now, with the added pressure to perform in class, he believes everyone is looking at him and seeing only an "Indian," not a whole person. In almost a whisper, he says that he hasn't been to classes in a week, can't stand the taste of the food here, and just wants to sleep all day, but can't. He looks you straight in the eye and says, "You tell those professors to ask Asian students to share what Asians think, and what White people and Black people think, because what they're doing to me is not fair."

Student Development Response

At first you are a little perplexed by Hodekki's situation. He seemed to be open to your suggestions and was willing to introduce himself to his professors and attend meetings of the Native American student group. Despite these efforts, Hodekki seems to be even more isolated, and now he is exhibiting signs of depression. You consider Hodekki's development, particularly as a Native American student.

The issue of identity among Native people is highly complex and politicized. With approximately 562 federally recognized tribes in the United States, each with its own distinct culture and history, much diversity exists among Native people. Native college students' development is tied not only to culture and ethnicity but also to history, tribal sovereignty, and the historical oppression of Native cultures (Torres, Howard-Hamilton, & Cooper, 2003).

Horse (2001, 2005) has described Native identity in terms of "American Indian consciousness" (p. 65). He explains that Native people see themselves as members of a specific tribe first, and that the consciousness of that membership is where Native identity begins (Horse, 2005). Furthermore, Horse (2001) explains, multiple layers exist in Native identity development: the family, the tribal group, and the larger general Native population. Horse's exploration of American Indian consciousness reveals five essential influences: (1) how well one is grounded in the Native language and culture; (2) whether one's genealogical heritage as an Indian is valid; (3) whether one embraces a general philosophy or worldview that derives from distinctively Indian ways or traditions; (4) the extent to which one thinks of him- or herself in a certain way, meaning one's idea of self as an Indian person; and (5) whether one is officially recognized as a member of a tribe by that tribe's government (Horse, 2001, p. 100).

LaFromboise, Trimble, & Mohatt (1990) developed a model of Native identity in terms of the extent to which a person adheres to traditional Native/tribal culture. Examining residential patterns, level of tribal affiliation, and individual commitment to maintaining tribal culture, LaFromboise and colleagues classify Natives into five categories or typologies of "Indianness":

- **Traditional.** These persons generally speak and think in their Native language and know little English. They observe old-time traditions and values.

- **Transitional.** People in this group generally speak both English and the Native language in the home. They question basic traditionalism and religion, yet do not fully accept the dominant culture and its values.

- **Marginal.** These persons may be part Indian, but because of their ethnicity they are unable to live fully within the cultural heritage of their tribal group. Neither are they able to identify completely with the dominant population.

- **Assimilated.** This group includes people who, for the most part, have been accepted by the dominant society. They generally have embraced the dominant culture and its values.

- **Bicultural.** These people are largely accepted by the dominant culture, but know and accept their tribal traditions and

culture. They can operate in either direction, from traditional society to the dominant society, with ease (LaFromboise
et al., 1990, p. 638).

This framework can help student affairs professionals understand that
Native students will exhibit different levels of "Indianness" and demonstrates
the wide diversity among these students. Note, the categories are descriptive,
not prescriptive; the goal is not to push Native students toward bicultural
status, but rather to better understand individual students. Observing and
understanding students developmentally and culturally is a central task for
college student personnel professionals; it is even more important in interacting with Native students. However, you need to balance the importance
of learning about Native students' lived experiences with respect for cultural
norms: Probing questions from a non-Native person can be intrusive and
inappropriate. Trust must be earned and built over time.

Comprehending the complexity of Native identity development is crucial. Understanding ethnic identity development in terms of marginality and
conflict with dominant culture is equally vital. Building on identity models
such as those of Erikson (1968), Marcia (1980), and Atkinson, Morten, &
Sue (1979, 1989), Phinney (1990, 1992) developed a three-stage model of
ethnic identity development. This model focuses on resolving two basic conflicts that youth encounter as a result of being members of a nondominant or
marginal group: (1) stereotyping and prejudice on the part of the dominant
White population and (2) conflict between the value systems of the majority
and minority cultures. Both conflicts influence the self-concept and sense of
ethnic identity of minority students. Phinney says that resolving the conflicts
yields three possible outcomes: (1) diffusion-foreclosure, (2) moratorium, or
(3) identity achievement (ultimately achieving a bicultural identity).

These models provide a context in which student affairs professionals
can approach Native student development. They illuminate the various levels of Native identity, as well as the issues involved in developing an ethnic
identity in relation to the dominant culture. Remember that while some
common identity issues affect many Native people, no one model fits all Na-

tive students. Identity among Native people is complex; theoretical models offer a basis from which student affairs professionals can begin to understand that complexity.

Counseling Response

You have already done something very important by creating a space in which Hodekki can speak. The fact that he arrives, frequently without an appointment, in your office means that he seeks your company and support. Despite the fact that you do not know a lot about his culture, Hodekki perceives you as caring, willing to learn, and connected to other resources. There is significant potential for building the affirming, long-term relationship you will need to continue to help him. Using the core conditions from the Person-Centered helping model in culturally appropriate ways can help you realize that potential.

Person-Centered Helping

The core conditions of genuineness, unconditional positive regard, and empathy can help you foster an open, safe atmosphere for Hodekki, allowing him to feel accepted for who he is. Recall that the central guiding question is "How does this person experience himself?" Thus, your initial focus should not be on how you assess his situation or what you can do to improve things for him; rather, you should focus on appreciating as fully as you can what Hodekki is experiencing. Although the core conditions will help you achieve that focus, they should not be applied in a rote manner. To be effective, you will need to adapt your use of the conditions with Hodekki, not because he is a special case as a Native American student, but because each student is unique.

Your first (and ongoing) task is to strive to understand how Hodekki experiences himself. You might ask questions to show your interest and invite Hodekki to share his experience with you. However, direct questions are not typical in the traditional Person-Centered framework, and they may be offensive to Hodekki. He has already conveyed discomfort with the questions some of his instructors

139

and classmates have asked. He seems to dislike being put on the spot to represent a singular Native American perspective; at the same time, questions about personal matters might feel intrusive to him.

For many Native Americans, personal information is shared only with intimates: family and close friends (Sue & Sue, 2008). Additionally, "learning occurs by listening rather than talking" for many Native Americans (Sue & Sue, 2008, p. 351), so Hodekki may not see value in extensive self-disclosure during his meetings with you. Still, respect for elders and authority figures is typically a cultural imperative for Native people (Sue & Sue, 2008). Thus, if you question Hodekki directly, you might be creating an uncomfortable situation for him. He might want to be respectful of you while simultaneously perceiving your requests for private information as inappropriate and not particularly useful.

You might wonder, "Well, if I'm not supposed to ask questions and he might not want to talk about personal matters, how is this supposed to work?" If you are reacting in that way, then you are likely discovering that you hold some culture-bound notions of helping (Sue & Sue, 2008). Many of the goals and processes in dominant helping models reflect the values and worldviews of White, middle-class people (e.g., Ponterotto, Utsey & Pedersen, 2006; Ridley, 2005). Emphasizing "verbal/emotional/behavioral expressiveness" (Sue & Sue, 2008, p. 142), self-disclosure, and a cause-and-effect orientation to problem solving (Sue & Sue, 2008) are common in the helping process among middle-class White people. Many cultural groups, including Native Americans, do not value those strategies in the same way. While they might seem perfectly reasonable to you, for Hodekki they may have little or no relevance. In fact, trying to use these techniques with him could actually reinforce his sense of isolation. While there is no simple solution, recognizing that these possibilities exist and staying open to Hodekki's preferences are steps in the right direction. Hodekki is already sharing information with you; allow him to continue do so at his own pace and to the extent he chooses.

Empathy is also essential to Person-Centered helping, and it is vital to your work with Hodekki. To help him, you need to be able to see his situation from his point of view. Many people on your campus might focus on Hodekki's receipt of a full scholarship as an unmitigated success—even you questioned whether his grandmother understood what an honor it is to attend Ivy. From Hodekki's perspective, his circumstances are not so clearly favorable. In fact, for Hodekki, all the gains that others see may be overshadowed by serious losses.

Empathizing with Hodekki means being able to recognize his grief. He has lost his day-to-day direct contact with his family, including his beloved grandmother; he cannot speak in his language, eat familiar food, attend spiritual ceremonies, or connect with nature as he normally would. His experience parallels what many international students go through: culture shock. It is an especially disorienting and difficult experience. Hodekki's struggles are made all the more painful in that he is expected to see himself as "fortunate" because he is attending a prestigious (predominantly White) college. The racism inherent in such an assessment may be largely invisible to many other staff members and most students at Ivy, but it is not to Hodekki. It adds a complicating, invalidating layer to his grief and loss.

Traditional Native curative strategies focus on restoring harmony and balance (Sue & Sue, 2008). You can help Hodekki generate ideas about how to achieve a balance in his life on campus, attending to mind, body, and spirit. There are several straightforward, practical ways to do this. Look with him at his schedule of studies, social activity, sleep, and the like, and support him in making changes that he thinks might help. Being indoors for long stretches of time is stressful for him; you might encourage him to spend more time outdoors by showing him the walking paths and parks in the area. He misses his favorite dishes; you can encourage him to get recipes from his grandmother and try a little cooking in the Native Student Center kitchen. You could offer to help, but only if Hodekki will tell you a story for every dish you prepare together. If he accepts the bargain, you will not only be sharing food; more important, you will be learning about his home and family. To help Hodekki increase his social connections, you and your office can reach out to him with support services and possibilities for social engagement. Among all these suggestions, listen intently for what he is willing to do and offer encouragement along the way.

Finally, strongly consider referring Hodekki to the counseling center. As with other cases in this text, timing and strategy will significantly influence whether or not Hodekki accepts the referral. Avoid referring him too quickly, as he might experience that as yet another rejection or judgment. As you build trust and gain credibility with him, you can begin a conversation about the services the center offers. Realize, however, that Hodekki may be wary about being "assessed." Ideally, you will know someone in counseling services who is a Native American or is sensitive to traditional Native cultural ways, and for whom you can vouch.

Sue & Sue (2008, pp. 356–357), after reviewing traditional Native American values, offer a list of implications for counseling Native clients. Nine of the thirteen points are adapted here, modified for student affairs professionals generally and for working with Hodekki specifically:

1. Explore ethnic differences. Be aware of your own cultural biases and how they might hinder your relationships with Native students. Ask yourself if you are working from shared values with students rather than imposing your values on them.

2. Explore the cultural identity of the individual student with whom you are working. Look particularly at tribal affiliation and level of acculturation. Hodekki is a top scholar, indisputably of very high intelligence. He is, however, much more traditional than the other Native students at Ivy, which sets him apart socially and isolates him, at least at this point.

3. Try to understand the history of oppression, and be aware of or inquire about local issues (e.g., mascot issues, disputed ownership of sacred lands, assumptions that all Indian students receive free higher education, etc.) that may affect Native students on your campus.

4. Expect that you will need to build trust over time, both for yourself and for any potential referral agency, office, or colleague. Reading about oppression is not the same as working with a traditional Native student. Hodekki is going to watch you closely. As a Lakota woman once said, "Do not assume,

nor disguise; a light flickers in your eyes" (Roberts, Harper, Caldwell, & DeCora, 2003, p. 27).

5. Be comfortable with silences or at least allow them, even if you are not comfortable. Productive silence, respectful silence, compassionate silence—all are important here. Hodekki may sometimes just want to be with you or take time to think with you. Stay out of the way by being silent so he can complete and reflect on his thoughts without interruption.

6. Keep in mind the cultural and experiential aspects of your student's situation. Hodekki is struggling to find his way in a very different culture on campus, while simultaneously staying true to his own culture.

7. If necessary, address basic needs. Hodekki is on full scholarship, but he may not know about certain social expectations on your campus. For example, he might not know that he'll need a tuxedo to wear to the honors banquet in November. You can help him navigate the campus system in practical ways.

8. Recognize that the campus environment does not feel inclusive to all students. Strategize with Hodekki about how to cope with or even change elements that are invalidating for him. While protecting his privacy and respecting what he has told you in confidence, you can consider how to advocate for him and other Native students.

9. Recognize that Hodekki is likely to be more holistic in his approach to change than many other students. Accept spiritual, intuitive, and nonlinear strategies he may use to cope with stress or feeling overwhelmed. In fact, Hodekki may already be using mindfulness strategies, although that might not be what he calls them. Existing in the moment, exercis-

ing nonjudgment, and practicing acceptance would probably be compatible with Hodekki's preferred coping strategies. Exploring and modeling mindfulness in your approach
with him could significantly strengthen your rapport. Sitting silently with Hodekki, inviting him to share what he
is experiencing in the present (if he wants to), and talking
with him about your own present-moment experience are
all potentially helpful strategies. Finally, if there is a campus
meditation group, you could suggest he consider joining; be
clear, however, that the group is not an attempt to influence
his well-established spiritual commitments.

Many non-Native people might read this case study and think about what a
privilege it is for Hodekki to attend such a prestigious school. Yes, there are benefits for him, but the notion that only Hodekki has something to gain is not only
inaccurate but racist. Other forms of privilege exist outside of power and status;
you can learn much from Hodekki. Your work with him could be transformative
for you if you open yourself to the possibility.

Discussion Questions

1. How might differing levels of Native identity or "Indian-ness" affect interactions between and among Native students? How might encounters with Native students of different levels of Indianness impact your effectiveness as a student affairs professional?

2. Referral to a mental health professional is or could be part of each case study in this volume. How does working with a student whose cultural background or level of assimilation is different from yours affect the referral process?

3. Recall any assumptions you may have made when you saw that the student featured in this case study is Native American. What did you think or feel as those assumptions were either validated or questioned?

4. What do you know about tribal people in the geographic area of your institution? How can relationships with indigenous peoples in your vicinity support your work with Native students on your campus?

5. How has your experience thinking through Hodekki's situation changed how you might work with students in the future?

References

Atkinson, D. R., Morten, G., & Sue, D. W. (1979). *Counseling American minorities* (1st ed.). Dubuque, IA: William C. Brown.

Atkinson, D. R., Morten, G., & Sue, D. W. (1989). *Counseling American minorities* (2nd ed.). Dubuque, IA: William C. Brown.

Erikson, E. (1968). *Identity: Youth and crisis.* New York: Norton.

Horse, P. G. (2001). Reflections on American Indian identity. In C. L. Wiyeyeshinghe & B. W. Jackson III (Eds.), *New perspectives on racial identity development: A theoretical and practical anthology* (pp. 91–107). New York: New York University Press.

Horse, P. G. (2005). Native American identity. In M. J. Tippeconnic Fox, S. C. Lowe, & G. S. McClellan (Eds.), *Serving Native American students* (pp. 61–68). San Francisco: Jossey-Bass.

LaFromboise, T. D., Trimble, J. E., & Mohatt, G. V. (1990). Counseling intervention and American Indian tradition: An integrative approach. *The Counseling Psychologist, 18*(4), 628–654.

Marcia, J. E. (1980). Identity in adolescence. In J. Adelson (Ed.), *Handbook of adolescent psychology* (pp. 159–187). New York: Wiley.

Phinney, J. S. (1990). Ethnic identity in adolescents and adults: Review of the research. *Psychological Bulletin, 108*, 499–514.

Phinney, J. S. (1992). The multigroup ethnic identity measure: A new scale for use with diverse groups. *Journal of Adolescent Research, 7*, 156–176.

Ponterotto, J. G., Utsey, S. O., & Pederson, P. B. (2006). *Preventing prejudice: A guide for counselors, educators, and parents.* Thousand Oaks, CA: Sage.

Ridley, C. R. (2005). *Overcoming unintentional racism in counseling and therapy* (2nd ed.). Thousand Oaks, CA: Sage.

Roberts, R. L., Harper, R., Caldwell, R., & DeCora, M. (2003). Adlerian analysis of Lakota women: Implications for counseling. *Journal of Individual Psychology, 59, 1,* 15–29.

Sue, D. W., & Sue, D. (2008). *Counseling the culturally diverse: Theory and practice.* (5th ed.). Hoboken, NJ: John Wiley & Sons, Inc.

Torres, V., Howard-Hamilton, M. F., and Cooper, D. L. (2003). *Identity development of diverse populations: Implications for teaching and administration in higher education.* San Francisco: Jossey-Bass.

CHAPTER 7

A Resident with Autism
Ellie

Hande Sensoy-Briddick, Emily Levine,
Ruth Harper, and Nona L. Wilson

Ellie is a 19-year-old Caucasian student who, weeks before the start of the fall semester, is accepted as a transfer student at a large university in the Southwest. Ellie was diagnosed with autism at age six. Because of her high intelligence and academic progress at a smaller college near her home, she was encouraged to transfer to further her education in the larger university's math department, where a gifted, celebrated scholar with Asperger's syndrome graduated and went on to doctoral-level studies just a few years earlier. Ellie's parents believe that the campus has much to offer their daughter.

Ellie is assigned to a double room in a co-ed residence hall. Her parents accompany her to campus to help with her transition to the university. Before leaving, they visit with Melissa, the resident assistant (RA) on the floor, to inform her about Ellie's condition. They ask Melissa to call them directly about any significant issues she observes involving their daughter. Melissa is uncertain about how to respond and encourages the parents to visit with you, the residence hall director (RHD).

As Ellie's parents discuss her needs with you, they note that, although she has challenges, their daughter is very bright and capable of handling challenging academic work. However, like many students with autism spectrum disorders (ASDs), Ellie has immature social skills and may need direct assistance or even instruction about how to interact with others. She comes across as painfully shy and socially awkward. Getting to know her can be difficult, because she prefers not to engage in conversation unless she has been around someone for at least a day or so. Even then, her parents explain, Ellie's conversations will be minimal, but eventually she will adjust and interact more easily. They encourage patience. They know that the friendly social chaos of a residence hall that many students thrive on can be almost toxic for students like Ellie, but she is willing to try it and wants to succeed.

In further discussion, it is clear that Ellie and her parents have connected successfully with the university's Office of Disability Services. To qualify for services, students must document disabilities, and Ellie has done so. She has been coached on how to approach her professors about accommodations and already has a student assistant assigned to her who will spend approximately 2 to 3 hours, Monday through Friday, helping with her daily responsibilities. The student assistant will ensure that Ellie follows a strict schedule and completes her assignments on time. Her parents indicate that Ellie has a very strong need for structure. Unless she follows a set daily routine, even basic life tasks (e.g., dressing appropriately, eating well) can overwhelm her. Ellie has signed a release of information form that allows college personnel to contact her parents with any concerns.

Ellie's roommate, Jane, a psychology major and a transfer student herself, is excited about sharing the room with Ellie. Jane readily reaches out to Ellie, inviting her to lunch and dinner at the Student Center. Jane is diligent in her efforts to help Ellie fit in, yet she is sensitive, going out of her way to avoid disrupting her roommate's routine. Wanting to be responsive to her roommate's needs, Jane makes necessary arrangements in the room so that Ellie feels at home. Initially, Jane, Melissa, and the student assistant are an effective support system for Ellie. Melissa frequently checks on Jane and Ellie to see that both are adjusting well to their new academic setting and to each other.

The first week passes without incident; however, the following two weeks are marked by noticeable changes in Ellie's behavior. Jane reports unusual episodes, such as waking up during the night to find Ellie standing by her bedside staring at her. On another evening, Ellie became extremely upset after not being able to find her syllabus for class. She had what Jane describes as a "meltdown," sobbing uncontrollably for about a half hour while rocking back and forth on the floor. The next week, Jane and two other residents tell Melissa that Ellie has started showering late at night, stripping off her clothes in her room and walking naked to and from the bathroom. Jane says that Ellie eventually gets dressed, but only after repeatedly being urged to do so.

Two female students on the floor seem protective of Ellie, referring to her as their "little sister." When they hear rumors of the incidents with Ellie, they speak to the RA on her behalf, saying that they think people in the hall need to be more understanding. Later that same day, other students on the floor report finding pieces of clothing in the bathroom and in the hallway that apparently belong to Ellie. Melissa quickly responds and talks to Ellie when she returns from class. Ellie states briefly that she misplaced her bathrobe. Melissa helps Ellie and Jane search for the bathrobe, which had fallen out of sight in the bottom of Ellie's closet. Jane later explains to Melissa that Ellie never mentioned the missing bathrobe and only shrugged when Jane tried to get her to put something on. After talking with Melissa and Jane and finding her bathrobe, Ellie seems better, although Jane is showing signs of frustration and fatigue.

Before the end of the first month of the term, after hearing that Ellie had left her room in the middle of the night and returned at dawn distraught and disoriented with cuts on her feet from walking around with no shoes, you decide that it is time to contact her parents. Meanwhile, Jane is exhausted and even a bit intimidated; she requests a room change, noting that stress from living with Ellie is starting to negatively affect her own academic work and social life.

Ellie's parents respond promptly. They hire a second student assistant for Ellie. Now Ellie is accompanied for approximately four hours a day. (At some colleges, students who request extra support pay an extra fee; in other cases, families directly hire aides for their students [*College transition programs launched for students with autism*, 2007]). With such extensive support, Ellie appears to do better and the worries subside. However, by returning to an uninterrupted, strictly monitored schedule, Ellie's connection with other residents deteriorates. The hall staff manages to maintain only minimal interaction with her, seeing Ellie in passing during the day and briefly in the evening on their rounds. Her "big sisters" on the floor have faded away, and Ellie now seems almost completely isolated.

Hall directors at your college receive midterm grade deficiency notices on their residents and check in with students who are struggling academically. In late October, you see that Ellie has deficiency notices in all her classes, even math. Ellie does not respond to repeated requests for a one-on-one meeting with you, and you can't seem to catch her coming and going, although you have her schedule and make several attempts. At the end of the semester, Ellie and her parents inform you that they are considering having Ellie transfer back to her former college closer to home. This arrangement, her parents believe, could be more conducive to her success. While you do not question their judgment, you know that Ellie will not be the last student with autism you will encounter.

Student Development Response

It is trying, at times overwhelming, to work effectively with students whose concerns require significant accommodation and support. Student affairs professionals will find that the major issues for students with autism generally have to do with social relationships, communication, and a need for structure and routine. Ellie poses unique challenges to residence life staff members, in part because meeting her needs entails creative responses and flexible thinking. Gwendolyn Dungy, executive director of NASPA, noted that autism is something colleges and universities are "very aware" of as the first big wave of children diagnosed with ASDs moves beyond high school. She said, "We want to establish a climate for success" (in Dutton, 2008, para. 8). Fortunately, many excellent resources are available to help you create such a climate.

Most research and writing about students with autism and Asperger's syndrome describe working with children (Smith, 2007). However, many strategies developed for younger students can be used with postsecondary students if they are adapted in respectful and age-appropriate ways. New resources are emerging as more students on the autism spectrum are pursuing postsecondary education (see, e.g., College Living Experience, n.d.; Palmer, 2005).

An important element of Ellie's success will be for you and your staff to acquire accurate information about ASD. Sometimes it will be hard to determine which of her behaviors you should be concerned about; the more you learn about autism, the better able you will be to conceptualize Ellie's situation. Personal accounts (e.g., Grandin, Duffy, & Attwood, 2004) can be extremely enlightening. If you have any responsibilities in the area of academic advising, as some residential life professionals do, you will want to know about the organization ASPIRES (Asperger Syndrome Partners and Individuals, Resources, Encouragement, and Support). Additionally, the Jed Foundation's publication *Student Mental Health and the Law* (2008) (which can be downloaded from www.jedfoundation.org/programs/legal-resource) is a primer of up-to-date information for higher education professionals working with students who have disabilities. It is particularly useful for navigating disability, mental health, and conduct issues.

Sanford and Schlossberg

As you learn more about ASD, you will begin to integrate this knowledge with what you know about student development. You might immediately think of Sanford's (1967) wise words about the need to balance challenge and support. Because college presents so many challenges for Ellie, she may require unusual levels of support to survive on campus (Brockelman, 2009, p. 274). "Creation of flexible support services" will help her "participate successfully in a typical college experience" (Dillon, 2007, p. 6).

It may also be helpful for you to look at Ellie in terms of Schlossberg, Waters, & Goodman's (1995) "4 S's" of situation, self, support, and strategies (in Evans, Forney, & Guido-DiBrito, 1998, p. 113). Schlossberg and colleagues' theory of transition proposes that students move in, move through, and move out of college environments. Ellie's **situation** is that she is in the midst of *moving in*, clearly a more complex process for her than for most students. Moving away from home and a uniquely supportive family environment is an enormous step for Ellie. The protective umbrella that her parents hold for her (Donovan & McKelfresh, 2008) is different from the umbrella other parents carry: larger, more flexible, and evident to others.

When working with Ellie, make no assumptions about what will or will not be obvious to her. What is obvious to the typical student may be significantly less so to her. The need to learn independent living skills, handle more complicated social interactions, and succeed in a more challenging academic environment may prove too much for Ellie to cope with all at once. And when students with ASD experience too much change or become overstressed, they demonstrate it behaviorally (Smith, 2007).

Ellie might struggle with sleep disturbances. Such struggles may be an indication of stress (Kadison & DiGeronimo, 2004, p. 106; Malow & McGrew, 2008) or they might represent a recurring concern, as they do for many persons with developmental disabilities. Check with Ellie's family about her habits, including her unusual behavior with regard to the shower. Has Ellie ever had to deal with a communal shower area before? Is she nervous showering around others? Is she afraid of making a mistake; is that why she is showering late at night? Could the problem be solved if she learns how to cope with this aspect of residence hall living? Or is the showering at night a sign of anxiety, and is the shower something Ellie needs to relax and cope with her anxiety about school? You and your staff members can explore these types of questions to help Ellie become more comfortable with residence hall living.

If Ellie's sleep disturbances are stress-related, or if the loss of self-care skills indicates a serious regression, transferring back to her first college and living at home may be a good option. The nighttime roaming and her inability to ask for help when she lost her robe may signal anxiety or may just indicate a need for higher levels of support, perhaps more than can be provided in a residence hall. Any unsafe student behavior must be addressed, but in Ellie's case, close monitoring is essential. It is no favor to allow her to do things that will get her in trouble or place her at risk. When Ellie walks around naked in the residence hall at night, she is not only inappropriate; she is vulnerable. This behavior must be addressed and changed to protect her and to keep other students from being uncomfortable.

To succeed in college, Ellie may require around-the-clock support from her family. If she moves home, it should be framed as "just for now" and not as a failure or an irrevocable choice.

Ellie's **self** brings unique gifts and challenges to your residence hall. She is academically talented and excited about her studies; she also presents some behaviors and concerns in the hall that you may not have previously encountered. It is important to remember that Ellie is not her disability; autism is one aspect of her identity. She is a young woman who loves math, music, and macaroni and cheese. She is completely devoted to regional indie bands and has a prodigious memory for groups and songs that others can never quite recall. She can be quirky in ways that are endearing as well as exasperating.

Numerous sources of **support** exist for Ellie. She has a highly engaged and supportive family. The Office of Disability Services and its allies will significantly contribute to her experience . The campus counseling center often has qualified employees who can provide not only counseling services for students with disabilities but also in-service training for staff. Additional resources may also exist. For instance, was Ellie involved in a church community at home? Does she engage in regular exercise? Would she enjoy participating in a small group of students with related disabilities to share ideas and have fun? Could her passion for music help her connect with other students? You will want to help Ellie consider all the possibilities.

In the hall, you may want to meet with Melissa (Ellie's RA) frequently or even schedule in-service training on autism and related disorders for interested residents and staff. Perhaps designating Melissa as the contact person with Ellie could reduce Ellie's stress by limiting the number of times she has to interact with unfamiliar people

Strategies for success are essential for Ellie. She has peer mentors and helpers to assist her in structuring her day and staying on track with both her studies and activities of daily living. Marshall University's Autism Training Center recommends a "positive behavior support approach . . . to assess each student's needs and develop appropriate academic, social, and life skills" strategies (2001, para. 1). At Marshall, college staff members regularly hold discussions to monitor progress, spot difficulties, and keep students working toward their goals. These tactics might be effective in your residence hall, or in collaboration with Ellie's academic advisor, peer mentors, and disability services staff members.

As noted, Ellie has difficulty managing personal boundaries with Jane. This is not a sign of pathology; it is simply Ellie's way of being with others. The residence hall staff could suggest using visual cues to delineate each roommate's side of their shared accommodations. Contrasting rugs, brightly colored floor tape, bookcases as dividers, or other physical barriers can establish clear, visual boundaries. Ellie might also benefit from written reminders to take her medication or lock the door to her room.

However, students with ASD commonly respond better to limited environmental stimuli, and can react negatively to even minor environmental changes, especially if they are surprised (Stokes, 2000). It is important to include Ellie in discussions about any change before it occurs. Explain that marking the floor and rearranging the furniture will help both roommates understand where their boundaries are and help them feel more comfortable. This is true and does not put the onus on Ellie. Acknowledging that both roommates have a right to privacy will help Ellie by making expectations explicit. Most people learn social conventions—what Myles, Trautman, and Schelvan (2004) call the *hidden curriculum*—without explicit instruction; persons with ASD may not be aware of these conventions unless they are specifically taught.

Generally, people with autism and Asperger's syndrome are visual learners (Stokes, 2000). "If it's important, write it down" is a good rule in working with students like Ellie who need frequent, concrete reminders and clarifications.

In conversation with students with autism, do not assume that discussion content will be processed, even if the student nods and seems to understand. Such signals may be a learned coping response to make the interaction end, not a sign of understanding (Myles et al., 2004). Verbal interactions should be calm and respectful, never condescending. Again, having written rules to refer to can be far less threatening than a lengthy discussion involving multiple people—a common occurrence in residence hall situations, especially during "interventions." One voice at a time or a quiet one-to-one chat will usually be much more effective (Myles et al., 2004).

Your approach to student involvement will be different with ASD students as well. Interactions that are meant to be supportive may actually be taxing and stressful for Ellie; she may require time alone to keep her energy up. For most students with ASD, socializing is hard work, not necessarily fun and relaxing (Winner, 2009). Schlossberg and colleagues (1995) also introduced the concepts of marginality and mattering. As a result of her disability, Ellie may feel marginalized in your hall and on campus. You, your staff, and other student affairs professionals can help her feel cared about and noticed in many positive ways.

Counseling Response

Person-Centered Helping

The core conditions of Person-Centered helping are appropriate to a wide range of students; with Ellie, you will need to use them in both highly focused and flexible ways. Seeing each person as unique is a hallmark of the Person-Centered approach, and that will work well with Ellie. She is not a representative of students with ASD; she is her own person, and you will want to focus on learning about her as an individual. Genuineness, unconditional positive regard, and empathy can help you understand her challenges without pitying her or thinking of her as "less than" other students. At the same time, learning about autism (while carefully taking cues from Ellie about what holds true for her) will be key to establishing a good working relationship.

You and your student affairs colleagues should sensitively explore what constitutes a developmental experience for her. What looks like dependency in a typical student may actually be a healthy coping behavior for her. For example, Ellie may need (and get) wake-up calls from her mother every morning. If Jane were getting such calls, you might become concerned; but for Ellie, the calls represent appropriate support.

Solution-Focused Helping

A Solution-Focused approach may be effective in helping Ellie make the most of her competencies and "do more of what works" (De Jong & Berg, 2008, p.

148) to succeed in college. Focusing on the problems or challenges Ellie is facing would be counterproductive; she is already all too aware of them. Rather, using a strengths-based perspective can be both encouraging and realistic.

As noted in chapter 2, Solution-Focused helpers are sometimes more directive than those using only Person-Centered techniques; often, Ellie will require direction. Imagine, for instance, that Ellie is arguing with Jane and that living together is becoming uncomfortable for them both. In talking with Ellie, you will want to listen carefully for what she wants (De Jong, & Berg, 2008, p. 21). Does she indicate a desire to be best friends with Jane? Or is sharing a small room with a virtual stranger very difficult for her? Your typical approach to roommate conflicts may not work in this situation. Ellie will probably find it nearly impossible to articulate her concerns directly to Jane, and she may need a different living arrangement (a solution of last resort in many residence halls). Instead of asking Ellie to talk it over with Jane or tell you what Jane does that is irritating, ask Ellie what living arrangement she would like.

Allow Ellie plenty of time to think this over; she may want to talk to her parents and peer helpers before deciding. Obtain as much detail as possible about her ideal outcome and then be realistic with her about possible changes. Asking "what and how questions" can work well (De Jong & Berg, 2008, p. 24). When she sees that neither she nor Jane is being blamed for the situation and that her wishes are being solicited, Ellie will be motivated to think about what she wants in her living arrangements.

Ellie has a track record of college success that you and other student affairs professionals can draw on to help her succeed at your campus. A Solution-Focused approach stresses building on previous success (De Jong & Berg, 2008). Therefore, find out what Ellie did well and enjoyed most at her former college. Did she take a reduced course load her first semester or two? Were courses in her major part of every term? Which courses did she excel in and like? Which student services were of most assistance? Do these services exist on your campus? How did Ellie find mentors, allies, and role models? How does she *like* to interact with peers? Can Ellie adapt what worked before to her current situation?

You will want to know whether a transition plan was created to help Ellie adjust to her new location. If so, are there elements of that plan with which you can help? Her advisor will want to learn about how Ellie was able to achieve the academic success that brought her to your institution. Ellie may need to connect quickly with professionals who can help her access adaptive technology, tutors, and other support

In co-constructing goals with Ellie, be clear about who is doing the work: It is her job to make it in college. You and others can help, but she must do everything she can. If you take on too much responsibility for her success, you could communicate to Ellie that you think she is incapable. Let her know how you can help while maintaining clear boundaries about who "owns" the achievements.

The Solution-Focused "miracle question" (De Jong & Berg, 2008, p. 85), in its traditional format (see chapter 2), might prove overwhelming to Ellie. Instead, the way you ask about her ideal living conditions and what worked for her at the other college are manageable ways of obtaining the same information. You might want to see if Ellie is willing to envision with you what it will be like for her at your college when she knows things are going well. As she creates and expands this vision, perhaps over time, both of you will see the seeds of her eventual success, whether on your campus or elsewhere. She might say, *"I will feel comfortable in my room. I will sleep well. I will not have to share a bathroom or shower. I will go to my classes and meet with my mentor every day. I will use my laptop to take notes in class and I will e-mail my prof if I have questions. I will not have meltdowns—I will think of something else to do, like walk away or call my mom. I will be more independent and not need my student assistants so much."*

As Ellie constructs the list of what constitutes success for her, you can reinforce her ideas and perhaps let her know that you'll give her a private signal occasionally as you see her doing things that support her goals. For example, when you see Ellie end a frustrating situation with a badgering student who thinks he's funny in the hall lobby, you can send her a text message acknowledging her triumph. When you do *not* find her name on the list of students with deficiency reports at midterm the next semester, you will ask her what she is doing to pass all her classes. If you miss running into her for a few days, you can check in on Facebook and say, *"Hey, Ellie. How's it going?"* or send a private message with the comment, *"I guess you must be working hard. Things seem to be going great!"*

Cognitive-Behavioral Strategies

Some Cognitive-Behavioral techniques can also help Ellie. As noted, visual cues in the residence hall room can be used to delineate appropriate boundaries between the roommates. Coping cards are another tool to consider. These cards can outline steps Ellie can take when she is overwhelmed or confused. You or others can help Ellie define a list of triggers for her panic attacks and meltdowns, and together come up with socially acceptable alternatives that are more adaptive. For example, if Ellie misplaces a syllabus or assignment, she can ask her student assistant for help, e-mail the course instructor, or call the disability services office. She could proactively organize her activities and commitments with a color-coded schedule. Her tests, projects, and papers also could be color-coded to help her focus and prioritize her work (College Living Experience, n.d., para. 3).

Help Ellie identify the physical feelings that she experiences when she feels she cannot cope, and generate possible responses she could use to help avoid a crisis. Does she feel hot? Have a knot in her stomach or become nauseated? Feel restless and unable to concentrate? What makes her feel better? Can she take a walk, call her parents, or listen to some of her favorite music? Ellie will be able to generate ideas after you share a few examples. Melissa and Jane could have a copy of this list and be aware of signs of distress that typically precede difficult reactions (Attwood, 2006).

Peers or helpers may be willing to model social skills and supervise practice. Ellie may not understand social subtleties or even hurtful remarks. She may take comments literally and completely misunderstand the intended message. For example, a student might say something to Ellie that sounds friendly but is not: "Hey, Ellie, cool pink pants! I had some like that in second grade." Ellie will not catch the irony and might even think this student wants to become a friend. "Verbal instruction, modeling, coaching, and personalized feedback to students with autism and Asperger's syndrome" are offered at some colleges, along with group discussions that "guide students in identifying social opportunities and provide a forum to experiment with functional and age-appropriate responses" (College Living Experience, n.d., para. 7).

Learning more about serving students with ASD is a challenge student affairs professionals can embrace. Emerging studies are beginning to establish best practices in this area (Dillon, 2007; Grandin et al., 2004; Smith, 2007). Integrating this knowledge with both student affairs and counseling models will promote adaptive services, advocacy, and leadership in student services.

Discussion Questions

1. After reading this case study, what questions do you have about working with students with autism spectrum disorders, and how will you explore answers to those questions?

2. What biases and prejudices might you hold toward students with neurological disorders? How will you grow as a professional by helping such students succeed in college?

3. Examine your own campus from the point of view of a student with Asperger's syndrome. What do you see as the biggest challenges and supports to students with autism spectrum disorders?

4. Not all students with autism are like Ellie. Describe experiences you have had with others "on the spectrum." In which ways are they similar to and different from Ellie? How would they require different interventions, resources, and responses?

5. Students like Ellie may require enormous amounts of staff attention to adjust and succeed in college. How will you balance helping such students with meeting the needs of all students?

References

Attwood, T. (2006). *The complete guide to Asperger's syndrome.* London: Jessica Kingsley.

Brockelman, K. F. (2009). The interrelationship of self-determination, mental illness, and grades among university students. *Journal of College Student Development, 50*(3), 271–286.

College Living Experience. (n.d.). Retrieved June 19, 2009, from www.cleinc.net/exceptionalities/autism_spectrum_disorders.aspx

College transition programs launched for students with autism. (2007, December 10). Retrieved June 30, 2009, from www.newswise.com/articles/view/536084

De Jong, P., & Berg, I. K. (2008). *Interviewing for solutions.* (3rd ed.). Belmont, CA: Thomson Brooks/Cole.

Dillon, M. R. (2007). Creating supports for college students with Asperger syndrome through collaboration. *College Student Journal, 41*(2), 499–504.

Donovan, J. A., & McKelfresh, D. A. (2008). In community with students' parents and families. *NASPA Journal, 45*(3), 384–405.

Dutton, M. K. (2008, July 8). *Autistic students get help navigating college life.* Retrieved June 19, 2009, from www.usatoday.com/news/education/2008-07-08-autistic-college_N.htm

Evans, N. J., Forney, D. S., & Guido-DiBrito, F. (1989). *Student development in college: Theory, research, and practice.* San Francisco: Jossey-Bass.

Grandin, T., Duffy, K., & Attwood, T. (2004). *Developing talents: Careers for individuals with Asperger syndrome and high-functioning autism.* Shawnee Mission, KS: Autism Asperger Publishing Co.

Jed Foundation. (2008). *Student mental health and the law: A resource for institutions of higher education.* New York: Author.

Kadison, R., & DeGeronimo, T. F. (2004). *College of the overwhelmed: The campus mental health crisis and what to do about it.* San Francisco: Jossey-Bass.

Malow, B. A., & McGrew, S. G. (2008) *Sleep disturbances and autism.* Retrieved June 30, 2009, from www.sleep.theclinics.com/article/S1556-407X(08)00033-7/abstract

Marshall University College of Education and Human Services. (2001). *West Virginia Autism Training Center model college program.* Retrieved September 19, 2009, from www.marshall.edu/coe/ATC/modelcollege.htm

Myles, B. S., Trautman, M. L., & Schelvan, R. L. (2004). *The hidden curriculum: Practical solutions for understanding unstated rules in social situations.* Shawnee Mission, KS: Autism Asperger Publishing Co.

Palmer, A. (2005). *Realizing the college dream with autism or Asperger syndrome.* London: Jessica Kingsley.

Sanford, N. (1967). *Where colleges fail: A study of the student as a person.* San Francisco: Jossey-Bass.

Schlossberg, N. K., Waters, E. B., & Goodman, J. (1995). *Counseling adults in transition* (2nd ed.). New York: Springer.

Smith, C. P. (2007). Support services for students with Asperger's syndrome in higher education. *College Student Journal, 41*(3), 515–531.

Stokes, S. (2000). *Children with Asperger's syndrome: Characteristics/learning styles and intervention strategies.* Written under a contract with CESA 7 and funded by a discretionary grant from the Wisconsin Department of Public Instruction. Retrieved June 30, 2009, from www.specialed.us/autism/asper/asper11.html

Winner, M. G. (2009). *Socially curious and curiously social: A social thinking guidebook for teens and young adults with Asperger's, ADHD, PDD-NOS, NVLD, or other murky, undiagnosed social learning issues.* San Jose, CA: Think Social Publishing, Inc.

CHAPTER 8

Returning Veteran with an Acquired Disability
Laurie

Kaela Parks, Nona L. Wilson, and Ruth Harper

T he student in the waiting area this morning sat with both feet flat on the ground and spine erect. She looked straight ahead and waited for her scheduled appointment with you, the director of disability services. This was not an appointment that Laurie wanted but, given her current situation, her VA counselor had told her it would be important for her to make this contact, so she was here. Laurie is a woman of action. She enrolled in courses at the college as soon as possible after getting back from Iraq. Although the personnel in the wounded warriors unit had encouraged her to wait until the following semester, Laurie had made up her mind: She was starting immediately.

The move from military life to that of a full-time student is not easy for Laurie. She has no family in the area. Her parents divorced when she was in elementary school and now live in different states. Her father is remarried and has a new family that she doesn't even know. Her mother is a semifunctional alcoholic, and her brother is a junior in a college somewhere in the Midwest. Like Laurie, he found a way out of the family early on; for him, it was a football scholarship. Laurie has known for some time that she must depend on herself alone.

This is her first semester in college, and Laurie has not been a student since she was in high school eight years ago. She was a senior when the news coverage of 9/11 reinforced her choice to join the Army; she served three years overseas before being injured. She considered herself lucky, since the blast that injured her had taken the lives of three other soldiers, and a fourth had received a very serious head injury.

After being discharged, Laurie completed extensive physical therapy (PT). During that time she began taking prescription pain relievers, and although she was offered a sleep aid, she tended to drink coffee and stay up late poking around the Internet rather than take the sedative. That choice was an attempt to avoid the nightmares that had plagued her since her return from the war. On the Internet, she spent most of her time blogging and chatting with other former military personnel. The jargon and sense of shared experience were soothing to her, much different than being around most of the students on campus.

The campus has a diverse student body with a relatively large percentage of older working adults who are attending courses on a part-time basis while supporting families. The college has a nontraditional student club and a division of commuter student services, as well as peer mentors from a variety of backgrounds. However, Laurie does not see this diversity and does not seek out others similar to herself. Instead, she focuses on the traditional college students who come straight from high school.

Laurie watches these students and thinks about how she is not like them. She does not slouch or cross her legs. She does not use her cell phone to text message during class or doodle pictures on her page of notes. These students always seem to be talking before class, in the restrooms, in the cafeteria. Laurie thinks they are whining and complaining about how hard this or that assignment is or how unfair this or that professor is. Their behaviors and attitudes make her cringe. From her perspective, they have no idea what real work is like, what true challenge feels like, or how unfair life can really be.

When Laurie hears traditional students complaining about mundane concerns, it brings up images of her fellow soldiers who lost their lives. She pictures their bodies all twisted and bloodied, and thinks about the families they left behind. She thinks about this and begins to hurt more and more, so she takes more pain medication. The pills help create internal silence, turning down the chatter in her head, blackening the disturbing images. Numbed and silent, she pushes forward.

The first time school came up in a discussion at the wounded warriors unit, Laurie decided that she would enroll. The college had sent a team—admissions, financial aid, and disability services personnel—to the unit. Laurie filled out her applications for admission and financial aid that day. The disability services contact person mentioned adjustments that could be made on an individualized basis, describing strategies such as note-taking assistance or the use of note-taking devices, reduced distraction testing environments or extended testing time, liaison services, and access to adaptive computing technology. The team distributed information for enrollment services, financial aid, disability services, the student health center, and the college counseling center.

The disability services staff member had brought a laptop to demonstrate technology that was available. Some of the soldiers had gathered around to see how Web pages, emails, even whole books in accessible text formats could be read out loud in a choice of voices. There were talking dictionaries and calculators, tools to summarize and annotate readings, or for recording lectures and notes, even software to dictate papers. Laurie noticed that some of the others in the unit were excited by these technologies, but she did not see herself as a person with a disability who needed special tools, or counseling, or anything else for that matter. She kept telling herself that once she got through her physical therapy she would be fine. She was one of the lucky ones, after all. Laurie took the information on enrollment services and financial aid but left the rest.

As she waited for the semester to start, her VA counselor stressed that Laurie still had a lot of PT to get through, and that she might want to wait for the following semester. Once Laurie made up her mind about something, however, there was only one way she saw to do it: full-bore.

She signed up for a full load of classes and took out a loan to pay for the expenses not covered through financial aid. The college had a Veteran's Affairs contact in the Financial Aid office, and some of the vets she talked to online had been able to navigate the system, getting the Pell Grant, scholarships, work-study jobs,

and GI benefits to all come together each semester and allow for full-time school-
ing without off-campus work. Most had managed pretty well, but that wasn't always the case. Some vets reported horror stories about not having enough money
with the benefits and aid alone, and then trying to work and getting behind in
studies. Laurie started the paperwork and hoped that she would be reimbursed
when the VA processed it all, but she decided to take out the loans and pay ahead
rather than wait.

When classes started, Laurie thought she was ready. She had her books and
supplies. She attended her classes, sitting up front but on the edge of the room,
near the door. But being in class and having the pen and paper were not enough.
Laurie listened to the lectures and wrote down what she thought were the important points, but then something the professor or a classmate said would remind
her of being deployed; her mind would wander and her notes turn into a mess. It
is impossible to study from them, and relying solely on her books does not work.
In one of her classes, the lectures do not seem to be related to the book at all, and
in two of the others the textbook writing is so dense that her eyes don't seem to
focus for more than a page or two. She finds herself rereading the same chapters.

Laurie failed two of her first exams. This was difficult for her to reconcile
with her beliefs about herself. She is not a failure. She is not an idiot. She is not a
weakling or a whiner. She is attending class but recently has been more and more
keyed in to what other students are doing. She looks at their notes and sees much
more detail, much more writing, than on her own pages. She watches them listening and realizes that she is not focused. Her situation feels unbearable.

Things have gotten worse over the course of the semester. Although Laurie's attendance has been mostly good, she missed several class sessions because of
medical appointments and PT sessions. She is staying up all night on the Internet
and finding it harder and harder to stay awake during the day. Her pain medication does not seem to be taking the edge off anymore, and it is very hard to focus.
She was unable to finish her last exam, getting through only the first two sets of
multiple-choice questions before time ran out. She grows increasingly disgusted
with the whining and childish banter of the students on the campus, and finds it
difficult to understand how she could be failing in this environment. She was a

soldier. She is equipped to handle adversity. Why can't she make this work?

The final straw came when her professor sent her an e-mail asking her to come in for a meeting. He wanted to discuss the exam she did not have time to complete. Laurie did not make the meeting and has not attended that class again. Instead, she withdrew from the course; because it is so late in the semester, she will not recover the tuition.

With these conditions in place—disconnected from the campus community; failing two courses, pulling a D in a third, and withdrawn from a fourth; experiencing intense pain and fatigue; and feeling numb to the entire process—Laurie is in your office but not entirely open to help. "To tell you the truth, I don't know why I'm here," she says. "My VA counselor told me to come in, but it's just protocol."

Laurie sits across the desk from you and barely listens as you outline rights and responsibilities and begin to make some recommendations. You know there are many options and resources for her. Possibilities such as a reduced course load, distance education so her PT sessions will not conflict with attendance, accommodations for exams to be administered in the lab with extended time, recording lectures, making use of tutors—all these would be helpful. However, looking across the desk, you see Laurie with her spine erect, her feet flat on the ground, and her jaw set tight.

Student Development Response

Your response to Laurie is informed by many variables. As director of disability support services on a campus with a large number of nontraditional students—many of whom are back at school after acquiring disabilities later in life—you are accustomed to meeting with students in transition. Some students are entirely comfortable with their status as persons with a disability and have a solid understanding of their strengths, allowing them to effectively navigate the accommodation process and advocate for themselves; but this is not always the case.

One of your first thoughts in meeting with Laurie is that she may benefit from participation in a new campus group being established. The group is composed of students who were active in the military but are now in civilian student roles. Like many colleges and universities across the country, your institution anticipated increasing numbers of student veterans and has been taking steps, backed by student development and adult learning theory, to improve their educational outcomes.

As noted by Schlossberg, Lynch, and Chickering (1989), adult students have diverse backgrounds with varied past experiences and multiple life roles. Student veterans, in particular, tend to have achieved a maturity beyond their years, coming to the university with a strong sense of responsibility and leadership (DiRamio, Ackerman, & Mitchell, 2008).

A rich set of life experiences can create tension when there is not a good fit between the person and the environment. The "fit" between students and the learning environment is vitally important in retention (Stoecker, Pascarella, & Wolfe, 1988). College and university environments are often geared more toward traditional students than toward adults (Tinto, 1987).

Adult students, especially veterans, can have a difficult time transitioning into college life, because they often are working through multiple transitions simultaneously. The transition into, through, and out of a military role, then into a student role, can include a significant amount of grief (Goodman, Schlossberg, & Anderson, 1997). When acquired disability is added to the equation, the transition can be even more difficult, and it does not necessarily unfold in a linear manner (Kendall & Buys, 1998). Seeing acquired disability as a time of transition rather than simply of loss is important (Ellis-Hill, Payne, & Ward, 2008).

If she becomes involved in the veterans' group, Laurie may gain the support she needs to move through her current transition. Student veterans with more semesters under their belts can help the newer members acclimate, recognize campus resources, and feel comfortable using them. By talking with other student veterans who have an acquired disability and who are using the accommodation process to mitigate barriers, Laurie may become more open to engaging in this process herself. Support is one of the key elements identified in transition (Schlossberg, 1981), and involvement itself is recognized as a strategy to gain traction in learning (Astin, 1999).

Adult nontraditional students are twice as likely as traditional students to leave school during the first year (NCES, 2002), although this does not necessarily mean that these older students are failing to meet their educational goals (Pappas & Loring, 1985). In Laurie's case, meeting with an academic advisor is a top concern. Clarifying her educational goal and developing a realistic game plan are steps that Laurie has skipped. As noted by DiRamio, Ackerman, & Mitchell (2008), it is important to take a holistic approach when working with student veterans. You know that one of the academic advisors is a veteran himself; rather than just pointing Laurie in the direction of the Advising Office, you call him while Laurie is in your office and introduce them so they can schedule the advising appointment. Laurie is in trouble at this point and, while your office can address some of the issues related to her disability, other connections will be vital to getting her back on track.

Your institution is concerned about retaining adult students. A majority of students enrolling in postsecondary education now possess at least one of the characteristics used to define nontraditional student status, but those who are considered highly nontraditional are most at risk of not attaining their educational goal (NCES, 2002). The reasons older students do not persist when it is their goal to do so are both similar to and different from issues identified as important to retaining traditional-aged students. Income, work schedules, family or medical concerns—all can be critical components in determining whether or not a student will stay in school. For students coming to campus from the military, there may be challenges in processing VA benefits, scheduling medical appointments, and coordinating with other ongoing military processes (DiRamio, Ackerman, & Mitchell , 2008). If a nontraditional student identifies the role of employee or soldier as primary, that person's role as student takes a lower priority. This relegation of education to a secondary role seems to be central to the challenges facing nontraditional students (NCES, 2002). While it is important to examine the overall combination of characteristics that define the individual student (Johnson, 1991), academic integration plays the largest role in determining whether students persist in their studies (Cleveland-Innes, 1994).

Academic integration can be defined as how well a student feels he or she fits into the academic life of an institution, and people who work with student veterans report that fitting in can pose a significant challenge for them (DiRamio et al.,

2008). Course selection will be important to Laurie's success in future semesters, and you hope that meeting with the advisor will be a step in the right direction. You recognize that an individual faculty member's instructional style can affect Laurie's classroom success—she might benefit from reviewing the student evaluations of faculty that are completed each semester and available through the campus library. You encourage Laurie to talk about her current classes—and the classes she is considering—in the campus veterans' group. She will be happy to learn that some staff and faculty members have participated in recent webinars and campus discussion groups focused on creating a more veteran-friendly campus.

Your institution, like many others, has tried to respond sensitively and responsibly to the recent increases in student veteran enrollment. The work is ongoing and not necessarily consistent across campus, but efforts are under way to make the learning environment more veteran-friendly; for example, identifying veteran staff and faculty members, creating the student veteran group, and hosting relevant webcasts and discussion groups.

These strategies are not novel. Established methods to improve nontraditional student persistence include recognizing the unique characteristics of subpopulations and encouraging advocacy in those groups, establishing related support services, and empowering staff to be aware of and sensitive to diverse student needs. Developing orientation or career counseling experiences specific to nontraditional students and encouraging faculty to develop inclusive learning environments are also recommended (Miller Brown, 2002).

The campus may have had multiple strategies in place to improve educational outcomes for nontraditional students, but the waves of returning soldiers require further efforts. To improve academic integration for student veterans, many campuses are developing student veteran groups that operate on a peer-to-peer basis (Student Veterans of America, 2009), and some campuses are establishing veteran one-stop shops and becoming more knowledgeable about and responsive to trauma and its consequences (Buck, 2009).

Although Laurie is not seeing all these efforts and has been experiencing difficulty in her transition, you hope her situation will improve as she gets involved in the student veteran group, establishes a connection with an advisor with whom she can relate, and considers accommodation strategies. In addition to the specific ideas you hope will be helpful to Laurie as a student veteran, you continue to engage in broader efforts for students with disabilities. You have worked for a number of years to foster a Universal Design approach that ensures the fullest access and richest engagement possible to the widest range of students (Burgstahler, 2009; CAST, 2009; CUD, 1997; Scott, McGuire, & Embry, 2002; Scott, McGuire, & Shaw, 2003). Such an approach is especially useful from a disability support services perspective, because it focuses on minimizing the need for accommodation. This is very important when students do not identify as having a disability yet face disability-related barriers that can impede academic integration (Buck, 2009).

An example of Universal Design that helps many people is the simple curb cut. Initially created to accommodate people in wheelchairs, curb cuts are used by people on bicycles and roller blades, those pulling wheeled suitcases or pushing baby strollers, and so on. "Accommodations" frequently benefit the population at large, not only individuals with disabilities, and this is true of a variety of academic accommodations as well.

The Universal Design workshops you hold on campus invite faculty members to bring specific courses to the table. Ideas can be shared regarding how flexibility can be built into a course without lowering academic standards. Professors who use emerging technologies are given ongoing technical assistance and encouragement. For example, more instructors are recording class sessions with course management tools so students can review the archived lectures if repetition is helpful to them. Faculty can choose to upload accessible class notes for each session, post grades regularly so that students can monitor their progress, and make sure that office hours include virtual hours so that students who work or have other obligations off campus can connect online.

In addition to the technology-based modifications discussed in faculty training sessions, workshops for faculty and staff focus on cultivating an open and responsive approach to teaching. Making sure students understand what is expected of them is important. It is also critical to design student services, academic courses, and other elements to be simple and intuitive to navigate.

173

You hope that by focusing efforts on the broader Universal Design approach and the more specific veteran-friendly elements in student affairs and academic affairs, your institution can ease the transition for students like Laurie. Proactive, holistic, universally designed learning environments that foster peer support will give all students a better chance to achieve academic integration and meet their educational goals.

Counseling Response

Clearly, you will need to refer Laurie to the campus counseling center. She is struggling with issues arising not only from her relatively recent military service and acquired disability but also from long-standing loss related to family-of-origin concerns. She has few social supports and significant academic and financial stress, and her coping strategies tend toward increasing self-criticism, diminishing self-acceptance, anger, drug use, and social isolation. When paired with her high self-expectations, these factors create a crisis situation for Laurie. For all these reasons, you will refer Laurie to your campus counseling center for professional assessment and services. It will not be easy to do so effectively for at least two reasons. First, you do not yet have Laurie's trust. She is skeptical and agitated, states of mind that do not foster receptivity. She has told you that she has come to see you because it is "protocol." In other words, she sees the meeting with you as a hoop through which she must jump. She does not expect to get help. Moving too quickly to refer her to someone else will only reinforce that belief and minimize the likelihood that she will accept the referral.

Second, Laurie is frustrated with herself. She is having a hard time understanding how she—a strong, competent soldier—can be struggling so much when she sees "weak and whiny" students apparently breezing through college. She believes she ought to be able to manage on her own. This kind of "fake it 'til you make it" attitude might be a coping strategy she developed early in life in response to her family difficulties. It is an attitude that she may have continued to practice in the military in response to the stressful, often traumatic, demands of service.

Laurie sees her struggles as indicators of failure. With this mind-set, she could easily hear a referral to the counseling center as yet another indictment—

that there is, in fact, something wrong with her, that she cannot make it on her own. Moreover, from Laurie's point of view, failing is not only perplexing and painful, it is shameful, and she wants to avoid thinking or talking about it. Thus, although making a referral to the counseling center is a priority, it is not going to be the first or only item on your agenda. Connecting Laurie with a counselor is important, but counseling is not a cure-all, and not all of her difficulties are best addressed in therapy. When students are in crisis, student affairs professionals need to see the whole student and resist the temptation to lay everything at the counselor's door, which not only needlessly pathologizes many developmental and transitional challenges but can ultimately reduce, not enhance, the support students receive. Yes, Laurie ought to see a counselor, but she also will benefit from study skills, classroom and testing accommodations, and the myriad other services and resources described in the student development response. Achieving some measure of relief and success in those areas could very well help motivate Laurie to consider counseling. Concepts and strategies from Cognitive-Behavioral approaches to helping will be especially useful in building rapport with Laurie, providing support services, and ultimately referring her to the counseling center.

Cognitive-Behavioral Helping

Collaboration

Cognitive-Behavioral helping encourages a focused, task-oriented, problem-solving orientation that will likely appeal to Laurie. A hallmark of the Cognitive-Behavioral approach is collaboration—partnering with students to help them solve their problems. Collaboration fosters co-ownership of the helping process, so that students are not passive recipients of campus services but active agents selectively using the services. Cognitive-Behavioral helping with Laurie might look like this:

You: *"I can appreciate how it might feel like protocol to come in to see me, since it wasn't your idea. But my sense is that succeeding in school is important to you; if you and I could figure out some ways to help you do that, would you be interested?"*

175

Laurie: "Sure, but at this point, I kind of doubt that's going to happen."

You: *"Okay, you're skeptical. But you haven't given up completely. You're here, and I'd like to help. So, would you be willing to use this time to see if we can come up with a strategy that might work for you?"* (Tone of voice is important here. Laurie's temperament and current mood suggest that a matter-of-fact, businesslike approach—as opposed to a more emotional, warm-and-fuzzy style—will be more comfortable for her. The key is to not come across as harsh, rejecting, or flip. Tone is a balancing act that gets easier with practice.)

Laurie: "I'm here. Might as well."

You: *"Good. I have some ideas about how to start. How about if I share them with you and you can decide what sounds good?"* (Because Laurie is skeptical and her motivation is low at this point, the collaboration begins with your offering ideas. If Laurie were more invested, it would be preferable to ask first about her ideas on how and where to begin.)

With this collaborative approach, you are bringing Laurie into the decision-making process right from the start, which is useful in several ways: (1) it shows respect for her perspective; (2) it is inviting without being pushy or overly solicitous (she is free to decline at any time); and (3) it begins immediately to foster a sense of agency and shared responsibility. Throughout the meeting, regardless of what concerns or services you are talking about, you can maintain a collaborative stance by weaving in the following kinds of questions:

- What ideas do you have about that?

- What have you tried before? What part of it worked? What didn't go as planned?

- Does that make sense to you? What part doesn't make sense?

- How might that be helpful to you? Is there anything about it that might not be helpful?

- Would working on improving that be useful to you?

- What would help you do that? What would prevent you from taking that step?

Such questions invite partnership and, by soliciting Laurie's perspective at each step in the process, help you understand how she is reacting to the meeting as it is happening. That kind of in-the-moment feedback makes it easier to notice and address misunderstandings or breaks in rapport relatively quickly.

Generate a Problem List and an Action Plan

Rather than quickly narrowing your focus to the first concern or two that Laurie mentions, from a Cognitive-Behavioral helping approach, you will want to work with Laurie to generate a fuller list of issues. After that, you can collaboratively decide how to prioritize and respond to them. Doing that might go something like this:

You: *"Since our goal today is to try to map out a plan to help you succeed at school, I think it would be useful to get as clear a picture as we can of what's getting in your way. Does that sound reasonable?"*

Laurie: "I guess. I'm not sure exactly what you mean, though."

You: *"Well, what I'm thinking is we could just start listing what's troubling you—create a problem list so we know what we need to address. You'll have to lead the way on this since you know what's going on, not me. But I've talked to a lot of students—a lot of student veterans—so I have some ideas, too, and I'll ask about some common concerns, okay? Then, once we have the list, we can prioritize and start identifying what can be done. Make sense?"*

Laurie: "I hope you've got plenty of ink in that pen."

At this point, you and Laurie will generate a problem list. You will let her take the lead, but you can encourage her to be thorough by asking, *"What else?"* It is also useful to have an organizational framework in your head that covers major life domains:

1. Health: sleeping, eating, exercise, medical conditions

2. School and work

3. Social and family relationships

4. Finances

5. Mood/emotions

6. Spiritual/religious practices

As Laurie describes what is troubling her, you can organize the list into these domains, asking about areas that she hasn't brought up. She may or may not have concerns in all the categories. Be careful to not push for a long list, but allow Laurie to include all the items she wants to. Remain interested and supportive but nonreactive (neutral). YOU are not going to address these issues. You are not exploring or discussing them. Rather, you are inviting Laurie to generate this list so you can refer her to the right services on campus to increase her chances of staying in school. If Laurie becomes emotional while generating the list, you could use that as opportunity to validate how tough things are for her right now and to begin the discussion about the counseling center.

Once the list is completed, ask Laurie to look at each item and identify the most pressing concerns as well as the ones she thinks would be easiest for her to deal with. This will allow you to begin collaborating on how she can proceed. At this point you can talk to her about which resources on campus can address certain items on her list, and she is likely to be much more receptive to hearing about them. By working together on the problem list and beginning to map out a plan of action that involves some help from you, some help from other offices on campus, and some self-help strategies, you likely have begun to build rapport with Laurie. At this point you are in a much better position to refer Laurie to the counseling center. First, you have demonstrated a willingness to work with her on her concerns, and have drawn on her perceptions of what is most pressing. Second, you have in front of you evidence from Laurie's own life, in her own words, of why she might benefit from seeing a counselor. Third, seeing a counselor is just one element of a larger plan and can be framed as part of the overall action she is initiating.

Together, these factors give you some leverage with Laurie. If she says that she does not want to talk to a counselor, you can more easily ask her to tell you what it is that prevents her from doing so. You have already asked this question about other issues and student services throughout your meeting, so there is nothing different or forceful here. You ask out of genuine curiosity and as an invitation to explore her point of view. Since you are collaborating, you can ask if it is okay if you share your ideas about how the counseling center can be helpful, reminding her that it is ultimately her choice and you will respect her decision.

Mindfulness-Based Strategies

Imagine that you refer Laurie to the counseling center and she starts to see a counselor who can help her with the more serious elements of her problem list. Even while Laurie is seeing the counselor, she may want to continue to check in with you about other issues on her list and how support services on campus are helping her. You could easily integrate some mindfulness-based strategies into your helping routine with her. If you are practicing mindfulness in your own life, you will be better able to model its benefits for Laurie. You might find, for example, that you are clearer-headed in your meetings with her, more aware of your reactions and impulses as they arise, and better at not acting mindlessly. As you notice these reactions, you could even discuss them with Laurie. For example, you could say, *"Laurie, as you describe the time you spend comparing yourself with other students, I find myself feeling like I just want to fix this for you. I know I can't, and it makes me feel a bit frustrated—but noticing that in myself helps me appreciate your frustration and desire to make things better."*

Modeling in this way allows you to (1) monitor your own reactions and increase your ability to be intentional; (2) share your present-moment awareness with Laurie in a way that expresses acceptance for yourself and her; and (3) invite her to use a similar sort of reflection with her experiences. You can ask her to do so during your conversations (*"What are you noticing right now?"*) and throughout the week. Laurie might benefit from more formal practice; if your campus offers a mindfulness group or yoga classes or workshops, you could encourage her to check them out. You could even contact the people running such groups and invite them to offer classes specifically for returning veterans.

Discussion Questions

1. How would a student like Laurie fare at your institution?

2. If a student clearly needs to see a campus counselor but is reluctant to do so, what are your options? What are your obligations?

3. What is your inclination when you begin working with a hesitant or skeptical student? How can the idea of collaboration help? What would you need to keep in mind as you strive to collaborate with a student like Laurie?

4. What can you do to ease the process of accessing multiple offices and services for a student who might feel overwhelmed or judged by multiple referrals?

References

Astin, A. (1999) Student involvement: A developmental theory for higher education. *Journal of College Student Development, 40*(5), 551–529.

Buck, R. (2009). *Psychological needs of returning veterans.* Webcast from Academic Impressions.

Burgstahler, S. (2009). Universal Design of instruction (UDI): Definition, Principles, and Examples. Retrieved October 27, 2009, from DO-IT faculty page website: http://www.washington.edu/doit/Brochures/ Academics/instruction.html

CAST. (2009). UDL Guidelines. Retrieved October 27, 2009 from National Center on Universal Design and Learning websitehttp://www.udlcenter. org/aboutudl/udlguidelines

Cleveland-Innes, M. (1994). Adult student dropout at postsecondary institutions. *The Review of Higher Education, 17,* 423–445.

CUD. (1997). *Principles of Universal Design.* Retrieved February 12, 2009, from Center for Universal Design at NC State University website: www. design.ncsu.edu/cud

DiRamio, D., Ackerman, R., & Mitchell, R. (2008). From combat to campus: Voices of student-veterans. *NASPA Journal, 45*(1), 73–102.

Ellis-Hill, C., Payne, S., & Ward, C. (2008). Using stroke to explore the life thread model: An alternative approach to rehabilitation following an acquired disability. *Disability Rehabilitation, 30*(2), 150–159.

Goodman, J., Schlossberg, N. K., & Anderson, M. L. (1997). *Counseling adults in transition: Linking practice with theory.* New York: Springer Publishing.

Johnson, D. (1991). *Formulating a conceptual model of nontraditional student attrition and persistence in postsecondary vocational educational programs.* Berkeley, CA: National Center for Research in Vocational Education.

Kendall, E., & Buys, N. (1998). An integrated model of psychosocial adjustment following acquired disability. *The Journal of Rehabilitation, 64* (3), 16–20.

Miller Brown, S. (2002). Strategies that contribute to nontraditional/adult student development and persistence. *PAACE Journal of Lifelong Learning, 11,* 67–76.

National Center for Educational Statistics (NCES) (2002). *Findings from the Condition of Education 2002: Nontraditional Undergraduates.* Washington, DC: U.S. Department of Education.

Pappas, J. P., & Loring, R. K. (1985). Returning learners. In L. Noel, R. Levitz, and D. Saluri (Eds.), *Increasing student retention.* San Francisco: Jossey-Bass.

Schlossberg, N. K. (1981). A model for analyzing human adaptation to transition. *Counseling Psychologist, 9*(2), 2–18.

Schlossberg, N. K., Lynch, A. Q., & Chickering, A. W. (1989). *Improving higher education environments for adults.* San Francisco: Jossey-Bass.

Scott, S. S., McGuire, J. M., & Shaw, S. F. (2003). Universal Design for instruction. *Remedial and Special Education, 24*(6), 369–379.

Scott, S., McGuire, J. M., & Embry, P. (2002). *Universal Design for instruction fact sheet.* Retrieved February 12, 2009, from University of Connecticut, Center on Postsecondary Education and Disability website: http://www.facultyware.uconn.edu/files/UDI2_Fact_Sheet.pdf

Stoecker, J., Pascarella, E. T., & Wolfe, L. M. (1988). Persistence in higher education. *Journal of College Student Development, 29*(3), 196–209.

Student Veterans of America. (2009). Retrieved May 1, 2009, from www.studentveterans.org Tinto, V. (1987). *Leaving college.* Chicago: University of Chicago Press.

Tinto, V. (1987). *Leaving college.* Chicago: University of Chicago Press.

CHAPTER 9

ADHD
Challenges
Austin

Linde Murray, Jody Owen, Ruth Harper,
and Nona L. Wilson

Austin is a 20-year-old White male student at a midsized public land grant university in the Midwest. He was raised in a rural farming community and attended a small local school system where everyone knew him. His working-class background has instilled in him independence, a strong work ethic, and a desire to achieve. Austin values money earned through hard work and has a part-time job as a welder at a factory to help cover college expenses.

In middle school, Austin was diagnosed with attention deficit hyper-activity disorder (ADHD). Symptoms of ADHD include "difficulty staying focused and paying attention, difficulty controlling behavior, and hyperactivity (over-activity)" (National Institute of Mental Health, 2008, p. 1). Austin struggled academically and even a bit socially, prompting his doctor to pre-scribe medication. This helped, as did working with a resource room teacher who advocated for him and helped him do well in school. When he entered college, Austin chose to discontinue medication because of its side effects;

his parents supported this decision. Austin believes that the occasional mood swings and insomnia he experienced on medication create greater challenges for him than ADHD. Currently, he is a sophomore, working to complete the requirements for a bachelor's degree in manufacturing technology, and you are his academic advisor.

The first thing you noticed about Austin at new student orientation last year was his friendly and outgoing personality. He wore a bright blue college sweat-shirt or T-shirt most of the time and seemed thrilled to be at "State." As you got to know him, you discovered that he enjoys being active; his favorite noncollege activities are working on his vehicle, hunting, and his welding job. In addition, Austin loves being with other students. He has social connections both on and off campus and has developed a group of close-knit friends who are all in the same academic program. These friends provide a strong academic and social support network for Austin. They enjoy taking courses together and often collaborate on group assignments and Manufacturing Technology Club projects.

Austin is aware of his strengths, and he excels at the activities and work that he likes. He tells you that he remembers information best when he can do something with what he has learned. Because of this, he identifies himself as a kinesthetic learner and believes this preference has an impact on his academic performance. The classes that are specific to his major tend to be hands-on; Austin enjoys these courses and performs well in them. In contrast, he experiences serious challenges with courses that require a great deal of reading and writing.

Certain general education courses (e.g., English composition, social sciences, and humanities) are required of all students. These classes are extremely difficult for Austin to complete at a satisfactory level. He has taken some of them twice and has not been able to pass all of them, which is causing him a great deal of stress. In addition, college algebra and chemistry, both prerequisites for more advanced courses in his major, are proving to be surprisingly tough for him. Failure to complete these courses on time will prevent Austin from progressing through major requirements with his peers. This is very worrisome to Austin for both academic and personal reasons. Not only will he no longer have study partners (a strong motivational force for him); he believes that he will be perceived as "such a loser."

Austin is disappointed with his lack of success in freshman-level courses and says that he feels like a failure. He believes he is letting down not only himself but also his friends and family. Because of these academic setbacks, Austin's self-confidence has diminished, and he questions his ability to succeed in college or in his chosen profession. "I guess I'm not 'college material,'" he sullenly tells you one day. "Maybe I should have gone to the tech school." As you listen, you think that if Austin continues to struggle so much in his gen-ed courses, you may want to talk with him about the technical school and the fact that it is an *excellent* educational choice for many people. That campus—about an hour away—has an engineering technology associate degree program that is very well regarded in the region and might be a great fit for Austin. For now, though, you believe that with adequate support Austin can succeed at your institution.

Unfortunately, when classes become difficult or when Austin begins to fall behind, he copes by shutting down. He becomes highly frustrated, stops trying in his classes, and avoids communicating with people, including those who can offer him support. This behavior exacerbates his situation.

As Austin's academic advisor, you regularly recommend that he seek assistance with his courses from professors, teaching assistants, and tutoring resources. You think about encouraging Austin to talk with his family physician about options for treating his ADHD and about working with the disability services office on campus, since his ADHD is documented. Unfortunately, he is completely closed to these topics when you gently approach them.

Austin believes that he should be able to do things on his own; it is extremely difficult for him to ask for help. In fact, he seems offended by any suggestion that he seek assistance from tutoring, supplemental instruction, or other help centers on campus. He thinks that accepting assistance means that he is not capable of earning a college degree on his own. Likewise, Austin is hesitant to ask for help managing symptoms of ADHD, although this condition seems to be part of the problem, especially with long reading assignments.

While Austin is resistant to obtaining formal support, he has taken some steps to improve his academic performance. Perhaps because of his excellent experience with a mentor in high school, he talks fairly often with you about his challenges, and he continues to study with friends. He says he uses study strategies recommended by his professors in class and in course syllabi. His biggest frustration is that he is working much harder than he ever did in high school, and he still cannot pass some of his classes. He also is putting forth more effort than most of his college friends, but they do not seem to be experiencing the same difficulties he is.

Student Development Response

In your academic advising role, you see Austin's talents and wish he were open to resources that could help him succeed. You know that many of the challenges Austin experiences—such as lack of academic success, low self-esteem, uncertain goals, difficulty with reading and writing, and sleep loss—are common for college students with ADHD (National Resource Center on AD/HD, n.d.). You draw on the seven vectors of student development (Chickering & Reisser, 1993) to better understand Austin's responses to your suggestions and to develop new strategies to support him.

You realize that Austin is having difficulty with **developing competence** (Chickering & Reisser, 1993, p. 45). His failure to pass certain courses and his comments about not understanding why he is struggling in those courses when he is working so much harder than he did in high school show that he is having trouble with the transition from high school academic expectations to college expectations. It is vital that Austin develop the academic skills to succeed at the university. On the other hand, Austin is doing very well socially and seems to have several healthy relationships.

A second developmental vector to consider involves **managing emotions** (Chickering & Reisser, 1993, p. 46). Throughout the semester, you definitely want to monitor Austin's tendency to shut down when he feels overwhelmed. In the past, handling frustration has been a challenge for Austin. For this reason, it is important for him to broaden his range of coping strategies for distressing emotions.

Difficulty with handling stress is a common challenge for students with ADHD. In fact, "students with ADD [ADHD] often *use* stress as a tool" (Quinn & Ratey, n.d., para. 1). Recognizing this, you take a proactive stance in advising

Austin. You help him learn to monitor his stress level, recognize potential stressors, and identify how stress affects his behavior. Together, you brainstorm options for overcoming those frustrations. This helps Austin tolerate stress without becoming overwhelmed. In addition, you recommend specific strategies that Austin can use when he notices his stress level is rising. These include taking care of himself through diet, sleep, and exercise; avoiding procrastination by developing daily and weekly study plans; and drawing on his strengths to overcome his challenges (Quinn & Ratey, n.d.). This process offers Austin alternatives to shutting down when he becomes frustrated, thereby increasing his effective coping behaviors.

You can continue to talk with Austin about his concerns about medication side effects. He would benefit from knowing that these effects often can be reduced or eliminated altogether by changing the medication or dosage, or by modifying behaviors, such as taking the medication with food or at a different time of day (Davis, 2005).

Because of Austin's opposition to using student support services, he faces a developmental challenge in **moving through autonomy toward interdependence** (Chickering & Reisser, 1993, p. 47). The fact that Austin is willing to meet regularly with you is a good sign, and you hope he will not shut you out when he needs help. Other assets for Austin in this area include the ongoing work with his study group and involvement in the student organization associated with his major. Reluctance to seek help and choosing to eliminate medication are typical behaviors for college students, who often feel that, as adults, they no longer need the same supports or treatments they relied on in high school (National Resource Center on AD/HD, n.d.; Quinn, 2007). In Austin's case, these decisions may be reinforced by his family values (e.g., strong urge to act independently). Austin may need more time before he is willing to rely on assistance from others. Recognizing that his commitment to independence is a long-held value, you will want to work slowly through his hesitation but eventually encourage him to take on leadership roles in the areas of his significant strengths, perhaps in the student organization.

One of the biggest challenges you face with Austin is helping him **establish identity** (Chickering & Reisser, 1993, p. 48). Here Austin faces two barriers: (1) his self-esteem is hurt by his poor academic performance outside his major, and

(2) he does not accept ADHD as part of his identity. His reaction is not uncommon: Persons with ADHD often experience low self-esteem. It is important to connect Austin with an appropriate resource to help him improve his self-image (NIMH, 2008). If low self-esteem becomes debilitating for him, you might suggest an appointment with a campus counselor.

Helping Austin accept ADHD as part of his identity may be difficult. High school students whose ADHD symptoms were managed well with medication and support may not realize the impact the disorder can have on their college lives if they stop their medication (Quinn, 2007). Since Austin discontinued treatment, he likely is experiencing himself in a new way. Talk with him about his success in high school and ask him to identify factors that played a role in that success. If he does not identify medication and other supports, you might introduce those ideas into the conversation. While Austin has established a strong, positive identity in many areas (as a hard worker, application-oriented thinker, responsible person, and social individual with many friends), the two barriers to overall identity achievement (low self-esteem and lack of recognition of ADHD as part of his identity) are significant. Not only will they interfere with Austin's further identity development; they also threaten to undermine the areas in which he feels competent and good about himself. As Chickering and Reisser note, identity is "a solid sense of self, . . . an *I* who coordinates the facets of personality, who 'owns' the house and is comfortable in all of its rooms" (1993, p. 49).

A final important area in which Austin struggles is **developing purpose** (Chickering & Reisser, 1993, p. 50), especially academically. He performs well in courses and activities in which he has a strong interest, typically those that match his kinesthetic and interpersonal learning preferences. However, he struggles—at times unsuccessfully—to pass other classes. To increase his motivation, you can help him find ways to make class content more meaningful. For example, you could help Austin connect with the purpose of the composition and public speaking requirements by discussing how learning to communicate better will help him succeed in his future career. Not every assignment will relate to Austin's personal interests or goals, but the skills he will develop are applicable to his future endeavors. Advisors regularly explain the role and importance of distribution requirements to students; in Austin's case, you may need to initiate such discussion repeatedly to maintain his motivation and support his success. In the future, he may become confident enough to talk with professors about how he learns best and how he might be able to make his assignments relate more directly to his interest areas. These strategies will help Austin find purpose not only in his current coursework but also in his personal and professional future.

Recall Sanford's (1967) observations about differences in individual student readiness for college and the need for student affairs professionals to tailor challenge and support interventions based on each student's situation and strengths. Your task as an active, committed academic advisor is to try to balance Austin's academic challenges with sufficient (neither too much nor too little) support in forms acceptable to him and in ways that communicate your faith in his abilities.

Counseling Response

Person-Centered Helping

Establishing trust and creating a safe environment will encourage Austin to talk about his experiences with ADHD and how the disorder affects him. You can start by clarifying and validating his concerns and connecting him with campus services. Convey genuine and consistent caring for Austin, as well as a shared commitment to his academic and personal success. Strive for congruence among your words, tone, and actions, even if Austin is sometimes inconsistent. For instance, Austin may joke around about failing courses that "don't matter." You will want to hear and respond to the full message conveyed by such statements. You might say, for example, *"Yes, it would probably be a relief to not care so much, wouldn't it?"*

Unconditional positive regard is essential. Austin already fears becoming "a loser," at least in some areas. He needs to know that your wholehearted acceptance of him is not contingent on his grades or anything else. You might assure him that most students struggle in one or more areas, and that student support services exist to address and mitigate those struggles. If Austin ultimately chooses to transfer to the technical institute, frame his decision as a choice for better fit, not a failure.

What you are both striving for is his success, and while being fairly direct with this student, resist "owning" his situation. Remain a supporter and express confidence in him, his abilities, and his worth as a person.

Solution-Focused Helping

Solution-Focused techniques and strategies will be very helpful with this student. Moving from problem solving to solution building is key to this approach and may appeal to Austin's active nature (De Jong & Berg, 2008).

Bringing a solution-building orientation to your work with Austin quickly communicates your confidence in him to address whatever issue brings him into your office. Austin is bright, motivated, and resourceful, and he wants to succeed. Instead of focusing on deficits, weaknesses, limitations, problems, and failures, a Solution-Focused helper dwells on competencies, strengths, and possibilities (of which Austin has many). By building on success and looking for exceptions to the problem, you can do many positive things: increase his optimism, create an atmosphere conducive to change, help locate resources, and give him control over whatever changes he makes.

From a Solution-Focused perspective, Austin is the expert on his life and experiences (De Jong & Berg, 2008, pp. 18–19). For example, you probably do not know what it is like for Austin to attend a college where there are more students in his residence hall than people in his hometown. You are even less likely to understand his reality as a student with ADHD who must focus intensely on his studies, particularly in areas that do not interest or seem relevant to him. As you adopt the "not knowing" attitude recommended by Solution-Focused thinkers, you will want to ask questions that allow Austin to tell you about his life and his challenges at college. Cantwell and Holmes call this "leading from one step behind" (1994, in De Jong & Berg, 2008, pp. 50–51).

Solution-Focused helping includes several important assumptions. First, small changes lead to bigger changes. If Austin is willing to work with just one tutor for one course, he will probably do better in that class. Second, people can't change the past, but they can change the future. Austin has failed several general education courses—but if he consistently uses some new strategies, he may pass them. Third, no problem exists all the time; exceptions exist and should be explored. Austin is a strong student within his major, and he has not failed all courses outside that department. What is happening when he is succeeding, especially in areas outside manufacturing technology? Invite him to talk as much as he is willing to about what is happening when he is successful, when the problem does not exist, or is not as severe (De Jong & Berg, 2008). Even Austin's relationship with you, a student affairs professional and helper, is an exception to his fierce independence and may set the stage for his collaboration with others who can assist him.

These strategies can also be used in the "managing emotions" or "managing stress" area of Austin's concerns. Have there been times when Austin, though frustrated, felt more in control of his emotions, or when he remembers being proud of how he handled a disappointment or setback? What was going on? What did he do that was different? Perhaps it was as a high school athlete, when he ran every day during track season. In college he has been too busy for sports, even intramural activities; but if he begins to see that daily exercise once helped him be more in control of his feelings, he might be motivated to find some time for running.

How to Begin

Start by inviting Austin to describe his situation. When you respond, use his language or paraphrase gently. For example, when he says, "I feel like such a loser," you can say, *"I can tell you feel pretty bad about your situation."* Notice something positive about him early in your conversation; for example, *"I'm impressed that you came to talk with me about the struggles you're having in some classes. This shows me that you're serious about figuring out a way to succeed, and we can work on this together."*

Next, ask questions and listen carefully for what he wants. Austin may not expect a 4.0; he may want to pass his general education courses and keep up with the cohort group in his major. Accept his viewpoint as valid and again offer assistance. As you sensitively pursue connecting Austin with student support resources, continue to listen to his comments about who and what are important to him and how he sees his situation.

Stages of Application

Your first goal, after establishing rapport and a working relationship, should be to identify a solvable problem. Austin wants to pass English composition this semester (in his second attempt). You could focus on this and cocreate goals. Austin must take the lead in generating meaningful, manageable goals, but you can help him create concrete, realistic goals that will require effort on his part (De Jong & Berg, 2008, p. 77).

When his goal is clear, cocreate interventions. Build on what Austin has successfully used before and also begin to offer information about relevant resources. For instance, if Austin says that in high school he got through English with the help of a friend, and that this was a comfortable arrangement for him, you could say that you are aware of peer mentoring services right across the hall. Assign strategic tasks. For example, you might offer to walk over to the peer mentoring office in the tutoring center with Austin and introduce him to the coordinator. She, in turn, could connect him with a peer mentor for English comp. Austin may prefer to do this himself. It doesn't matter who does what—what matters is a clear plan for follow-up action.

Assume that Austin meets with a peer mentor. Your role then becomes one of reinforcing and encouraging this behavior, and keeping an eye out for positive results in the class by asking Austin how he is doing. Another Solution-Focused tenet comes into play at this point: If something is working, do more of it (De Jong & Berg, 2008, p. 229). This does not necessarily mean that if Austin's grades in English improve, he should see his tutor more often. Rather, it suggests that if this strategy is effective, he should consider other ways to use it. For example, perhaps he could find a peer mentor in sociology as well.

You can help Austin build on his strengths and do more of what works by recommending strategies that match his learning preferences. He might be able to develop hands-on ways of studying to accommodate his kinesthetic preferences; he might also want to continue to work with study groups to maintain social connections and academic support. As your discussions with Austin progress, you can suggest other strategies known to help students with ADHD, including creating to-do lists, developing a scheduled routine, using a planner, and breaking large tasks into smaller, more manageable units (NIMH, 2008). Over time, your goal will be to shift accountability so that Austin takes increasing responsibility for monitoring his own progress.

Miracle Question

Another Solution-Focused strategy is the "miracle question" (de Shazer, 2007, p. 38). For Austin, the question might be stated this way: *"Austin, if you could create a miracle and things here at college were exactly as you'd like them to be, what would be happening?"* Austin is likely to respond, *"Well, I'd be passing all my classes, doing really well in my major, spending time with my friends, and making enough money to get by."* You could then follow up with questions that elicit additional details in all areas of Austin's "miracle," and note that many aspects of what he wants are already present in his life.

As Austin's advisor, you could steer the conversation to the "passing all my classes" portion of his idealized world. Carefully "refrain from interpretations and unsolicited suggestions while remaining attentive to every verbal and nonverbal nuance of the [student's] unfolding description" (de Shazer, 2007, p. 38). You might say, *"Tell me more about what would be happening if you were passing all your classes. You lit up when you said that. What would your English professor notice was different?"* Austin might reply, *"Well, I would be friendlier, for one thing. I get so tense in that class that I don't look at anyone or talk to anyone. And I suppose I could talk with the prof about the book list and find a book I can actually stand, not just take the first one and hate it."*

Austin could generate many ideas that contain the foundation for his future success, given time and encouragement: *"Well, obviously, I have to go to class to pass. I have to read the material and turn in all the assignments, even the ones I think are dumb. But I'm pretty much doing that already, unless I start thinking that I'll fail no matter what I do. I guess I have to do better on those darn assignments!"* You can reinforce what Austin is doing well by saying, *"It's terrific that you are already going to every class meeting and doing the work. That's huge. Now what else have you done before that led to passing grades, or what else have you thought about doing?"* Go on a "collaborative search in the [student's] real, everyday world" to uncover and highlight what Austin has done or will consider doing to pass the courses that are hard for him (de Shazer, 2007, p. 39).

As Austin clarifies his "miracle" and identifies strategies that will work for him, you can use a scaling question to gauge his level of motivation to act on his intentions, perhaps pertaining to just one class (De Jong & Berg, 2008, p. 108): *"Austin, you've come up with some really good ideas here. Now let's think about that English comp class for a minute. On a scale from 1 to 10, where 1 means you really don't plan to do any of this (work with a peer mentor, talk with the professor, etc.) and 10 means you are already putting some of these strategies into your planner, where do you put yourself?"* Imagine that Austin says, *"Well, you know I want to pass that class. It's driving me crazy. I'm pretty motivated. I'd say I'm at an 8."* You respond, *"An 8? That's terrific! It tells me that you are very committed to passing the course. Why do you say you're at an 8? What puts you there?"* Austin says, *"I need that class behind me; I just have to pass it this time. I'll do whatever it takes—but I'm not perfect, and I don't like to talk to English professors, so I didn't say 10."* He laughs when he says this, and you sense that Austin is sincere. He fully intends to use all available resources to pass the composition class, and your interest and support can help keep his motivation at that level throughout the semester.

Reframing

Reframing involves offering a different, more positive view of something the student perceives as a fault (Welfel & Patterson, 2005, p. 91). For instance, Austin might say, *"I'm that dumb guy with ADHD."* You could reframe that image by reflecting, *"You have to work harder in certain areas, and you're smart enough to know what you need to do—and even smarter for doing it."* Reframing is not about denying what students tell you about their experiences, but it invites them to see those experiences in a different light.

Compliments

Frequent, meaningful compliments based on observable behavior can encourage students (De Jong & Berg, 2008, p. 116). To Austin, you might say, *"You got a B on that paper? Fantastic! I guess working with your peer mentor really paid off! Way to go!"* Because Austin is easily discouraged when things do not go well, you will want to celebrate his successes, small and large. You could use questions to encourage him to identify and amplify his strengths and review what is going well for him. When Austin scores well on an exam, you could ask, *"Great! How did you make that happen?"* or *"What did you do that worked so well this time?"*

Person-Centered and Solution-Focused strategies, along with Austin's evident willingness and commitment, could increase his chances for success in college and give him a greater sense of accomplishment and self-efficacy. Both approaches help you focus on student strengths and offer reality-based encouragement for challenging situations.

Discussion Questions

1. What is your opinion of "intrusive advising" (defined as "proactive interactions with students, with the intention of connecting with them before a situation occurs that cannot be fixed [Varney, n.d., para. 2])? Do you think the advisor in this scenario is too directive? How do you monitor when and how much to help a student?

2. How do you help students cope with stress? What kinds of activities or suggestions would you share with students? Reflect on how you operate in your own life, and consider what you model in the area of stress management.

3. What assumptions do you have about working with a Solution-Focused approach? Do they hold up with this student? In what types of situations might they not hold up or not be the most effective approach?

4. Austin has a variety of strengths and wants to succeed in college. Think of a more challenging situation, such as working with a student whose strengths are harder to identify. How might you use a Solution-Focused approach with a less motivated student?

References

Chickering, A. W., & Reisser, L. (1993). *Education and identity* (2nd ed.). San Francisco: Jossey-Bass.

Davis, J. L. (2005). Tips to reduce the side effects of ADHD medications. *WebMD*. Retrieved April 27, 2009, from www.webmd.com/add-adhd/guide/reduce-side-effects-adhd-medications?page=3

De Jong, P., & Berg, I. K. (2008). *Interviewing for solutions* (3rd ed.). Pacific Grove, CA: Brooks/Cole.

de Shazer, S., with Y. Dolan, H. Korman, T. Trepper, E. McCollum, & I. K. Berg. (2007). *More than miracles: The state of the art of solution-focused brief therapy*. Binghamton, NY: Haworth Press.

National Institute of Mental Health. (2008). Attention deficit hyperactivity disorder (ADHD). Retrieved June 3, 2009, from www.nimh.nih.gov/health/publications/attention-deficit-hyperactivity-disorder/adhd_booklet.pdf

National Resource Center on AD/HD. (n.d.). College issues for students with ADHD. Retrieved June 3, 2009, from www.addresources.org/article_adhd_college_chadd.php

Quinn, P. O. (2007). Top ten things I wish students with ADHD knew. Retrieved June 3, 2009, from www.addresources.org/article_adhd_students_quinn.php

Quinn, P. O., & Ratey, N. (n.d.). How college students with ADD (ADHD) can manage stress. Retrieved June 3, 2009, from www.addvance.com/help/young_adults/stress.html

Sanford, N. (1967). *Where colleges fail: The study of the student as a person*. San Francisco: Jossey-Bass.

Varney, J. *Intrusive advising*. Retrieved September 15, 2009, from www.nacada. ksu.edu/AAT/NW30_3.htm#10

Welfel, E. R., & Patterson, L. E. (2005). *The counseling process: A multitheoretical integrative approach*. (6th ed.). Belmont, CA: Thomson Brooks/Cole.

CHAPTER 10

Male Social Development
Matthew

Jason A. Laker, Ruth Harper, and Nona L. Wilson

Matthew is a Caucasian first-year college student. He is 18 years old and from a middle-class suburban background. The Campus Security Department has referred him to you, his residence hall director (RHD), for a disciplinary meeting following an incident that took place over the weekend.

According to the report, two security officers (a male and a female) encountered Matthew behind the Student Center at 2:30 a.m. on Saturday night/Sunday morning, where he was urinating on the side of the building. Matthew was reportedly intoxicated (watery eyes, slurred speech, trouble walking, smelled of alcohol) and was quite dirty, as if he had fallen onto wet ground more than once. The report further states that when the officers confronted him, he ran away, but tripped and fell. He struggled with the officers, swearing abusively at them (e.g., quoted in the report as calling them "F---ing rejects," "little b--ches," and "I'll f---ing own you—you're fired, a--hole!").

Because Matthew remained aggressive and uncooperative, the local police were called. They gave him the choice of spending the night in jail or going back to his campus residence and staying quiet. The report states that Matthew started to lose consciousness, so the police took him to the detox facility at the hospital. He spent the night there and the resident assistant (RA) reported to you that Matthew's roommate picked him up the next morning. The RA remarked that Matthew has had at least one other incident in which he required assistance from floormates after drinking to the point of intoxication. It was not dealt with formally because the RA heard about it two weeks after it happened. The RA indicates surprise at the details of this incident, as Matthew is generally pleasant and mostly keeps to himself. Occasionally he is seen with floormates, and he has never publicly used abusive language in the hall.

As RHD, you send Matthew a note telling him that he is required to come speak with you about the episode. On the day of the meeting, Matthew sends you an e-mail saying he has a doctor's appointment and can't meet with you. He doesn't mention when he will next be available, so you check his class schedule in the database system and call him in his room the next morning at 8:30. Matthew has a 9:00 class, but when he answers the phone, it is clear that the call has awakened him. He agrees to meet with you that afternoon. You ask him to repeat the agreed-upon meeting time, since he sounds tired, and he repeats that he'll be there.

At 3:00 that afternoon, Matthew enters your office, sits down, and looks at the floor. You try to strike up an informal conversation to get to know him. In response to your questions, he tells you that he is a first-year student intending to study management. You work fairly hard to elicit anything more than two- or three-word responses, but are able to surmise that Matthew finds being at school generally "okay." His first-term grades are not as good as he expected, but he is passing all his courses. Eventually, Matthew warms up a bit and the conversation relaxes.

About 15 minutes into the discussion, you say that the two of you have some business to address in terms of the incident report. Matthew replies, "Yeah, I was really stupid . . . sorry." You answer, "Well, you don't seem stupid, but it seems you were very drunk. And you said some pretty nasty things to the officers." Matthew says, "Yeah, I didn't know I drank that much. Guess it got away from me. I don't even remember what I said."

You decide to try an approach you have used with other young men. You look at Matthew and say, *"Matthew, I'm confused. Can you help me understand something?"* This catches his attention and he looks up. You ask, *"Well, may I be blunt?"* Matthew nods, so you proceed. *"I read this report to you and, well, the guy described in it sounds like a total jerk. But I've been here with you for about 15 minutes and you seem like a perfectly nice guy. Can you help me understand the discrepancy between the two? Who's the real Matthew?"*

Matthew does not seem offended but rather struck by what you have said. He thinks for a moment then says, "Yeah, I'm not usually like that. I'm usually kinda quiet, but when I drink, the guys think I'm funny, and sometimes it gets outta hand." You nod with understanding, then respond, *"May I ask you one more question?"* He says, "Sure, I guess." You continue, quietly but seriously, *"When did you first decide you weren't worth being around unless you were drinking?"* Matthew is stunned, and his eyes fill with tears. He puts his head in his hands for what seems like a long time; it is a full minute before he looks up and says, "I don't know."

Your impression of Matthew is that he has strayed completely off course at college, and you say, *"Let's set aside the incident report for a minute—you seem really lost to me . . . what's going on?"* At this point, tears well up again in Matthew's eyes. He is quiet for a moment, and then starts talking. He speaks for about ten minutes, which is notable, given his quiet manner earlier.

In the conversation, you learn that Matthew is the first person in his family to go to college. His parents divorced a year ago, and his mother pressured him to go to counseling. The counselor was not particularly helpful, in his view, but the family physician was aware of the divorce and diagnosed Matthew with depression. He has a prescription antidepressant that makes him feel better, but since arriving at college he has taken it sporadically, because he forgets sometimes. He is worried about his younger brother and sister, who live with their mother in his hometown, which is about three hours from campus by car. Matthew doesn't get to see any members of his family very often. His younger siblings have been feeling stressed and upset about the fighting between their parents over custody and child support. Matthew tries not to think about it, but it's difficult, because his siblings call him to unburden and his mother is unhappy that he doesn't return her messages. He describes her as "really emotional" and a "hassle" to deal with. Matthew relies on her and his dad for college expenses, and has to "play games" to get them to pay their share without them "using it against each other."

Matthew has a girlfriend whom he started dating in high school; she is a year younger, still in 12th grade. He says he doesn't know what to do about her, either, because she keeps calling and wants to come stay with him for the weekend, but her parents won't allow it. "Besides," he says, "she doesn't understand college and I'm sick of the high school bulls--t." He elaborates on that last point to the effect that he thought college would be different, but he sees a lot of the same "s--t" here as he did there. He says he's sick of everything being "so f---ed up" (then interjects an apology for all the swearing).

During his disclosures Matthew continues to look at the floor, his demeanor wavering between obvious sadness and being overwhelmed by waves of frustration and anger. When he finishes his narrative, he says he's sorry for causing trouble and that it won't happen again. You ask him how often he drinks, and he says, "Not much . . . maybe three times a week, with some friends, but they drink more than I do."

Looking thoughtfully at Matthew for a moment, you observe, *"Wow. You're really carrying a lot of pressure. Where are you getting support?"* At this point, he is unable to speak because he is again fighting tears, wiping his nose and eyes on his shirt. All he can manage to say is "I don't know." You offer, *"Matthew, you know, you just talked to me for almost 15 minutes, completely sober, and I appreciated listening to you. It helped me get to know you. I was not at all bored, and I didn't wish you would be funny or drunk. Is it possible that your friends, I mean your real friends, would appreciate you for who you are, too, without you drinking, and without you being out of control?"* Matthew considers this a moment and says, "I guess I never thought about it that way." You suggest gently, *"Well, I'm glad you're thinking about it now. Let's talk about how to make things right with the Security staff and the rest of it, in terms of this incident, and then make a plan so you can get the support you need to be successful here at school and more comfortable personally. What do you say?"* Matthew smiles for the first time, and responds, "Yeah, okay, that sounds good."

Student Development Response

The themes in Matthew's story are fairly common: negotiating the transition from high school to college personally and socially, contending with mixed messages and experiences with alcohol, and issues relating to his home and family situation. The issue that is less commonly discussed with male students is that of gender identity development. However, O'Neil, Helms, Gable, David, and Wrightman (1986) developed a conceptual framework called the Gender Role Conflict Scale that sought to describe not only the significant themes in men's gender role socialization but also the tensions between the dominant scripts and the lived experience of being male. They contend that a conflict exists between what a man is told he should be in society and the human emotions and personal struggles he may encounter on a personal level that often do not fit neatly into that stereotype.

Student affairs graduate programs include material on seminal theories of student development, but despite using male subjects, this material rarely discusses men and male identity overtly. Meth and Pasick (1990) point out that, although this literature intended to describe students in general (albeit using exclusively male norms), it did not intentionally "explore what it means to be a man" (p. vii). In other words, just because the research subjects were male does not mean that the theories explain men's gender identities or experiences. Much of the research in student affairs over the past 20 years has focused on particular student subpopulations to correct the problem of students whose identities have been marginalized in earlier research. Ironically, few researchers contemplated the fact that while the early theories didn't marginalize men, they didn't particularly address them, either. Only recently has research on male students as gendered people become more common in student affairs circles, and it is still rarely included in professional preparation or staff training programs.

O'Neil and colleagues (1986) posed four themes associated with male gender identity development. The first is **restrictive emotionality**, referring to the emotional rigidity men are expected to exhibit. The second is **socialized control, power, and competition**, referring to the ways in which men are expected to have their life issues and responsibilities in order and be in command at all times. The third is **restrictive sexual and affectionate behavior**, referring to expectations that men will demonstrate their masculinity (and prove their heterosexuality) through sexual prowess and multiple female partners, and, in so doing, adhere to a narrow and impersonal range of romantic expression. The fourth theme is **obsession with achievement, work, and success**, in which manhood is tied to constant striving to realize and maintain professional and financial eminence.

Consider Matthew's situation. Look, for example, at the offensive comments he made to the Security guards (e.g., "F---ing rejects," "little b--ches," and "I'll f---ing own you—you're fired, a--hole!"). Each of these statements was abusive, and together their content sought to assert dominance and power. They were not only hypermasculine but antifeminine (related to but not the same as "antiwoman"). These hateful statements reflect a great deal of insecurity and rage—not surprisingly, since they were uttered at a time when authority figures found Matthew doing something he should not have been doing.

Also, consider Matthew's remarks about his family and girlfriend. He didn't say, "I'm sad" or "I'm grieving" over his parents' divorce or his distance from his girlfriend. Instead, he expressed anger (the one emotion allowed to men in this script) and dismissively asserted that, "she doesn't understand college and I'm sick of the high school bulls--t," which actually reveals a great deal of sadness and grief. His overt dismissal is a tool to attempt to regain control—but it doesn't work in your office.

As a brief aside, student affairs professionals often deal with the "emotional fallout" of college-age students whose parents divorce. Young adults can experience "a profound sense of loss" (Cain, 1990, para. 9) when this occurs, especially if it is unexpected. Because parental divorce sometimes "represents the first sobering crisis" college students experience, it can carry tremendous impact, and can "mark the end of an era of trust" (para 12). Matthew may be in the throes of such an emotional transition.

It takes an enormous amount of energy to pursue the four themes identified by O'Neil and colleagues. When a male student lets down his guard, it is important to validate and invite more conversation, rather than to shut it down. Because these moments often happen during disciplinary or other seemingly negative encounters, professional staff may miss the opportunity to connect and focus more on correcting or even chastising the student. This has the effect of prohibiting vulnerability, shaming the student, and even entrenching the restrictive socialization that contributed to the problematic behavior in the first place. Davis and Laker (2004) describe this as a "bad dog" situation, referring to the way a dog's owner might yell at it for a transgression; to be effective with a student, there must be a connection between the rebuke or challenge and support. Student affairs professionals purport to have expertise in balancing the two; they ought to do better than bad dog scenarios. This is not to diminish or dismiss Matthew's accountability for his actions. Rather, it is to invite the practitioner to help Matthew become accountable in an authentic manner, in which there is room for a genuinely corrective experience: to grow as a person and as a man.

Being transparent with Matthew (and with students in general) about our agenda and goals is worthwhile. For instance, sharing the four themes with Matthew could help him name his experiences and generate agency in his own development. Discuss how drinking is dangerous when combined with his medications and how it could lead to an incident that would cause his dismissal from school. Even these messages relate to the themes of masculinity: Choosing not to drink in the face of overwhelming pressure to do so requires great courage.

In situations like Matthew's, an alcohol education program or even an alcohol assessment performed by a mental health professional might be recommended or required. One approach that has achieved positive outcomes is called Brief Alcohol Screening and Intervention for College Students, or BASICS (Dimeff, Baer, Kivlahan, & Marlatt, 1999). BASICS takes a nonconfrontational approach aimed at students who are experiencing problems associated with their drinking. Drawing on extensive research at the University of Washington, BASICS is both developmental and motivational, stressing a "harm reduction" approach. Since Matthew is not old enough to drink legally, engaging with him in developing strategies for less risky or moderate drinking poses ethical challenges. However, other student-generated goals drawing on the BASICS format can be useful. As an alternative, it could be beneficial to refer Matthew to the health promotions area—maybe even encouraging him to volunteer with them as part of the resolution to this case (assuming this option has been prenegotiated between your department and health promotions as an acceptable sanction).

Matthew did not find the counseling useful during his parents' split, but he accepted the prescription for antidepressants from a physician. The stigma associated with seeking mental health counseling is significant for men, but they might see going to the family physician differently—particularly if a physical examination is not required. It is important for campus health centers and counseling services to work closely together to determine how male students (and certain other populations, such as international students from countries where mental health issues are stigmatized) might present with something like trouble sleeping or headaches, when in fact they are struggling with anxiety or depression. For this reason, you could revisit the issue of support structures with Matthew, reframing the idea of counseling.

You could say that it's one thing when your parents demand that you talk with a counselor they have chosen. It's quite another when you choose to go to a counselor at the college who has expertise in the issues you're facing (especially when your student fees are already paying for it). Make sure that Matthew understands confidentiality—that the counselor will not share information about him with anyone. Describing help-seeking as an act of agency can support Matthew's sense of masculinity, of taking ownership and control over his life.

Finally, you might try to get Matthew to tell his friends that he will not be drinking for a while, so he can get focused. Even if he is not ready to do this, schedule a follow-up meeting with him so you can reinforce the agreements you make and the relationship you are building. You will want to become part of his support base. Such a relationship can increase his accountability to the rules and reinforce his exploration of more sustainable ways of being a man.

Counseling Response

You have made tremendous headway with Matthew in just one meeting by using what you know about male socialization to challenge his assumptions about being entertaining, interesting, or worthwhile only when drinking. You have also introduced the idea that it is okay, even desirable, for a man to seek help when he is overwhelmed or struggling. This brief discussion has helped Matthew to begin to think about what kind of man he wants to be and become. He indicates that he does not want to get into further trouble.

You have used effective nonverbal behaviors that communicate respect: a gentle, accepting tone of voice; appropriate eye contact; occasional nods and smiles; and a physical posture that indicates that you are listening carefully (Okun, 1992). To work effectively with men, Pollock (2001) recommends creating a safe space, allowing time for comfort in expression, being active while talking, listening without judging, and offering affirmation. In subsequent encounters with Matthew, both formal and informal, consider what a Solution-Focused approach could add to your work with him.

Solution-Focused Helping

A strengths-based approach to campus judicial meetings provides a format for university personnel to deal effectively with policy violations while maintaining a focus on solutions, as opposed to concentrating on the consequences of student misconduct. This method helps students think about times when they are *not* in trouble, helps them plan realistically to avoid policy violations in the future, and increases students' confidence they will not return for another judicial hearing. In judicial meetings handled in a strengths-based manner, students are less defensive and more open to addressing and changing their problematic behavior (Trenhaile & Harper, 2005).

Policy violation discussions can be challenging and uncomfortable for both students and university personnel. Students are often defensive or even angry; Matthew certainly entered the conversation in a closed, guarded manner. The experience can be stressful for all participants, perhaps as a direct result of the typically problem-focused nature of such meetings. Understandably, when a judicial conversation does not go well, the student may leave frustrated and with negative attitudes toward those enforcing policy and issuing sanctions. Once a student has a negative interaction with a judicial representative, future interactions likely will be negative as well. In contrast, you have opened your conversation with Matthew by attempting to get to know him and not looking exclusively at the problem that triggered the meeting.

Solution-Focused thinking, like the constructivist assumptions on which it is based, does not pathologize Matthew's situation; rather, it sees him as capable of creating or constructing a different, more positive reality. It also calls for a collaborative approach to change, which seems particularly appropriate with Matthew, who appears to become motivated as you talk with him. Solution-Focused therapists often pose a friendly yet serious "challenge" at the conclusion of a first conversation, such as *"Between now and the next time we meet, I want you to observe, so that you can tell me next time, what is happening in your life that you want to continue to have happen"* (Molnar & de Shazer, 1987, in Guterman, 2006, p. 25). Mathew might notice relaxing times with friends that do not include drinking, or e-mail, phone, or text exchanges with his family that feel good, not strained.

Matthew has a problem that brought him to your attention; he violated the alcohol policy and was highly disrespectful to security personnel. But as a consequence of your initial positive dialogue, the two of you may emerge from the meeting with a coconstructed goal. This goal might consist of Matthew's being able to have fun with friends without drinking and, further, to explore campus resources that will help him be happier in other areas of life as well. Much of this will be beyond the scope of your duties as an RHD; for example, Matthew may, in time, choose to talk with a campus counselor about his family and relationship issues. In fact, you will want to encourage this contact, as Matthew was previously diagnosed with clinical depression and is still clearly struggling emotionally. In the meantime, however, and well within the range of your responsibilities, you can work with Matthew to explore other ways to relax, to interact with peers, and to be himself (his nondrinking, "real" self) in the residence hall.

Identifying and Amplifying Exceptions

Focusing on the issue of enjoyable peer interaction that does not involve alcohol, you will want to ask Matthew about exceptions: times when he has had fun with friends while sober. Since Matthew does not drink all day, every day, there will be identifiable exceptions to his idea that he must drink to be perceived as a worthwhile companion. Because of their mundane nature, these exceptions are frequently not noticed or are "written off" as unimportant. In fact, the exceptions are very important and can hold the key to future success. Frame questions about exceptions in open-ended ways, such as "*Tell me about a recent situation when you had a great time with someone when you were not drinking.*" This works more effectively than the similarly worded but closed question "*Has there been a time when you had fun without drinking?*" Sometimes students are so problem-oriented that they dispute the existence of any exceptions. If this were to happen with Matthew, you could ask a different question, using what de Shazer (1988, in Guterman, 2006, p. 51) called the "crystal ball technique": "*What will it be like when you are having fun without drinking?*" or "*Envision a situation where you're having a great time but no alcohol is involved. What's happening?*"

As Matthew identifies exceptions, listen very carefully and emphasize, through amplifying questions, what he did at those times that worked well for him. Suppose Matthew comes up with three recent circumstances in which he had fun and did not drink: a "family weekend" on campus when his younger sister and brother visited and attended a dinner and basketball game with him; his regular Tuesday night study group for calculus (which has become surprisingly social and fun for him, as it involves some "pretty cool people"); and a weekend night when he and his floormates impulsively went to the midnight show of the new Harry Potter film. Your immediate reaction could be one of pleased surprise: "*Wow. I'm kind of amazed that you were able to come up with three examples so quickly—and that they involve family, friends, and your studies. Apparently there are many exceptions in several areas of your life.*"

Your task, at this point, is to ask additional amplifying questions to help Matthew more fully explore the differences between times when he has the problem (thinks he must drink to be fun or even acceptable) and times when the problem does not exist. The following are frequently used amplifying questions (Guterman, 2006, p. 52):

- "How did you make that happen?"

- "How did it make your day (or evening or weekend) go differently?"

- "Who else noticed?"

- "How is that different from how you've dealt with the problem in the past?"

- "What did you tell yourself to make it happen?"

- "What does this say about you and your ability to deal with
this problem?"

- "What are the possibilities?"

Each of these questions is designed to elicit positive statements from Matthew. Notice that none of the questions is focused on "not drinking." Rather, all
your attention goes to how he has done things differently; in other words, how he
has chosen positive options and obtained positive results. While Matthew's situation is complicated and will not be easily resolved, these kinds of questions, over
the course of several conversations, could help him take steps toward his goal and
recognize his own central role in rewriting his circumstances.

Because the incident that brought Matthew to your office had to do with
weekend intoxication, you might choose to ask more about the late-night movie with his floormates, because that situation offers the clearest exception to his
drinking. How did he choose to stay sober the night of the movie? As a result,
how was that experience different? What did his friends think and how did they
interact with him? What did he tell himself to stay sober that night? What are
the possibilities for future fun-yet-sober interactions? Assume, for example, that
Matthew tells you that he and his friends wanted to have fun but it was a Sunday
night, so they chose to go to the movie instead of drinking to avoid being hung
over on Monday morning. In that decision, his friends were communicating, even
if indirectly, that they can appreciate him sober. They were saying to each other
that they can enjoy being together sober. Ask Matthew what was different about
that experience as a result of not drinking. He may say, "*Well, we had a blast. It was
an awesome movie with incredible special effects. Nobody threw up or got obnoxious,
including me. None of us got in trouble with the law or the college rules. And I felt
pretty good on Monday morning.*"

Co-constructing Competence

Solution-Focused work also builds on strengths. What are Matthew's strengths? From this brief case study, you can infer several. He is social (wants to be liked); "generally pleasant" (well-mannered); responsible (doing fairly well academically and showed up for his appointment with you); goal-oriented (has declared a major in management); remorseful (apologizes for his actions); responsible (is concerned about his siblings); responsive (takes in your questions about who he really is); capable of sharing honest emotions (tears up in your presence); independent (has not sought help); and open to changing his life in positive ways (did take antidepressants and see a counselor, and has a meaningful conversation with you). He is likely to possess several additional strengths as well, such as high intelligence, resiliency, and a desire to succeed. All of these traits represent significant assets on which to draw in working with Matthew. He may not be aware of or in touch with these strengths, however, so point out the skills, talents, and positive characteristics you see in him.

Imagine that you and Matthew decide to meet on a weekly basis for the next month; also picture asking him to note changes in the coming week that he would like to maintain. At some point during the month, you may wish to use a scaling question to determine his commitment to his goal of having enjoyable experiences with peers without drinking. You might ask, "*Matthew, on a scale of 1 to 10— where 1 means that you're totally certain that you and I will not ever have another meeting about an alcohol violation and 10 means you're pretty sure you will soon be back here in my office because of another incident of drunkenness, public urination, and abuse of college staff members—where do you see yourself?*" In this scenario, Matthew may respond, "*I see myself at a 3.*" You will want to react very positively to this ranking: "*A 3? Considering that you were here only two weeks ago because of your behavior, I'm impressed. What tells you that you're at a 3 now?*" Matthew may say, "*Well, you really got my attention. I thought you were just going to yell at me, but you didn't. I was on the edge of doing something that would get me kicked out of here for good. I really don't want that to happen. I don't have everything figured out by any means, but I want to stay in school and get my head together. Drinking doesn't help any of that, not in the long run, anyway.*"

Matthew's concerns are common ones for college students. A strengths-based or Solution-Focused manner of dealing with judicial violations can change the tone and, more important, the results of disciplinary meetings. Likewise, understanding the role of alcohol in the male socialization process—particularly how high-risk drinking is linked to traditional masculinity—can substantially improve your ability to respond effectively. By approaching Matthew in such a positive way, you can engage him in the meaningful work of becoming a man.

Discussion Questions

1. What assumptions do you have about working with male students? When and how do you question those assumptions?

2. Describe the most stressful or unsuccessful judicial hearing or "enforcement" situation you have witnessed or handled. In what ways might a Solution-Focused or strengths-based approach have changed that interaction?

3. The caring conversation described in the case study works very well to reach Matthew and students like him. What are other ways to help a student connect with his or her best self?

4. Matthew responds favorably (even remarkably) to the scaling question posed here. What if he had responded less positively; for example, "If a 10 means I'm back here next week with another violation, I'm at a 9. Basically, I just hope I don't get caught again. If you think you can talk me out of drinking, you're sadly mistaken." How does that response change what you do with Matthew?

References

Cain, B. S. (1990). The price they pay: Older children and divorce. *New York Times Magazine*, 2/18/90, retrieved July 10, 2009, from www.nytimes.com/1990/02/18/magazine/the-price-they-pay-older-children-and-divorce.html

Davis, T., & Laker, J. (2004). Connecting men to academic and student affairs programs and services. In G. Kellom (Ed.), *Designing effective programs and services for men in higher education* (pp. 47–57). San Francisco: Jossey-Bass.

Dimeff, L. A., Baer, J. S., Kivlahan, D. R., & Marlatt, G. A. (1999). *Brief alcohol screening and intervention for college students: A harm reduction approach.* New York: Guilford Press.

Guterman, J. T. (2006). *Mastering the art of solution-focused counseling.* Alexandria, VA: American Counseling Association.

Meth, R. L., & Pasick, R. S. (1990). *Men in therapy: The challenge of change.* New York: The Guilford Press.

Okun, B. F. (1992). *Effective helping: Interviewing and counseling techniques* (4th ed.). Pacific Grove, CA: Brooks/Cole.

O'Neil, J., Helms, B., Gable, R., David, L., & Wrightman, L. (1986). Gender role conflict scale: College men's fear of femininity. *Sex Roles, 14,* 335–350.

Pollock, W. S. (2001). *Real boys workbook: The definitive guide to understanding and interacting with boys of all ages.* New York: Villard.

Trenhaile, J., & Harper, R. (2005). *Strengths-based judicial conversations.* Unpublished manuscript.

CHAPTER 11

Relating to Parents
and Family
Natalia

Jody Donovan, Nona L. Wilson, and Ruth Harper

As the director of parent and family programs at Regional University (RU), you are charged with supporting and educating students' parents and family members. Your position is fairly new at the university, and you take your role very seriously, hoping to build your professional credibility among parents and families, your colleagues, and the administration. Rather than criticizing the stereotypical "helicopter parent, " you focus on the positive support "umbrella families" (Donovan & McKelfresh, 2008) can provide. You have taught families to equip their students with their own figurative umbrellas. Then, if needed, families can stand beside their students, holding the umbrella of support so the students can use their energy to conduct their academic and personal business on campus. You have cautioned families not to run after their students, holding an umbrella over their heads "just in case."

For the most part, you have been successful with the majority of parents and families. As you review your workload, you realize that you are most successful with college-educated parents and families. You have had some challenging cases involving families with blurred or nonexistent boundaries (Minuchin, 1974), but the situation with Natalia and Cecelia Romero is especially troubling.

Cecelia Romero is calling your office yet again about her daughter, Natalia, a sophomore, first-generation, limited-income Latina student. Cecelia is insistent. "I am her mother! I love my daughter. She is everything to me and to her *abuela*. Natalia is the future of our family. She refuses to answer my phone calls and has not been home in over two weeks. Maybe I should hurt myself, and then she will have to come home." Kathy, your administrative assistant, patiently explains, not for the first time, "I'm sorry, Señora Romero. We cannot give you any information about Natalia without her permission. We will pass along another message to Natalia to call you. And please, don't hurt yourself." After listening to Señora Romero's non-stop verbal barrage for about ten more minutes, Kathy politely but firmly states, "I'm sorry I can't be of any additional help to you. Perhaps there is someone in your community who can better support you. I must end this phone call." Exasperated, Kathy hangs up the phone and logs this as the fifth call from Ms. Romero this week. Twenty minutes later, you open your inbox to an e-mail from Ms. Romero with "URGENT! HELP ME AND MY DAUGHTER!" as the subject line.

Earlier this week, you asked Natalia to stop by your office for a visit. She scheduled an appointment for today at 1:30 p.m. You have about 15 minutes between appointments to prepare for Natalia. Checking her RUWeb student information system account, you see that she is academically successful, earning a 3.75 GPA over the past three semesters. However, she has changed her major four times: from pre-med to business to vocal performance, and now to Spanish. She is a resident assistant and works part time in the math tutoring lab on campus.

Arriving a few minutes early, Natalia says hello to Kathy and takes a seat in the reception area. She apologizes again for her mother's behavior, explaining, "*Mi madre* is not well. She worries about everything and has to go to the hospital a lot because she gets out of control. It's just me, *mi madre*, and *mi abuela* at home. I'm so sorry for all the trouble I've caused." Kathy assures Natalia that all mothers worry and that it is important for students to touch base with their families on a regular basis.

Natalia appears to have dressed up for this appointment, has a pen and notebook out on the table, and seems to be a bit nervous. Entering your office, she apologizes again for her mother, assuring you that she will ask her mother to refrain from bothering the college. You tell Natalia that you want to learn more about her and how she's doing at Regional University.

During your conversation, you learn that Natalia has many talents and interests. She is overwhelmed with the choices and options at college, including majors, courses, student organizations, and social opportunities. Natalia is also anxious about her financial situation and feels pressured to maintain good grades to keep her scholarships and financial aid. She works two jobs to pay for her living expenses and send some money home to her mother and grandmother each month. Natalia shares that she is learning about social justice, being an ally, and exploring all aspects of her identity, including religion, sexual orientation, and cultural heritage. Her eyes light up as she talks about all the possibilities that await and engage her.

You guide the conversation to Natalia's relationship with her mother. Immediately you notice the change as she lowers her eyes, slumps back in her chair, and crosses her arms tightly against her chest. "*Mi madre* has always been sick. She has a hard life, supporting both me and *mi abuela*. I worry about her all the time and then feel guilty when I have fun here at RU. *Mi madre* hurts herself to make me come home. Sometimes she takes too many pills or cuts herself or stops eating so the police take her to the hospital. I always have to tell her how much I love her and how I will never leave her. Everyone in my hometown knows about *mi madre* and looks down on our family. I was so glad when I got accepted to Regional University."

Natalia continues, "*Mi madre* thinks I should be a doctor or do something in business because I will make a lot of money. *Mi abuela* loves my singing voice and I bring her such happiness when I sing to her over the phone." Natalia sighs. "What I really want to do is just travel. I want to escape my life. I hope to save enough money to study abroad next year so I can be on my own and *mi madre* can't find me." Breaking down in tears, Natalia asks forgiveness for saying such bad things about her mother, begging you to not tell her mother anything you've talked about. She then asks about this thing she heard about called the "Buckley Amendment . . . something you can put on your record so no one can find you, and the school can't tell anyone that you are enrolled."

217

Student Development Response

Natalia's situation is complicated and presents a number of challenges for you. While your role is to support and educate students' parents and family members, your interactions with Cecelia Romero, as well as Natalia's description of her, indicate that Cecelia's needs go well beyond what you can address. You can, however, offer important assistance to Natalia by helping her negotiate her changing relationship with her mother. You can help her clarify her goals and concerns, acknowledge the impact they have on her (and her relationship with her mother), and identify and access available resources (internal, on campus, and in her home community). But before beginning that work, you will need to review the policies and procedures that define the professional parameters within which you must work.

You will want to be sure that you fully understand your institution's philosophy and practice in dealing with students' parents and families—particularly in situations, such as this one, that involve parental mental health issues. Specifically, you will need to know your institution's interpretation of the Family Education Right to Privacy Act (FERPA), because it will shape your interactions with Cecelia. You will also want to know whether Cecelia claims Natalia on her income tax forms and if she is listed as an emergency contact for Natalia.

Finally, although neither you nor any other staff member at Regional University can provide mental health services for students' parents and families, Cecelia has threatened her own personal safety. You should immediately consult with your supervisor and the campus counseling center to discuss your obligations and options in this situation. A call to a local community mental health facility might be appropriate to enlist community resources to help Cecelia. Your supervisor and the counseling center can help you determine when such a call might be necessary and who should make it. Clarifying these policies and procedures will allow you to establish the institutional context for your work with Natalia; some of this you may need or want to discuss with her, while other aspects you can address with professional colleagues and supervisors.

The issue at hand is how to respond to Natalia during your first meeting. The pressure and distress Natalia is experiencing in her relationship with her mother—

and her mother's dramatic statements to you and your assistant—could easily capture your attention. You will want to address these matters, but keep in mind that Natalia's mother, however central she might be, is only one aspect of Natalia's life. Natalia is bright, hardworking, curious, passionate about learning, and, thus far, overwhelmingly successful in her transition to college life. She also has a lifetime of experience with her mother. Keeping Natalia's strengths and experience in the forefront of your thinking will help both you and Natalia as you work together. Moreover, despite Natalia's statements that she wants to "escape" from her family, she obviously has strong bonds with her mother and grandmother. Validating both her commitment to being a student and her sense of loyalty to her family will help you build trust and rapport, and help Natalia approach problem-solving efforts in a way that acknowledges all of what she values.

Many students feel alone in their struggles. This might be especially true for Natalia, given the social stigma associated with mental health concerns and what she has described about being looked down on in her hometown. She might be worried that the stigma is following her to campus. You can help dispel the idea that she is unusual by using developmental and descriptive models to point out the ways in which her experiences parallel those of many of her peers.

Although Natalia's circumstances are more complex because of her mother's mental health concerns, the core issue is a classic developmental challenge: renegotiating the changing parent-child relationship. Natalia is enjoying the rites of passage that characterize young adulthood: having increased freedom from her mother and grandmother, engaging in new activities, and developing new relationships that open up fresh possibilities for her sense of who she is and who she can become. She is also struggling with the challenges that passage inherently brings: loss of previous structure, insecurity, and a desire at times to race past the process and arrive at the conclusion ("I want to escape my life."). Drawing her attention to the ways in which her concerns with her mother reflect widely shared developmental challenges can help both of you keep her situation in perspective and avoid needlessly pathologizing her mother and their relationship. While there are serious concerns with her mother, not *everything* about Natalia's struggle has to do with her mother's issues.

Some aspects of Natalia's concerns are typical for first-generation college students. Although her mother and grandmother are very proud of Natalia, they do not have a framework for understanding the systems she must navigate and the enormous and rapid changes that may be happening for her. Nor, perhaps, do they have the skills to mentor her through many of those changes. This gap between what Natalia is experiencing and what her mother understands about it may be creating anxiety for her mother and fueling the incessant phone calls and e-mails to your office. If so, this is exactly the sort of situation your office is designed to respond to, and you can share information with Natalia and her mother that might help ease tensions.

Natalia's mother might surprise you and Natalia by responding well to the idea that there are ways she can be helpful to Natalia. And in learning to do such things, Cecelia might obtain the increased attention and affection from Natalia she seeks. Until you have evidence to the contrary—and you do not yet—consider the possibility that Natalia's mother is frightened by the unknown and that with accurate information she can better support her daughter. Information will not resolve Cecelia's long-standing mental health issues, but it might help her feel more assured that her daughter is safe and that she can be part of this new phase in her daughter's life.

You can help Natalia recognize that she is not alone in needing to find mentors beyond her immediate family to help her through this transition. Together, you could identify possible sources for mentors: Residence Life, the Academic Advising Center, the Multicultural Center, the Women's Center, the Career Center, and her work-study supervisor.

As you discuss the potential benefits of finding campus mentors, you might encourage Natalia to pay particular attention to at least two aspects of her identity: her experiences as woman and as a Latina. Natalia could be emerging from a somewhat unusual type of foreclosure status (Josselson, 1996) in which she unquestioningly accepted her ongoing role as supporter, even rescuer, of her mother. However, it is also possible that your seeing Natalia's role with her mother as a "rescuer" is a culturally bound interpretation that does not fit for Natalia. That is, traditional Latino culture strongly values loyalty to parents, so Natalia's relationship with her mother must be understood within the context of her cultural heritage as well as her individual circumstances. Her desire for increased independence and individuation appears to cause Natalia feelings of guilt.

Thus, her development as a student and woman may be complicated by cultural conflicts as she figures out how to integrate her established identity as a Latina with her emerging identity as a college student. Natalia will need to explore the personal and cultural implications of the choices she is considering and discern which aspects of her culture are integral to her identity. A Latina role model will be very important as she moves toward identity achievement in ways that honor her heritage yet are flexible enough to support her new aspirations. Campus groups such as Chicanos in Action (CIA) and other local Latino/Latina organizations are avenues through which she can seek potential mentors and establish supportive peer relationships.

Natalia has a wide range of strengths and assets. Moreover, many aspects of her concerns are neither unusual nor limited to students whose parents have mental health issues. Keep these truths in the forefront of your discussions as you support her in renegotiating her relationship with her mother and exploring her emerging identity as a young adult.

Counseling Response

As noted with other case studies in this text, students of color may prefer more active and direct forms of helping (Sue & Sue, 2008). Incorporating Cognitive-Behavioral strategies into your relationship with Natalia could be helpful because she might respond well to the active, collaborative approach to problem solving that characterizes this kind of helping (Seligman, 2006).

You could begin by adopting an empathically curious attitude that forms the foundation for **guided discovery**. That is, convey a genuine sense of concern and support to Natalia while acknowledging that you do not yet understand what troubles her most about her situation and indicating that you would like to work with her to find out. Recall that the first two steps in **Socratic dialogue** are **asking informational questions** and **listening**. The process might go something like this:

You: *"It sounds like this is both an exciting and a challenging time for you. I hear at least two things happening that seem to be concerns: First, you worry about your mom. You care about her and you feel responsible for her. Second, you're trying to move forward with your own life and you have goals here that you're trying to pursue. Trying to deal with both of these things is hard right now. Is that right?"*

Natalia: "Yes. I just don't know what to do. Mostly I want to run away from the whole situation with my mother . . . but then I feel so guilty."

You: *"Sure . . . because both your family issues at home and your own life at college matter to you, it's hard to see how to handle them at the same time. Could we take just a few minutes to talk about each part—your concern for your mom, your goals here at school—so I can better understand?"*

Natalia: "Okay."

You: *"Good. Which one should we start with?"*

Natalia: "My mom, I guess. I DO really love her . . . it's just . . . it overwhelms me sometimes. I don't want her to think I don't love her . . . that I don't appreciate all she's done for me and how hard things are for her. But sometimes she embarrasses me, like calling here. It's never enough with her. I can't help it. I want more than just taking care of her. I just want to get away. I think sometimes I have to just run away."

Notice how Natalia has difficulty staying with one topic. This is quite common when people are upset—especially when they are anxious—because talking about what makes them anxious increases their anxiety. Her inability to focus, combined with her distress and her mother's history of mental health issues, could lead you to prematurely conclude that you need to limit your conversation and refer her to the counseling center.

While you eventually will refer Natalia to the counseling center, you will want to be careful about the timing of that referral. Natalia might be especially sensitive to the idea that *she* should see a counselor. Referring her at the first sign of distress could have several negative consequences: It may offend her if she feels misunderstood; it could create a barrier to your ability to offer the services you are equipped to provide; and it might erroneously confirm a hidden fear she might harbor about her own risk for mental health problems as the child of someone with such issues. When the time is right to mention seeing a campus mental health professional, you can let Natalia know that counselors often help students with normal developmental issues and also can be of great assistance to family members of those who suffer from a mental illness. So, rather than quickly moving to "you should see a counselor," maintain a collaborative spirit, acknowledge the difficulty she is having, and gently try to focus the discussion.

You: *"It seems really hard for you right now. Neither taking care of your mother nor focusing exclusively on yourself seems entirely right. You like it here and want to do well, so you start to really move into that, but then you feel bad for your mom. You try to respond to her, but then you think about your own life. Does that sound about right?"*

Natalia: "Yes, it's just the same thing over and over. I'm stuck in a loop."

You: *"There might be things that my office can do that would be helpful. What you're describing actually happens more than you might think, especially for first-generation students whose families don't really understand what going to college is like. I wonder if we could make a list—with one column focusing on your mom and one column focusing on school—and get a clear idea of what you need help with so we can start to get you unstuck. Does that seem useful?"*

Working together on this kind of list accomplishes several important steps in the helping process: (1) Natalia is able to voice her concerns (in whatever way they come up, and you can check which side of the list they should be recorded on)—that alone might offer some relief; (2) as she shares her concerns, you can be supportive and attentive to build trust and rapport; and (3) you can use the list to begin talking about services your office can provide and other resources available on campus. Introducing the counseling center, then, becomes just one item on a menu of options available to her and might be less threatening.

The National Alliance on Mental Illness (NAMI, www.nami.org) offers resources for people with serious psychological issues and their families. Also, the National Network of Adult and Adolescent Children who have a Mentally Ill Parent (NNAAMI, http://home.vicnet.net.au/~nnaami) has excellent resources online that Natalia could explore on her own. These websites might enable Natalia to learn more about her mother's mental illness and help her understand it.

As you discuss the "school" side of the list, you might want to address Natalia's difficulty deciding on a major. If she has not brought it up, you can ask about it. You can encourage her to visit the Career Center, letting her know that it has inventories that help students examine the reasons they are indecisive, as well as inventories that identify student aptitudes, interests, and values (Krumboltz & Vosvick, 1996).

The key elements of a valuable response to Natalia include an active, collaborative stance; a sincere effort to normalize the aspects of her experience that are common developmental transitions; and acknowledgement of the unique challenges she faces. Generating a "problem list," identifying the items to which you can respond, being direct about the ones you cannot address, and seeking to connect Natalia with other campus services would likely strike an effective balance between support and action.

Discussion Questions

1. What are your immediate reactions to this scenario? What are your thoughts about Cecilia? What are your concerns for Natalia? What do you believe to be your strengths and your challenges in this situation?

2. Which resources will you draw on as you proceed?

3. What expectations about increased independence or individuation in young adulthood—versus loyalty to family—do you hold?

4. Have you had a close family member with mental health issues? How might your experiences influence your work with Natalia and her family?

References

Donovan, J. A., & McKelfresh, D. A. (2008). In community with students' parents and families. *NASPA Journal, 45*(3), 384–405.

Josselson, R. (1996). *Revising herself: The story of women's identity from college to midlife.* New York: Oxford University Press.

Krumboltz, J. D. & Vosvick, M. A. (1996). Career assessment and the career beliefs inventory. *Journal of Career Assessment, 4*(4), 345–361.

Minuchin, S. (1974). *Families and family therapy.* Florence, KY: Routledge.

Seligman, L. (2006). *Theories of counseling and psychotherapy: Systems, strategies, and skills.* New Jersey: Pearson Prentice Hall.

Sue, D. W. & Sue, D. (2008). *Counseling the culturally diverse: Theory and practice.* (5th ed.). Hoboken, NJ: John Wiley & Sons, Inc.

CHAPTER 12

Microaggressions on Campus
Experiences of Nontraditional Age Women of Color[1]

Annemarie Vaccaro, Nona L. Wilson, and Ruth Harper

You are a relatively new staff member at Hampton Community College (HCC), an institution that enrolls 3,000 students, a large proportion of whom are nontraditional age students. The institution is committed to diversity and enrolls 40% students of color. Hiring employees of color is also a priority, but a less successful one: Only a small number of staff and faculty members are people of color. As the student life advisor, you work closely with student government. In this role, you meet Jade.

Jade, a 34-year-old African American woman, has recently been elected as

---

[1] While the names have been changed, the women depicted in this chapter are real. They shared their experiences and reactions in an unpublished qualitative study about racism and microaggressions at an evening and weekend college for women.

a representative to student government. She has had some transition issues in coming to college after being in the world of work. Even though the school is somewhat racially diverse, it does not always feel like the most welcoming place. Jade is very alert to unwelcoming aspects of student life at HCC. You notice that she gradually befriends two other nontraditional age women of color (Kendra and Mia) who have similar feelings. One day these three decide to plan a coffee hour for women of color. They hope the event will serve two purposes. First, it will be a place where women of color can meet one another. Second, it will offer a forum for dialogue about women's experiences at HCC. Because Jade trusts you, she invites you to attend as an observer.

The night of the event, Jade, Kendra, and Mia are pleasantly surprised that 18 women attend. They self-identify as six Black women, five Latinas, three Asian American women, two Native American women, and two biracial women. There is positive energy in the room as the women informally begin introducing themselves. They say things like, "I've seen you around campus" and "Weren't you in my Introductory Psychology class?" Fairly quickly, the discussion turns to the women's collective experiences with racism on campus. Specifically, they begin to talk about the things that make them feel unwelcome or uncomfortable at HCC.

Alicia says, "It's those subtle, everyday interactions with White faculty, staff, and students that wear me down." Brenda concurs. "It is the snickers, looks, and closed-minded comments that grate on my nerves." Carmen adds, "And because racism can be subtle, it's hard to address." "Absolutely!" says Dana. All the women start to nod their heads, and Jade invites each woman to share a recent experience on campus with racism.

Lydia offers to go first. She explains how she hears a lot of comments in classrooms, hallways, and the cafeteria that she considers offensive. One prominent place where racism and ethnocentrism show up consistently is in Spanish class. Lydia feels that her peers are intolerant of cultural differences. When a White classmate said, "They say everything backwards!" Lydia retorted, "'To us it's not backwards; in fact, to us *you* speak backwards!' It stuns me how narrow-minded some people can be." Many heads nod in unison.

Onida shares how White students often try to strike up conversations with her by mentioning their supposed knowledge of or interest in Native American culture. Just last week in math class, a White person mentioned that he had talked to an Indian shaman while on vacation in Arizona and that he had Cherokee relatives. Onida listened for a few minutes, then asked him to stop talking. She says, "It drives me up the wall when people who know nothing about my culture pretend to know all about Native cultures—especially people who believe they're open-minded and educated!"

Mia describes how a White student used the words "those boys" to refer to members of the school's basketball team in a class presentation. She says to the others, "It was just her normal way of communicating. I don't even think that it was a conscious act of devaluing African American men." Some of the other women agree that such comments and actions often occur unintentionally, but are painful nonetheless.

In one of her global studies classes, Lupe says that she heard a small group of White women talking about their solution to poverty in developing countries. One White student argued that poverty could be alleviated if "they'd stop having so many kids!" Lupe was very offended. Feeling disrespected is an everyday occurrence for Lupe and many others in the group. They note that disrespect comes in many forms: biased or ignorant comments, exclusion from group projects, disapproving looks, and being treated as if they are invisible. The most difficult incidents, the women agree, are those that are subtle and likely not intentional or deliberate. And most disappointing, they all agree, is the fact that faculty and staff members do not speak up when these incidents happen. "Do they even realize what's going on?" Kendra wonders aloud. "Or do they agree?"

In addition to the closed-mindedness of peers, many of the women report less than positive interactions with faculty and staff. Many feel that White professors routinely ignore or even put down their class contributions. Patience talks about the subtle things that professors do in the classroom. On a number of occasions, White peers had made comments almost identical to the ideas Patience had shared. The White students received praise for "great ideas," while Patience received no reinforcement for speaking. Jackie also says that professors devalue her contributions. During group discussions, professors say, "We need to speed it along" or glance at the classroom clock when she or other women of color are talking. Conversely, professors never seem to rush even the most long-winded White students. Jade adds that her professors seem surprised that she's "so articulate." She adds, "I'm getting pretty sick of that so-called compliment."

Most of the women admit that they share their negative experiences only with family or friends outside of school. Elisa says, "Most people, particularly White Americans, are not aware of the racism. They're oblivious to it, and they get offended if you bring it up." Very few of the women discuss their experiences with White people they consider friends. Lola explains, "I have some friends who are White, and they have been very supportive and stuff. But, I don't know how to describe it. The knowledge isn't there. They may like us, but they don't really *know* us." Tai exclaims, "They *don't* know us! And it is not something that's ever going to change." Only two of the women have talked to university personnel about their experiences with racism. Shawna says, "I don't think I've ever said anything to a teacher . . . because I think they're not going to get it, or not understand it, so I just don't bother."

Further discussion reveals that these women have developed a host of coping mechanisms to deal with racial microaggressions at HCC; some look for peer support, others rely on internal strength, while some challenge incidents as they occur. Some women, like Cara, say that on the first day of class they look for a seat next to another woman of color. Lupe says, "So when you walk into a room and there is another person of color there, you're like, 'Oh, I know you understand. I'm going to sit right next to you.' You know? You start a sentence . . . and they can practically finish it for you." While women like Cara and Lupe find comfort in connecting with students of color, others rely on an inner strength that has developed from years of dealing with racism. Suki says she has become so accustomed to everyday racist occurrences that she's learned to "tune them out." Soledad concurs. "Because of the world we live in, I automatically look past racism or people just being biased, because that's the way I have to live every day. You live around it." A few women nod in agreement. However, Jesse says, "We shouldn't have to deal with it, look past it, or live around it!" Chara agrees, "Other people's close-mindedness should not be our burden as women of color." Jade exclaims, "You're right!"

After two hours of lively sharing, Jade, Kendra, and Mia ask the group what they should do as "next steps." As a student government representative, Jade feels a responsibility to bring these experiences to the administration. University leadership should know that women of color consistently experience covert racism on campus. Five women support Jade's suggestion, while four others doubt it will make a difference. The rest of the women admit that they have little time or emotional energy to explain their experiences (and defend their feelings) to the predominantly White, male administration. As the mother of two, Lisa uses her emotional energy to support her children, who also experience overt and covert racism. Last week, she spent an hour with her son's middle school principal, trying to get the principal to reconsider a decision she felt was racially biased against her son and his friends.

At the conclusion of the meeting, Jade, Kendra, and Mia ask the group if they are interested in creating a formal student organization for women of color. Six of the women, plus the three organizers, say that they are very interested in such a group. They appreciate the idea of a safe space where they can talk about the impact of racism in their lives without the fear of offending White people. Three young mothers claim they could not dedicate themselves to an official group. They aren't sure they have the time or energy. The remaining six women have mixed feelings. They are busy with families and full-time employment, but they really enjoyed this meeting with other women who have had similar experiences. This coffee hour was one of the most validating experiences they have had at HCC. However, they wonder if positive change can happen unless they bring White peers and administrators into the dialogue. These six women believe that a campuswide conversation with people from all races is essential to create a welcoming climate. Thus, they ultimately decide that a group solely for women of color is not right for them.

Jade, Kendra, and Mia are perplexed. They wonder how 21 women can have similar experiences with covert racism but not agree on whether or how to address it. While the women share similar experiences, they have different ideas about what should happen next and how much time and emotional energy they can contribute to future efforts.

Student Development Response

Your mind might be racing through all the student development theories you learned in your graduate preparation program. With 21 students in the room, a variety of theories could be applied. Certainly, many developmental concepts are relevant to this case, including adult development, racial identity, ethnic identity, gender identity, and women's ways of knowing. The women in this case study represent a myriad of cross-cutting developmental stages. Jones and McEwen's (2000) model of multiple identity development may be useful as you interact with this group. That model calls attention to distinctions that women may make between their "inner" identities and their "outside" identities (Jones & McEwen, 2000, p. 408). That framework effectively captures one of the central themes that emerges among the women: not being understood for who they truly are. Models that consider specific aspects of identity—such as race, gender, and decision making style—might be especially instructive. Because racism is a recurrent concern for the women, exploring racial identity is a good starting point.

In your graduate program, you were probably encouraged to explore issues of diversity so you would be a more culturally competent practitioner (Pope, Reynolds, & Mueller, 2004). Ideally, you learned (and may have experienced) that discrimination in the 21st century is covert and at times unintentional. Instead of facing overt racist events, people of color face a consistent pattern of covert and seemingly small, yet painful racist happenings called microaggressions (Pierce, Carew, Pierce-Gonzales & Willis, 1978; Solórzano, Ceja & Yosso, 2000). Three decades ago, microaggressions were defined as "subtle, stunning, often automatic, and non-verbal exchanges which are 'putdowns' of blacks by offenders. The offensive mechanisms used against blacks are innocuous. The cumulative weight of their never-ending burden is the major ingredient in black-white interactions" (Pierce et al., 1978, p. 66.)

More recently, Sue, Bucceri, Lin, Nadal, & Torino (2007) referred to microaggressions as "brief, commonplace, daily verbal, behavioral, and environmental indignities" (p. 72). Constantine (2007) describes them as "subtle and commonplace exchanges that somehow convey insulting or demeaning messages to people of color" (p. 2).

Research has shown numerous negative effects of microaggressions on people of color: feelings of invisibility, self-doubt, frustration, exhaustion, helplessness, and racial tension (Constantine, 2007; Franklin & Boyd-Franklin, 2000; Solórzano et al., 2000). All the women in this case had experienced some form of microaggression. As a student affairs practitioner, you have a responsibility to offer a developmental response to the group as well as to the individual women. While it is beyond the scope of this chapter, you should also be concerned about larger issues of campus climate.

Schlossberg's (1989) ideas of marginality and mattering are also relevant to understanding these students. The women in this scenario feel marginalized at HCC. Whether or not the behaviors of their peers, faculty, and staff are intentional, the women experience marginalization. Jackie describes a specific instance when she believed her class contributions did not matter to her professor. From her point of view, if her ideas were truly valued, the professor would not have asked her to "hurry it along." Microaggressions such as this one contribute to women's sense of marginalization.

Rendón's (1994) notion of validation—"an enabling, confirming, and supportive process initiated by in- and out-of-class agents that foster academic and interpersonal development"—is especially relevant here (p. 46). This group of women experience invalidating environments inside and outside the classroom. You should keep in mind the ways *your* actions (or inactions) will directly affect their sense of mattering and validation.

Women's experiences of and responses to marginalization and validation are shaped by their stages of racial identity. Racial identity relates to "the sense of group or collective identity based on one's perception that he or she shares a common racial heritage with a particular reference group" (Helms, 1993, p. 4). In this case, racial identity describes the processes by which people of color deal with marginalization, internalized racism, and other effects of living in an oppressive society. This group of women experience marginalization on campus and invalidation in the classroom. While there was agreement about the widespread existence of microaggressions, individual women responded to these incidents in diverse ways. Further, at the end of the coffee hour, the women could not come to a consensus about future steps. These differences could indicate various racial identity stages as well as varying internal psychological resources.

A variety of racial or ethnic identity models might be useful for practitioners at HCC (Banks, 1981; Cross, 1971; Ferdman & Gallegos, 2001; Gibbs, 1974; Horse, 2001; Jackson, 1975; Kim, 2001; Milliones, 1980; Phinney, 1990). It would be impossible to detail all the differences between and within races in this short case study, but it is important for you to consider multiple racial identity models in your response. No single theory would be appropriate for a diverse group of 21 women. One way to begin thinking about racial identity is to consider some of the hallmarks of racial identity theory. In her analysis of identity models for marginalized groups, Sleeter (2001) found many consistent themes across these theories. These themes were likely inspired by Cross's (1971) model of racial identity and are reflected in more contemporary racial identity models (Banks, 1981; Cross & Fhagen-Smith, 2001; Hardiman & Jackson, 1992).

Some of the steps, stages, or phases noted in racial identity theories are (a) little awareness of oppression; (b) recognition of and opposition to oppressive systems; (c) immersion in one's community or culture; (d) integration of a particular identity into one's whole being; and (e) a commitment to fighting all forms of oppression. Cross and Fhagen-Smith (2001) suggest that people can "recycle" through these stages more than once as they build an enhanced racial identity. The women in this case were likely in a variety of places along this continuum, some for the first time and others through recycling.

As adults, these women are unlikely to be in the earliest stages of racial identity development. Persons in early stages have little recognition of oppression—all these women recognized experiences with covert racism. Those who were most interested in a group solely for women of color may have been in the immersion stage. Women in this stage may also have been least interested in working collaboratively with Whites to address racism. Conversely, women in later stages of racial identity development might believe that bringing White faculty, staff, and students into the conversation is essential. Persons in later stages of racial identity typically see themselves as part of a positive collective, with Whites as potential allies. By the time people reach the final stages of racial identity, they have developed ways of dealing with racism that do not harm their inner being. Suki and Soledad talked about being able to "live around" or "tune out" racism. Over time, they have learned to cope with microaggressions in ways that protect their inner selves.

Gender is also salient to this scenario. A number of student development theories describe the unique ways women develop, make meaning of the world, and make decisions. While one describes a psychosocial model and the other a cognitive structural model, both Gilligan's (1993) and Josselson's (1973, 1987, 1996) research found issues of care, connection, and relationships with others to be central themes in women's lives.

In your study of student development, you likely used Gilligan's theory to analyze moral dilemmas. Whether or not you consider the decision to address racism a moral decision, key concepts from Gilligan's theory may be useful in your response in this case study. Gilligan's ethic of care in moral decision making can help you understand the variety of individual responses to microaggressions and the diversity of thought that emerged in the discussion of potential "next steps." While women could be anywhere along Gilligan's spectrum, level 2, the second transition, and level 3 may be of particular interest to you as a practitioner.

Women in Gilligan's second level place the needs of others above their own. Lisa talks about not having time or emotional energy to confront racism on campus because she focuses her fight against racism on issues that affect her children. Disequilibrium between individual needs and the needs of others can push women into a second transition, in which they begin to question the assumed dichotomy between responsibility to others and self-sacrifice.

Gilligan's third level of moral development is characterized by a balance between a woman's own needs and the responsibility she feels to others. Women's moral decisions are made by achieving balance between care and supportive relationships and protecting oneself from exploitation and hurt. Many of the women in this case study negotiate a delicate balance among care for self, emotional support of family, and the emotional time and energy needed to address racism on campus. The 21 women likely embody many combinations of Gilligan's foci of care.

As you work with these women individually and as a group, you may use parts of many developmental theories. While the women all experience covert racism and microaggressions, their reactions to those experiences vary. The lack of consensus regarding what to do about racism on campus reflects the multiple and cross-cutting issues related to identity, which include, but are not limited to, race and gendered decision making. As you work with the group, you will need to help the women find solutions that meet their group and individual needs. For instance, women in early stages of racial identity development and later stages of women's moral development have different needs than women in later stages of racial identity but early stages of women's moral development. Further, women with partners or dependents (such as children and aging parents) might think differently about the time and emotional commitment needed for the "next steps" than women without such relationships.

It will be no easy task to respond in a developmental manner to 21 women who present a variety of developmental identities. However, if you stay mindful of how crucial it is to help women and underrepresented students of color feel validated, you can convey to these women that their experiences and concerns matter to HCC.

Counseling Response

For some, it might be tempting to draw the "diversity box" around the group and to think or act in a different way with these women. But if you do that, all that follows will be problematic. The concepts and skills needed to work effectively with this group must be central to your professional practice, not add-on models or skills that you use in certain circumstances. If your initial reaction to the scenario is to notice differences between yourself and the women, and to think "I don't know what to tell them—what they should do, what they need," that's good. In fact, that is the mind-set you should cultivate in every encounter with every student you help. This is not "I don't know" in the closed—"don't know, don't need to know, someone else should do this"—sense, but rather an open, tentative, receptive, mindful "not-knowing" (De Jong & Berg, 2008, p. 20).

Conversely, if your initial reaction is to think you understand well what these women are going through because they seem similar to you, be cautious. Similarities—not just differences—can get in the way of truly hearing someone's experience, and these women are clearly saying that they need to be heard. The awareness of self and others required to hear and help them is a model for all effective helping, and the counseling frameworks presented in chapter 2 will be useful.

Before considering how specific counseling concepts and skills can support your work, look at two models for thinking about diversity that provide a helpful overarching framework. These models can help make the myriad issues you will need to consider a bit more manageable. The first comes from Savin-Williams (2001). Although his work focuses on homosexual youth and their families, he advocates a point of view that has broad application. Savin-Williams suggests that we work from an assumption that people (1) are all the same; (2) have group differences; (3) have differences within groups; and (4) are unique. That is, using yourself as the subject, you would find that certain elements of your experience and identity are universal; others are shared by people with similar characteristics (race, gender, sexual orientation); some elements of your experience and identity are quite different from those of people outsiders might easily label as the same as you; and some elements or aspects of your experience and identity are unique to you.

This framework is especially relevant to this case study. It underscores a central truth: No matter who you are and what your background is, there will be points of similarity and connection between you and the women, and points of difference and departure. That is also true for the women in relation to each other. They may share a common concern and a similar perspective about some of their experiences, but each woman is unique. Keep these truths in mind as you work with them.

The second model, developed by Hays (2008), provides a system for organizing similarities and differences that is both comprehensive and user-friendly. Her model, the ADDRESSING model, recognizes that all of us have multiple identities, the salience of which varies from person to person, across the lifespan, and in response to life circumstance. Using her model, you would strive to understand each woman's identity in terms of the following factors (p. 4):

- Age and generational influences

- Developmental and acquired Disabilities

- Religion and spiritual orientation

- Ethnicity and racial identity

- Socioeconomic status

- Sexual orientation

- Indigenous heritage

- National origin

- Gender

Each of these aspects of identity can be a source of privilege or oppression, and each can significantly influence a person's life story. Some of these aspects are more readily observable and can end up as the focus of attention when other, less obvious, aspects of identity are more personally significant. In other words, although the women in this group have come together around issues related to their status as women of color, their individual identities are complex and fluid. The ADDRESSING model is a useful way to attend to that diversity without singling out one aspect that you happen to notice or ascribe significance to and using that as the defining characteristic of the person, when that aspect of identity might not be the most relevant or meaningful to her.

This model is a useful tool for enhancing your self-awareness as well. Considering your own identity status across the ADDRESSING elements and your own experiences with privilege and oppression can help you anticipate potential strengths and challenges that may arise in your interactions with students. As a whole, this group expresses a fair amount of anger at White people, at the ignorance that often accompanies privilege, and at the burden of having to continually educate others about their experiences with little benefit in return. If many aspects of your identity have traditionally been privileged, you may find it challenging to listen to the group's anger. You could get defensive, even subtly, and wish to move them too quickly to problem solving or focusing on positives. In return, they might they feel—even if they trust you—that their experience with you simply replicates their experience on campus: They may feel called on to take care of you, educate you, or assure you that you are okay.

Conversely, if you are identified primarily with traditionally marginalized groups, the group's anger might echo your own frustrations, and it might be easy to hear their complaints as "the same" as yours. It might be easy to encourage them to take action that you believe should be taken. In either case, you must be intentional in noticing how your own concerns can be triggered and finding ways to deal with the concerns that support your personal and professional growth, and that allow you to be mindful and purposeful in your work with the women.

Person-Centered Helping

You have been invited to the group meeting to listen; first and foremost, that is what you should do. Core ideas and skills from Person-Centered helping will be useful. When you speak, focus on reflecting what you hear the women expressing. As noted in chapter 2, the central question in Person-Centered helping is "How does this person see him- or herself?" (Fisher, 2007). Sharing with the group what you hear as their answers to that question will help them feel understood. Fisher's instructions to (1) respond to what is personal rather than what is impersonal; (2) respond rather than lead; and (3) respond to feelings, not just to content (p. 432) are ideal suggestions for your role with this group.

Responding to what is personal rather than what is impersonal will mean keeping your focus on what the women are saying about their experiences. Be especially careful not to allow your attention to shift to people outside the group—even when the women themselves are describing others' actions or attitudes. If that happens, your conversation with them will be more about others and less about them. When the women share experiences that involve details about what other people have or have not done, be purposeful in keeping your attention on what those experiences are like for the women speaking. With you—if nowhere else—other students, faculty, and staff members are secondary characters; these women are center stage.

The second step is responding to rather than leading the speaker. This means refraining from stepping in to direct them. You may have great ideas and suggestions, but the group is just coming together and their voices need to emerge. Allow them to discover their own courses of action. This may be challenging, since the women have already begun to reveal that they are not necessarily drawn to the same ideas about how to respond. Moreover, they are a diverse group and thus will not only bring different backgrounds, life experiences, and perspectives, but will also have different interpersonal and communication styles. Some of the women may prefer a faster paced conversation that allows for a fair amount of verbal overlapping and open disagreement; others may need more silence and prefer to avoid direct disagreement. Overall, the women are indicating that they feel misunderstood and devalued. You will want to help them come together in ways that minimize the chance of repeating those negative experiences and that do not, even subtly, pressure them to conform.

One way you can help, if the group continues to meet, is to suggest many different ways the women can express themselves and share their ideas: in the large group, in smaller groups or pairs, individually, orally, and in writing. Another is to keep in mind that not everyone values "verbal/emotional/behavioral expressiveness" (Sue & Sue, 2008, p. 142). Some cultures value restraint, so you will want to be careful not to impose "openness" as a value on any of the women.

The third recommendation is to respond to feelings, not just content. This will be easy enough to do when the women directly identify what they are feeling. Often, however, it can be hard for persons in the midst of an emotionally intense experience to identify and articulate exactly what they are feeling. Frequently, people will talk around their emotions—suggesting what they feel indirectly through tone, rate of speech, facial expressions, and body language. Some of the women may not have precise language to describe the extremely complex emotions they are feeling. As a listener, you will need to carefully attend to them to hear the emotion that is perhaps embedded but not directly expressed in their stories. To do this well you must be able to separate your reactions from theirs; so, again, self-awareness is key.

Finally, remember that not everyone expresses emotion the same way. What you initially interpret as anger or disinterest (because a woman will not look at you, for example) could be reserve or respect—or something else entirely. What you might think is agreement (because a woman smiles or laughs) might be confusion or discomfort. Be tentative in your interpretations, verify them with the women, and be willing to be wrong and make adjustments. That kind of openness actually garners more trust and credibility than always being right.

Solution-Focused Helping

Several concepts and techniques from Solution-Focused helping are relevant for supporting this group of students. The women will benefit from clarifying their goals, maintaining and enhancing their sense of competence, and finding exceptions to the invalidating environment that surrounds them. Helping them do those things, however, will require considerable thoughtfulness on your part. The more identified you are with traditionally privileged groups, the more care you will need to take in the timing and tone of these strategies. For example, if, as a White woman or man, you move too quickly or forcefully to discussing what the women can do to cope with or change their experiences on campus, you run the risk of being another source of invalidation. As discussed earlier, you might prefer to avoid their anger. Even if that is not your motive, as a person with a history of privilege, you can easily, prematurely, shift the focus. However, staying "safe" yourself by avoiding any sort of assistance that might call your motives into question can actually short-change this group. If you are a person of color, you could run a similar risk of pushing too quickly or forcefully for solutions and might be seen as denying the truth of oppression. Shifting the students' talk from concerns to solutions requires trust and rapport so the women will feel supported and heard.

There is no magic formula here—or in any direct work with students—for calculating the balance of support and challenge. That balance is always a negotiation, worked out in relationship. Often it requires student affairs professionals to take risks, to be vulnerable, to make mistakes and learn from them. You can educate yourself, use your best skills and sharpest judgment, and still make mistakes. You will want, then, to be observant as you use Solution-Focused concepts and techniques. If used skillfully, they can be very helpful.

241

Cocreating Competence and Finding Exceptions

These women are extremely competent. They bring considerable life experience to their roles as students, and they have already indicated that they are using several effective coping strategies, such as peer support, drawing on internal strength, and challenging offensive incidents. Bringing attention to their strengths and competencies, and encouraging them to notice what they are doing well, can be validating and empowering. Particularly in an environment that does not adequately support or acknowledge these women, amplifying their strengths is important.

Bearing in mind all that has been said about privilege, ask these women about times when the microaggressions do not occur or occur less frequently. Looking for exceptions may identify potential allies. One woman might say, "Dr. Jenks in the Business Department shows a real interest in all his students. I never feel unheard or devalued in his classes." Jade might observe, "I expected the student government reps to be a bunch of pseudo-leader types, you know, just pumping up their résumés and not really interested in anything or anyone. But I've been surprised, especially since I got on the Executive Committee. These people are not all young or self-centered. I actually look forward to the meetings."

Other group members may notice that what *they* do makes a difference; for example, one student shared that she intentionally sits by another student of color in her classes. "It's harder for that math instructor to overlook both of us, ha! And when she does, we just look at each other and instantly know what we are both thinking. It helps." A woman might note that talking to an instructor outside of class seems to break the ice and show her interest. You can ask the students if they are willing to pay attention in the future and notice what is happening when things are going well.

At some future point, it might be an interesting intellectual challenge—as well as a productive discussion topic—for the group to consider the miracle question: *"If a miracle occurred here at Hampton Community College and it became an affirming, inclusive environment, what would that look like? What would be happening?"* Remind the students to put their responses into "I" statements, such as "I would be comfortable being myself in all my classes" or "I'd walk into the cafeteria and feel like I belonged." As the students enumerate images, they can also be generating ideas for how to turn the images into reality: "I will have strategies for engaging faculty members as well as other students, and I will be empowered to know what to say and how to say it when I'm mistreated" or "Those white cafeteria walls will be covered with bright, colorful murals that welcome all people and set a different mood—and I know who can get that done!"

Cognitive-Behavioral Helping

Counseling literature strongly suggests that "American Indians, Asian Americans, Black Americans, and Hispanic Americans tend to prefer more active-directive forms of helping than nondirective ones" (Sue & Sue, 2008, p. 177). Active-directive and influencing skills include sharing personal perceptions, being more active in the conversation, offering suggestions, and teaching skills—or what might be summed up as "becoming a partner to the client" (p. 147). The literature supports many of the cardinal features of Cognitive-Behavioral helping, and you many want to consider integrating Cognitive-Behavioral strategies into your work with this group.

Collaboration is the centerpiece of Cognitive-Behavioral helping. The spirit of teamwork—of joining with the students to help them identify, examine, and resolve their concerns—should characterize every aspect of Cognitive-Behavioral helping. As noted in chapter 2, **Socratic dialogue** is a major tool in collaboration and entails a balance between nondirective skills (listening and summarizing) and more directive skills (asking informational and synthesizing questions). You can tailor your collaborative efforts to suit the individual women in the group by noticing which women are more responsive to the nondirective elements and which women are favorably inclined toward the more directive elements. Adjusting your style to the preferences of individual students while remaining congruent is not only respectful but can help you build strong working relationships.

You can use Socratic dialogue to encourage meaningful conversations among the women. Some members of the group may be interested in moving forward toward problem solving. Socratic dialogue provides a structure for doing so that is at once active and deliberate, focusing the conversation on what the women know from their experiences to help them identify potential strategies.

The first step in Socratic dialogue involves **asking informational questions** to help clarify student concerns and begin to tease out specific details that can be addressed. Such questions might include *"What situations on campus are most upsetting for you? What stands out to you about those situations? What are aspects of those situations that are common for you as a group? Are there experiences that you believe only you have encountered? If so, what are they?"* A useful follow-up for any question in this group is *"What else?"*

The second step is **listening** for elements that seem to be especially important to the women, even those that might be glossed over. While you listen, strive to remain open, to allow the unexpected to register with you, and to resist listening only for those things you might expect to hear.

The third step, **summarizing**, brings together what you have heard in a succinct way so that the group members can take in the big picture. Remember, however, that even in summarizing, you will want to maintain a collaborative relationship. Ask questions such as *"Is that right?"* or *"What have I missed?"* or *"How would you say that in your own words?"* Your role is not to decide for the group members what their concerns or priorities are, but to help them clarify those priorities themselves.

The final step, **asking synthesizing questions,** invites the members to consider the information they've shared in new ways; ideally, they'll notice aspects that reflect their own statements and experiences but to which they had not previously fully attended. This can open up opportunities for responding to their concerns. With this group, asking synthesizing questions might look something like this:

You: *"When we started the conversation, there was a lot of agreement about the problems with acceptance and recognition on campus—and that really held up throughout the discussion. It also seems like everyone here really appreciated the chance to talk to each other. As you discussed what would help, however, the idea of a support group for women of color got only mixed support. How do you put together those two things: a consensus around the concerns but not around the support group?"*

Jade: "Well, I think this is part of why things are so slow to change . . . it's hard to find something everyone can agree on."

You: *"Right . . . so ONE option isn't likely to work for everybody. Kind of like ONE way of doing things on the larger campus doesn't work for everybody."*

Kendra: "Yeah, maybe we could think about different options . . . going back to the stuff we identified tonight and generating options."

Mia: "Right, because while not everyone wanted a support group for women of color, nine of us did. And that's something."

Jade: "I guess it also has to do with what's going in everyone's lives . . . some women are married, are mothers, have other obligations. But some of us do have time and energy, and maybe we can do some things that would be useful to those who don't have the time."

At some point, the group as a whole—or individual members—might want to discuss specific actions they can take immediately to cope with the stressors they experience on campus. The three Cognitive-Behavioral strategies described below might be especially useful for them. Although the strategies would not result in change on campus, they could help support these women, provide some respite or relief from the burdens they bear, and help shore them up for taking more direct action against discrimination on their campus.

1. Risk/resource balance. Engaging the members in a discussion of the balance between their risks on campus and their resources for handling those risks could be empowering for them. During the meeting, the members appear galvanized around their shared experiences with microaggressions and take some comfort in having their concerns validated. While sharing their concerns can be essential, focusing only on the risks and not the resources could diminish their ability to respond to the problem. Considering the balance between risk and resource offers several potential benefits. The process (1) gives the group an opportunity to do a reality check (*"How bad is the situation?"*); (2) engages the group in searching for resources, allowing them to brainstorm all the sources of strength and resistance they can identify—both internal and external; and (3) sets up an opportunity to discuss how to minimize the risks and magnify the resources.

2. Distraction is a temporary but often useful strategy. The consequences of suffering repeated microaggressions are significant. The incidents themselves may be fleeting, but the compounding negative effects are not. At the same time group members are organizing to respond to discrimination—by writing letters to the administration, forming a support group, confronting offenses when they occur—they could benefit from finding ways to purposefully disengage. In other words, you might help the group generate a list of ways to give themselves "time outs" from the burdens of being students at a predominantly White campus. You might initiate the process simply by asking the group, *"What allows you to set this aside, even briefly, and refuel?"* Encourage group members to generate as many ideas as they can, moving into things they could do but have not yet tried.

Once they have generated a list, invite them to discuss how those things— events, practices, relationships, or self-talk—refuel them. You might ask, *"When you do those things or spend time with the people you've identified, what improves for you?"* Again, generate a list, then ask the group to consider how being intentional about including these things in their weekly schedules might help them to take constructive action on campus. You can also invite them to talk about what happens when they stay focused on the problems for long stretches without any relief or time out.

3. Coping card. Some members of the group might be experiencing microaggressions that are especially difficult for them to handle. There might be situations that repeatedly disrupt their days, interfere with their ability to study, or simply linger and hurt deeply. There might be other situations that—although both you and the students wish you could instantly resolve them—may not immediately stop and for which a coping plan might be helpful. Consider sharing the five-step coping card technique with the group or with individual members:

1. Acknowledge your feelings.

2. Remember, the intensity is temporary.

3. Identify your resources.

4. Identify constructive action that you could take right now.

5. Imagine what you would tell a friend who is feeling what you're feeling.

Jade, or any of the other women in the group, might create a personalized coping card that reads something like this:

> "Right now I am SO ANGRY and SO TIRED. I am sick of always having to deal with other people's ignorance! I am HERE and I want to be acknowledged! I also know that there are times—not enough of them, but there are times—when I do feel acknowledged and I don't always feel like I'm on fire like I do right now. I need to remember that I'm a strong, smart, capable, creative, resourceful woman who has a lot to offer. And I have a LOT of people who love me for me. Right now, I could call Mia or Kendra, call my sister, go exercise, say a prayer, put on my iPod, or write in my journal. I can also remember that if Mia or Kendra were this angry right now, I'd tell them, 'Channel your energy! Channel your energy! Do NOT let people pull you down or get you to act in ways that disrespect yourself or hurt you in the long run.' They'd laugh, but we'd all know it's true."

Jade can keep the card with her and pull it out during particularly distressing times. The process of reading through it could help soothe her agitated feelings and remind her of actions she could take right then to help get her through the difficult time. The card incorporates distraction (step 4) and, in doing so, can help create some breathing room for Jade. It reminds her of her own priorities and values, as well as her many resources and supports.

As this response demonstrates, each of the counseling models—Person-Centered, Solution-Focused, and Cognitive-Behavioral—has something to offer. And many of the concepts and skills can be used together to enhance your support of this group. The important common threads throughout each of the models are (1) to listen for student concerns and strengths, and (2) to respond in ways that allow students to feel heard and valued.

Discussion Questions

1. Considering the options described from the three counseling models, how would you proceed with the various members of this group?

2. Imagine that a support/sharing group for women students of color is formed. How might you support its members if they decide to try to raise awareness of the concerns they have identified? Do you think White allies could or should be involved with the group? Why or why not?

3. The concept of collaboration should help you act as an advocate or teach advocacy skills without "taking over" the problem. What would that look like?

References

Banks, J. A. (1981). The stages of ethnicity: Implications for curriculum reform. In J. A. Banks (Ed.), *Multi-ethnic education: Theory and practice* (pp. 129–139). Albany, NY: State University Press.

Constantine, M. G. (2007, January). Racial microaggressions against African American clients in cross-racial counseling relationships. *Journal of Counseling Psychology, 54*(1), 1–16.

Cross, W. E., Jr. (1971). The Negro-to-Black conversion experience: Toward a psychology of Black liberation. *Black World, 20*(9), 13–27.

Cross, W. E., Jr., & Fhagen-Smith, P. (2001). Patterns of African American identity development: A life span perspective. In C. L. Wijeyesinghe & B. W. Jackson III (Eds.), *New perspectives on racial identity development: A theoretical and practical anthology* (pp. 243–270). New York: New York University Press.

De Jong, P., & Berg, I. K. (2008). *Interviewing for solutions* (3rd ed.). Belmont, CA: Thomson Brooks/Cole.

Ferdman, B. M., & Gallegos, P. I. (2001). Racial identity development in Latinos in the United States. In C. L. Wijeyesinghe & B. W. Jackson III (Eds.), *New perspectives on racial identity development: A theoretical and practical anthology* (pp. 32–66). New York: New York University Press.

Fisher, D. (2007). *Communication in organizations.* (2nd ed.). Mumbai: Jaico.

Franklin, A. J., & Boyd-Franklin, N. (2000). Invisibility syndrome: A clinical model of the effects of racism on African-American males. *American Journal of Orthopsychiatry, 70*(1), 33-41.

Gibbs, J. T. (1974). Pattern of adaptation among Black students at a predominately White university: Selected case studies, *Journal of Orthopsychiatry, 44*(5), 728–740.

Gilligan, C. (1977). In a different voice: Women's conceptions of self and morality. *Educational Review, 47,* 481–517.

Gilligan, C. (1993). *In a different voice: Psychological theory and women's development.* Cambridge, MA: Harvard University Press.

Hardiman, R., & Jackson, B. (1992). Racial identity development: Understanding racial dynamics in college classrooms and on campus. In M. Adams (Ed.), *Promoting diversity in college classrooms: Innovative responses for the curriculum, faculty, and institutions* (New Directions for Teaching and Learning, 52, pp. 21–37). San Francisco: Jossey-Bass.

Hays, P. A. (2008). *Addressing cultural complexities in practice: Assessment, diagnosis, and therapy.* (2nd ed). Washington, DC: APA.

Helms, J. E. (1993). *Black and White racial identity: Theory, research, and practice.* Westport, CT: Praeger.

Horse, P. G. (2001). Reflections on American Indian identity. In C. L. Wijeyesinghe & B. W. Jackson III (Eds.), *New perspectives on racial identity development: A theoretical and practical anthology* (pp. 91–107). New York: University Press.

Jackson, B. (1975). Black identity development. In L. Golubschick & B. Persky (Eds.), *Urban social and educational issues* (pp. 158–174). Dubuque, IA: Kendall Hall. :

Jones, S. R., & McEwen, M. K. (2000). A conceptual model of multiple dimensions of identity. *Journal of College Student Development, 41*(4), 405–414.

Josselson, R. (1973). Psychosocial aspects of identity formation in college women. *Journal of Youth and Adolescence, 11,* 293–299.

Josselson, R. (1987). *Finding herself: Pathways to identity development in women.* San Francisco: Jossey-Bass.

Josselson, R. (1996). *Revising herself: The story of women's identity from college to midlife.* New York: Oxford University Press.

Kim, J. (2001). Asian American identity development theory. In C. L. Wijeyesinghe & B. W. Jackson III (Eds.), *New perspectives on racial identity development: A theoretical and practical anthology* (pp. 67–90). New York: New York University Press.

Milliones, J. (1980). Construction of a Black consciousness measure: Psychotherapeutic implications. *Psychotherapy: Theory, research and practice, 17*(2), 175-182.

Phinney, J. S. (1990). Ethnic identity in adolescents and adults: Review of research. *Psychological Bulletin, 108*, 499–511.

Pierce, C., Carew, J., Pierce-Gonzales, D., & Willis, D. (1978). An experiment in racism: TV commercials. In C. Pierce (Ed.), *Television and education* (pp. 62–88). Beverly Hills, CA: Sage.

Pope, R. L., Reynolds, A. L., & Mueller, J. A. (2004). *Multicultural competence in student affairs*. San Francisco: Jossey-Bass.

Rendón, L. (1994). Validating culturally diverse students: Toward a new model of learning and student development. *Innovative Higher Education (19),* 33–52.

Savin-Williams, R. C. (2001). *Mom, dad, I'm gay: How families negotiate coming out*. Washington, DC: APA.

Schlossberg, N. K. (1989). Marginality and mattering: Key issues in building community. In D. C. Roberts (Ed.), *Designing campus activities to foster a sense of community* (New Directions for Student Services, 48, pp. 5–15). San Francisco: Jossey-Bass.

Sleeter, C. E. (2001). *Culture difference and power*. New York: Teachers College Press.

Solórzano, D. J., Ceja, M., & Yosso, T. J. (2000, Winter-Spring). Critical race theory, racial microaggressions, and campus racial climate: The experiences of African American college students. *The Journal of Negro Education, 69*(1/2), 60–73.

Sue, D. W., Bucceri, J., Lin, A. I., Nadal, K. L., & Torino, G. C. (2007, January).

Racial microaggressions and the Asian American experience. *Cultural Diversity and Ethnic Minority Psychology, 13*(1), 72–81.

Sue, D. W., & Sue, S. (2008). *Counseling the culturally diverse: Theory and practice.* (5th ed.). Hoboken, NJ: John Wiley & Sons.

CHAPTER 13

Working Together to Help Distressed Students on Campus

Dan Wilcox

My colleagues and I[1] at Kansas State University Counseling Services welcome invitations to talk with faculty, staff, and students about what we do to help students who may be struggling psychologically. Not surprisingly, we have fielded more and more of these requests since the high-profile tragedies at Virginia Tech and Northern Illinois University. In addition to basic information about our services, members of our campus community want to know how they can be helpful with struggling students. By now, most student affairs professionals and faculty members are aware of the mounting evidence that more students are coming to college with psychological wounds and are experiencing some form of psychological challenge (Benton, Robertson, Tseng, Newton, & Benton, 2003; Kitzrow, 2003; Soet & Sevig, 2006). Understandably, college personnel are primed to react with suspicion or concern to behavior that seems questionable,

Portions of this chapter were originally published in the National Academic Advising Association (NACADA) webcast *College Student Mental Health: Information and Suggestions for Academic Advising* (Wilcox, Harper, & Herman, 2007). Reprinted with permission.

outward displays of emotion, or written work that is laced with violent or grandiose imagery. And if it hasn't happened already, they know that it is just a matter of time before they encounter these students. Whenever we get a chance, we remind them that they can contact us if they feel uncomfortable or don't know how to approach a student with their concerns.

I am pretty sure that if you look on your university or college counseling services website, you will find a link to a page with advice for how to help troubled students. Most counseling services consider it part of their role to help faculty and staff members know what to look for and how to identify signs that concern is warranted. Because approaching such students can present multiple challenges, most college counseling centers also make it a point to share ideas about how to talk with students who appear to need help. If further assistance makes sense, guidance is provided on how to make appropriate referrals. This chapter on how to identify, approach, and guide distressed students to helpful resources is an addition to a growing body of literature and to conversations that I hope are already occurring on your campus (Allen & Trimble, 1993; Ellingson, Kocheneur, & Weitzman, 1999; Sharkin, 2006; Wilcox, Harper, & Herman, 2007).

I've said it before and I'll say it again: Counseling center professional staff members like hearing from members of the campus community. We welcome their interest in and concern about students and their willingness to take some action. We want to work hand-in-hand with faculty and staff to support students and help them succeed in college. But while we applaud faculty, staff, and students who want to get involved, we also worry about a tendency to overreact. Given recent events and the call to be on guard, we are concerned that idiosyncratic behaviors or age-appropriate acting out may be labeled, stigmatized, or pathologized.

What is the norm for college students today? How much leeway in behavioral expression are we willing to grant before we think, "That's just too weird!" Some students like to dress in black and sport multiple piercings and tattoos. Others can't seem to recognize common sense social cues and appear awkward or ill at ease in most group or social settings. If, during a new student orientation, the quiet student in the back of the room stands up, raises his voice, and passionately makes his point during a discussion of the dangers of Facebook, do we need to be concerned? In his excellent resource guide for helping students, Bruce Shar-kin's reply to a similar question is "My answer is an unequivocal maybe" (Sharkin, 2006). My response is "Consult, consult, consult." If you are pondering, flum-moxed, or bewildered by a student's behavior, don't hesitate to call your campus counseling service or another trusted mental health resource.

Gary Pavela, a teacher in the honors program at the University of Maryland, College Park, and author of *Questions and Answers on College Student Suicide: A Law and Policy Perspective*, warns us that we are on shaky legal ground if we limit access to college for people with mental disabilities (Pavela, 2000, 2008). Further-more, he reminds us that students with psychological disabilities are a part of the creative diversity that we value on our campuses. His words make sense: "We seek a diversity of insights, ideas, and experiences—including, perhaps, the experience of learning how to adapt to a mental disability and to turn the adaptation into a worthy career or creation" (Pavela, 2008, para. 7).

Wouldn't it be convenient if there were a simple blood test or an X-ray that could identify psychological problems and help us predict who will attempt suicide or engage in violent behavior? Instead, mental health experts agree that it is difficult to accurately diagnose a psychiatric disorder. Experts also agree that there is no de-finitive way to predict who will be dangerous or violent. A large-scale study reported in the February 2009 issue of the *Archives of General Psychiatry* acknowledges that mental illness alone will not predict future violent behavior. Combining mental ill-ness with substance abuse adds some predictive power, but not much, according to the study (Elbogen & Johnson, 2009).

The developmental tasks of the college years add to this challenge. For many students, college is a time to experiment and explore in ways that lead to age-appro-priate growing pains. These growing pains are not necessarily depression, anxiety, or some other mental illness. Excessive drinking, sexual experimentation, and a preoc-cupation with appearance that lead to food and mood issues are part of college life for some students. I'm sure that when many of us reflect on our own experiences as undergraduates, we recall how we learned to become more interpersonally compe-tent and to manage negative or disruptive emotions. What we may forget is how some of what we learned came from being with others who shared our struggles.

When it comes to succeeding in college, stress (not depression or anxiety) is the biggest threat to today's college students. According to annual surveys conducted by the American College Health Association (ACHA) since 2000, stress is the number one impediment to academic success for college students. Annually, ACHA asks students to think back over the past year and choose from a list of 25 factors the one that contributed most to academic problems, such as receiving an incomplete or dropping a course, receiving a lower grade on a test or for a course, or experiencing a significant disruption in dissertation, research, or practicum work. The results of the latest survey echo previous outcomes (ACHA, 2009). Stress consistently leads the list of offenders, which includes Internet/video games, sleep difficulties, work, cold/flu/sore throat, relationship difficulties, and depression/anxiety.

Stress is worn like a badge of honor by many of today's high-energy, hyper-involved college students. "If I'm not stressing, I'm not achieving" seems to be the mantra. Students struggle with high expectations and a perceived need to be all that they can be. College is the time to launch these success/achievement projects, and the pressure to make perfect decisions about majors, internships, extracurricular activities, and all the right experiences is definitely present. The contemporary college student has many choices to make with much at stake, and there is no assurance that things will work out. The focus is squarely on the future, and the future is uncertain. Is it any wonder that we are seeing more stressed-out students?

It has always bothered me when people talk about college life as if it were a fun, summer camp-like break before real life begins. I've talked to parents who are well aware of the stressors facing their young adult child. I've also talked to my share of parents who hear that their son or daughter is struggling in college and say something like "Wait until he [she] gets a real job, then he'll [she'll] know what stress is all about." I do my best to be diplomatic and helpful, but sometimes I feel like saying, "How would you like to work a part-time job, work with three different groups on three different projects, meet multiple deadlines, and study for and take tests—all on very little sleep and a diet of Froot Loops and 'box mac'?"

We want more of these stressed-out students to come to counseling services. Most counseling services have excellent interventions and strategies for helping students manage their stress. If students learn to deal with the stressors of college, they will have a valuable set of skills for life. At counseling services, we would like to see the stressed-out student before the consequences of stress become debilitating. Thankfully, many students do meet with us when they are stressed and overwhelmed. Residence hall directors, faculty members, academic advisors, and even friends often recognize stressed-out students and refer them to us.

Unfortunately, many students wait until they are in crisis before coming for help (University of Michigan News Service, 2007). A 2006 survey highlighted what many of us have observed about students' attitudes and beliefs about seeking help for mental health issues: It's the stigma thing (MTVU College Mental Health Study, 2006). This study found fear of embarrassment as the top reason students do not seek help for emotional issues. Seventy-seven percent of students surveyed do not want friends to know they are going to a counselor to work on emotional issues. Interestingly, half would encourage a friend to request counseling, but of that half, only 22 percent would seek assistance for themselves.

Chronic stress, left unmanaged, can have bad outcomes. Zeke was stressed out and did not know that assistance was available to help him cope with his persistently negative thoughts and feelings. Things spiraled downhill for Zeke. He was a high achiever, an "A" student who strived to be and do his best. Like many students, Zeke was competitive and looking for the edge that would lead to a high-paying job after college. He had a part-time job, was active on campus, and tried to spend time with his friends and take advantage of extracurricular activities on campus.

As Zeke added more activities and responsibilities, he started to worry more. He wondered if he had what it took to be successful. If he couldn't hack his schedule, live on four hours of sleep a night, and get good grades, what did this mean for his future? Zeke began to question his ability to succeed, and his doubts inflamed his anxiety. He responded to the worry and pressure by doing what he had always done—he worked harder. However, this time his hard work did not lead to success; in fact, it seemed that the harder he worked, the less he accomplished. His worrying increased, and he paid less attention to his physical health and well-being.

His personality seemed to change to the point where he had no motivation at all. He felt guilty, but he did not have the energy to do anything about it. Sometimes he couldn't sleep; other times, he would sleep too much. Zeke's thinking patterns became pervasively negative and pessimistic. He lost interest in activities that used to give him pleasure. He started to believe that things weren't ever going to change.

This case highlights a downward spiral of stress leading to depression. There is good and bad news about depression. The bad news first: **Depressed people often wait to get help.** Depressed people are stuck with their negative thoughts and pessimistic predictions. When they think about seeking help, they wonder, "What good would that do?" Zeke thought, "I don't want to be told that I'm depressed." It is the nature of depression that the afflicted person tends to deny him- or herself the very things that would be most helpful, including counseling. There is even sadder news about college students and depression: Most students who commit suicide never talked to a counselor (Gallagher, 2005; Kirsch, Leino, & Silverman, 2005).

The good news about depression and anxiety: **Most people get better**. In fact, disorders related to depression and anxiety are among the most treatable of all psychiatric illnesses. Talk therapy and medication options abound, and both get high marks for helping people deal with these mood issues, especially if they are used in combination (Seligman, 1995). Most students on college campuses have relatively easy access to these treatment modalities. Speaking on behalf of college counselors across the country: We want to see students before they spiral down into a depressive crisis. We want to prevent or treat mood disorders and help students cope effectively with their emotional experiences. We hope that helping college personnel recognize general warning signs will contribute to this preventive effort. By the nature of their work, advisors of student organizations, residence hall and wellness staff members (and other student personnel staff members who are not counselors) are positioned to be first responders for students in distress.

Students tend to share their problems with people they believe will listen and care. Many college personnel are in this category. Inevitably, at one time or another, student affairs staff will hear students talk about the following:

- Death or serious illness of a family member or close friend

- Parents' divorce

- Personal illness

- Severe homesickness

- Anxiety about choosing a major or career direction

- Fears around graduation and plans for the future

- Financial problems

When personal and emotional problems start to intensify and the meetings with students are dominated by accounts of these kinds of problems, student affairs professionals should recognize that it is time to make a referral to counseling services.

Student affairs professionals and faculty members witness academic, behavioral, and interpersonal problems that may signal that help is needed. When distress becomes a problem academically, students will struggle to stay on task and sustain progress. Behaviors to watch for include these:

- A dramatic decline in academic performance

- A pattern of dropping classes or asking for extensions

- Missed deadlines

- Excessive, unexplained absences

- Frequent requests for special attention or consideration

- Severe reaction to a poor grade on a test or paper

- Extreme fear of speaking up in class or approaching the professor

- Persistent doubts about the student's ability to succeed in school

Out-of-character behaviors can also be a sign that a student is distressed. If an upbeat, positive student starts to sound negative and pessimistic, and look sullen and downcast, a more serious problem may be the cause. If this kind of behavior persists, consider it a red flag. Unusual or disruptive behaviors such as the following suggest underlying problems:

- Dependency: the student wants to be around you all the time or makes excessive appointments to see you

- Loss of interest in activities that used to be engaging

- Significantly increased activity (e.g., extreme restlessness, nonstop talking, inability to relax)

- Suspiciousness or feelings of being persecuted

- Inappropriate or bizarre conversation (e.g., talking nonsense or being unable to carry on a coherent conversation)

- Unusual irritability, outbursts of anger, unexplained crying, aggressiveness, excessive worrying or anxiety; significant decline in personal hygiene, standard of dress, or grooming

- A change from normal, socially appropriate behavior (e.g., becoming disruptive or aggressive, persistent lying or stealing)

Students who are distressed often struggle in their relationships. They may have obvious difficulty getting along with other students. They may wear friends out by constantly ruminating about problems. Some students may have a difficult time making friends or struggle mightily whenever they are called upon to interact in the student union, participate in residence hall activities, or speak in class. Things to look for:

- Extreme shyness or lack of social skills

- Inability to make friends

- Roommate conflicts

- Problems in dating or marital relationships, and overreacting to them

- Too frequent, too lengthy visits in your office

- Attitude of blaming others, not seeing one's own role or taking responsibility

- Threats regarding others

- Total social isolation

Of course, not all students are going to be as transparent or up front about their personal problems. Many are unable to recognize that they may be in trouble, or they may have difficulty connecting their personal problems with their emotional or situational adjustment difficulties. Such a student might suddenly start crying uncontrollably during a one-on-one advisor meeting or even during a class. He or she might seem uncomfortable or refuse to answer your questions, or may startle you with a rambling, incoherent discourse.

I understand that some student affairs professionals will be uncomfortable approaching a distressed student. Believe me, I have encountered student behavior in my office that has made me uncomfortable. I'm not ashamed to say that under certain circumstances I may have thoughts like "Just go away" or "Why me?" Trying to be helpful with some students can feel like trying to lasso a tornado. If you have questions about a student, or if you want some tips on how to approach a student who may need help, don't hesitate to call counseling services or contact other resources.

The following are some general guidelines for approaching students if you feel comfortable doing so.

Approach and talk with students in a supportive manner. Be sensitive to time and place. Ask to meet with the student at a mutually agreeable time when there will be enough time for an extended discussion. Meet the student in a relaxed, private setting. This minimizes the potential for embarrassment and demonstrates your willingness to help. Be up front about your reasons for meeting with the student, and share your observations in a nonjudgmental fashion.

Try saying something like *"I've noticed that you've looked kind of down lately, and I'm concerned. Do you have some time to talk? We can meet in my office."* Or *"I've heard that you've stopped going to class and are sleeping through meals. Your friends tell me that you've stopped talking to them and going out with them. They're very wor-*

ried about you, and frankly I am, too. I wonder if there's something bothering you or worrying you. I know we don't usually talk about personal matters, but I'd really like to try to help. Can we talk?"

Listen to the student's thoughts and feelings in a sensitive, nonthreatening way. It's impossible to overestimate the power of good listening. In fact, just a few minutes of effective listening on your part may be enough to help the student feel cared about and more confident about what to do. Your student will know you are listening when you invite him or her to talk with gentle encouragers such as *"Tell me more about that." "Try to put your feelings into words." "What else?"* Note how these questions are open-ended and don't elicit a yes or no response. Open-ended questions feel a lot less judgmental than yes or no questions, and they reflect a caring, concerned listener who really wants to help.

Communicate understanding by repeating back the essence of what the student has told you. Try to respond to both the content and the emotions behind that content. Here are examples of how you might communicate understanding:

- *"It sounds like you're not accustomed to such a big campus and you're feeling left out of things."*

- *"I can see that it's hard to talk about your feelings. Take your time."*

- *"You certainly have a lot going on right now. I imagine you feel overwhelmed."*

- *"You and I haven't talked about these issues before. Is it difficult to talk about these matters with me? Perhaps it would be easier to talk with a counselor, privately and confidentially."*

Instill hope and reinforce your students' help-seeking behavior. Tell them that taking the initial step to seek help is often difficult. Once a student decides to reach out for assistance, things often improve. At the counseling center, we often talk about how a student will show up for the first appointment and say, "I feel so much better than when I called to make this appointment; I almost called to cancel." For many students, especially depressed students, talking to someone marks the point when they start to take action on behalf of their desire to feel and do better.

Working with students to identify options for helpful action is another big hope booster. Distressed students want to feel better, but they are confused about how to make that happen. For such students, creating possible pathways is creating hope. One caution: Be careful not to minimize concerns with *"You have nothing to worry about"* or *"Everything will be fine."*

Finally, asking students what they have done so far to cope with the problem or to feel better reminds them that they have their own ideas and strategies that work. Find out what has worked before, even just a little bit.

Maintain your boundaries, and be frank with the student about the limits on your ability to help him or her. Don't try to do too much. A desire to become a surrogate counselor can turn into a complicated situation and even lead to a rupture in the relationship you have with the student. In talking with advisors and faculty on my campus, I've become aware that some of them have learned this lesson the hard way. After months of trying to help her struggling student with weekly meetings at the coffee shop and through e-mail, the academic advisor is in over her head. For the distressed student, it's just more bad news from a trusted source of support: *"I really don't think I can help you."* Reassure your student: *"There are people who know much more about this than I do. Why not give them a try?"*

Refer your student to counseling services or another mental health professional when you feel the student needs their help. Your experiences with students have probably taught you that the referral process can be simple or quite complicated. Some students will readily accept your invitation to seek help. Others will hesitate or reject the suggestion outright. Students vary in their openness and readiness to seek help or counseling (Prochaska, Norcross, & DiClemente, 1994). A number of factors influence students' receptivity. Most mental health professionals are aware of these factors and are ready to engage with students, wherever they are on the readiness spectrum.

Here are some general guidelines for making referrals that will help both eager and not-so-eager help seekers. These guidelines work best when there is no sense of urgency. (What to do when there is evidence that the student may be thinking about suicide or violence is described later in this chapter.)

Get to know your referral sources. Your knowledge of campus services can ease a student's discomfort about seeking help. Visit the counseling center offices and websites and learn who works there, what they offer, and how to make contact and schedule appointments. Find out about their hours of operation, eligibility for services, and whether fees are involved. Most counseling services offer initial consultations at no cost to the student. Find out if your institution's health and counseling services offer psychiatric services and consultations with students about the use of medications.

If your campus does not have a counseling center, you will have to go the extra mile to find out about community mental health or private practice resources off campus. Knowing something about these resources will help your students feel more comfortable about seeking help off campus. In addition to general information about staff and services, find out if they accept health insurance and if they have a sliding-scale fee for students. Do they have experience working with college students? What is the typical wait for a first appointment?

Listen to how your students talk about counseling and seeking help. Ask your student, *"What do you think about counseling?"* Listen for negative connotations or biases about counseling. You can help with gentle challenges and by normalizing help-seeking behavior. You may know students who benefited from seeing a counselor. Share their stories. From the data we've collected over the years at our counseling center, we know that students with higher GPAs tend to seek help in greater numbers than those with lower GPAs. We believe that successful students are willing to seek and make use of helpful resources, including counseling.

Increase student confidence and expectations about seeking help. Your knowledge of referral sources and your ability to talk authoritatively about the people and services and how they are tailored to address a student's specific concerns will go a long way to build student confidence in those resources. Research has shown that client confidence in the counselor is related to positive outcomes. Believing that competent professionals are available to address psychological issues goes a long way to generate a student's expectation that things will get better.

"Give it a try." Students may not know that they are in charge of the process.

They might think that once they start counseling there's no turning back. Reluctant students might be relieved to know that they can speak with a counselor on a one-time basis without making a commitment to ongoing counseling.

Remind students that counseling services are confidential. Students may be concerned about how information they share in counseling will influence their status in the college or university. They will be relieved to hear that any information they share is kept strictly confidential by on- or off-campus counseling services and will not be disclosed to parents, faculty, other university departments, or even you, without the student's written permission. The general requirement that counselors keep information confidential does not apply when disclosure is required to prevent clear and imminent danger to the individual or to others, or when legal requirements demand that confidential information be revealed. Counselors will clearly explain these limits to students.

Tell students what to expect. Most students will not have been to a counselor or therapist before, so it can be helpful to provide a sense of what to expect. Here again, your knowledge of the people and services will come in handy. Knowing the names of staff members and their areas of expertise will help you make the student feel that he or she will be dealing with a "known quantity." Your familiarity with the ethnicity and gender of counseling center staff will enable you to direct students to specific counselors, for example, a woman or a person of color.

Some students are not sure they will be accepted, even at their campus counseling services. Some GLBT students or students with certain religious beliefs may not trust psychological counseling. Your ability to reassure students by telling them about the people who sought counseling and got the help they wanted will help pave the way for these and other reluctant students.

Talk about what happens at the first visit. Most students will appreciate knowing about the intake process and what to expect when they go to the counseling center for the first time. The process is fairly standard and straightforward for most counseling centers. Typically, there are some forms to fill out or complete online. Students will share basic demographic information and will be asked to write briefly about what brings them to counseling. Most likely there will be some kind of symptom checklist or a way for students to indicate which issues are interfering with their academic and social progress. This is not much different from what is asked of anyone who visits a health care provider.

While there is variability among counselors and the way they work with students in the first appointment, most counselors want to hear students talk about what brought them to counseling and what changes they hope to see as a result. Whatever the approach, most counselors will do their best to gather information in a respectful and sensitive manner. This includes questions about suicidal ideation or behavior, other forms of self-harm, drug and alcohol use, and other aspects of the student's life on campus.

What you can do when there is a sense of urgency. You may believe it would be in the student's best interest to be seen by a mental health professional right away. Most counseling services offer on-call or walk-in services for students when there is a sense of urgency. This means that counselors are available to meet with the student right away. We advise faculty and staff to make this type of call from their office. Often, your student will agree to call on his or her own. Many college personnel offer to escort the student to counseling services. (This works even when there is no sense of urgency.) This gesture of support can be reassuring to the student, and knowing that your student is in competent hands adds to your peace of mind.

When a student makes references to suicide or danger to others, there are things you can do to help. If the student appears to be in imminent danger of hurting him- or herself or others, call counseling services or the campus police immediately. Tragic, highly publicized events on college campuses have highlighted the need for campuses to develop crisis response teams and communication networks. Make sure you know the resources on your campus for dealing with this situation.

Surveys suggest that many students think about suicide and even attempt it. Paul S. Appelbaum, a professor of psychiatry at Columbia University and a past president of the American Psychiatric Association, has written, "Two large-scale studies generated nearly identical findings. Roughly 10 percent of college student respondents indicated that they had thought about suicide in the past year, and 1.5 percent admitted to having made a suicide attempt" (Applebaum, 2006, p. 915). Given the scope of these studies, these percentages represent a large number of students. Applebaum continues, "Combining data from the available studies suggests that the odds that a student with suicidal ideation will actually commit suicide are 1,000 to 1." Still, all overt references to suicide and hurting oneself must be taken seriously.

Some students keep these suicidal thoughts to themselves or cloak their despair. You may need to ask these students directly if they are thinking about hurting themselves. The American Foundation for Suicide Prevention has developed an excellent film, *The Truth About Suicide: Real Stories About Depression in College* (2004). I highly recommend this film as an adjunct to efforts on your campus to raise awareness and do something about this serious issue. In the film, a student who struggled with depression and considered suicide said this: "I would much rather have someone ask me about suicide when I am feeling okay than not ask me about suicide when I am suicidal."

Remember, there is no infallible way of determining who is thinking about self-harm or suicide. A student may be experiencing a combination of the general academic, behavioral, and interpersonal factors listed earlier, and also may be considering suicide. Ask about suicide if you see signs of depression or hopelessness. Students with a history of depression or attempted suicide are at higher risk. Don't hesitate to share your concerns when you hear a student say something like "What's the point of living?" or "I'd be better off dead." Even if the student is not considering suicide, he or she may have other issues and could benefit from counseling.

What if the student refuses to seek help? No matter how distressed they are, some students will refuse to make that call or go to counseling services. Don't panic; if the student does not appear to be a danger to self or others, it is okay to let him or her go, then contact someone from the office of the dean of students or speak with a staff member from counseling services. The student may already have been identified as "struggling" in the residence hall or may already be a client at counseling services. On our campus, it is not unusual for the assistant dean of student life to hear about such students from advisors, staff in residence halls, teachers, or Student Union personnel. She is not bound by confidentiality and can gather information from different resources and make sure that lines of communication stay open. She is in an excellent position to intervene and ensure that the student is assessed and gets help. The assistant dean on your campus is likely in a similar position.

Many campuses have some type of crisis or behavioral intervention team consisting of members of various offices (e.g., Dean of Students, Counseling Center, Residential Life, Safety and Security) that is notified when a student appears to be functioning very poorly or is perceived to be at risk. Cornell University's alert team is an example (Bernstein, 2007). Because of rules regarding confidentiality, the counselor is usually the "silent member" of the committee; he or she receives but does not share information about students. However, this interdisciplinary, campuswide approach allows for appropriate information sharing across functional lines and allows administrators to "compare notes on signs of student emotional problems" (Bernstein, 2007, p. A1).

Follow up with the student. There is one more step in the referral process. Following up is often overlooked or neglected, but it is important. Students don't always do what they say they will do. Make arrangements with students to check in with you a week or two after you make the referral.

I have worked with faculty and advisors who talk to the counseling center about the student. Sharing information with the counseling center can be very helpful, although counselors cannot reciprocally share. Just say that you wish to provide information about a student who may be a client. I'm okay with this, and so are my colleagues. Don't forget to address the issue of confidentiality with the student. If you want to verify that the student met with a counselor, the student must sign a consent form at the first appointment to release this information to you.

In conclusion, think about counseling services and referring a student if—

- The problem is more serious than you feel comfortable handling.

- You are very busy or stressed and cannot find the time to deal with the problem.

- You have helped as much as you can, and further assistance is needed.

- You think your personal feelings about the student will interfere with your objectivity.

- The student admits that there is a problem but doesn't want to talk to you about it.

- The student asks for information or assistance that you are unable to provide.

Counseling services personnel appreciate how often student affairs professionals serve as our eyes and ears on campus. We want you to know that we support your efforts with students who can use our help. We also understand what a challenge it can be to work with students in psychological distress. Struggling students face complex mood and situational concerns, and they also may deal with a stigma about seeking help. Without your guidance, they may fail to connect with critical helping resources. Let's work together to help each other and to help our students—including those with mental health issues—succeed.

References

Allen, D., & Trimble, R. (1993). Identifying and referring troubled students: A primer for academic advisors. *NACADA Journal, 13*(2), 34–41.

American College Health Association (ACHA). (2009). American College Health Association/National College Health Assessment spring reference group data report [electronic version]. *Journal of American College Health, 57*(5), 477–488. Retrieved September 17, 2009, from www.acha-ncha.org/docs/JACH_March_2009_SP08_Ref_Grp.pdf

American Foundation for Suicide Prevention. (2004). The truth about suicide: Real stories of depression in college [DVD]. Author.

Appelbaum, P. S. (2006). Depressed? Get out! Dealing with suicidal students on college campuses [electronic version]. *Psychiatric Services 57*(7), 914–916. Retrieved September 17, 2009, from http://psychservices. psychiatryonline.org/cgi/reprint/57/7/914

Benton, S. A., Robertson, J. M., Tseng, W. C., Newton, F. B., & Benton, S. L. (2003). Changes in counseling center clients' problems across 13 years. *Professional Psychology: Research and Practice, 34*(1), 66–72.

Bernstein, E. (2007, December 28). Bucking privacy concerns, Cornell acts as watchdog. *Wall Street Journal*, p. A1.

Elbogen, E. B., & Johnson, S. C. (2009). The intricate link between violence and mental disorder: Results from the national epidemiologic survey on alcohol and related conditions. *Archives of General Psychiatry, 66*(2), 152–161.

Ellingson, K. T., Kocheneur, E. O., & Weitzman, L. M. (1999). University counseling center consultation: Developing a faculty orientation program. *Consulting Psychology Journal: Practice and Research, 51*, 31–36.

Gallagher, R. P. (2005). National survey of counseling center directors, 2005. Retrieved April 14, 2009, from www.iacsinc.org/2005%20National%20Survey.pdf

Kirsch, J., Leino, E. V., & Silverman, M. M. (2005). Aspects of suicidal behavior, depression, and treatment in college students: Results from the spring 2000 National College Health Assessment Survey. *Suicide and Life-Threatening Behavior, 35,* 3–13.

Kitzrow, M. (2003). The mental health needs of today's college students: Challenges and recommendations. *NASPA Journal, 41*(1), 167–181.

MTVU College Mental Health Study: Stress, depression, stigma, and students: Executive summary. (2006). Retrieved January 22, 2008, from www.halfofus.com/_media/_pr/mtvUCollegeMentalHealthStudy2006.pdf

Pavela, G. (2008). Commentary: Fearing our students won't help them [electronic version]. *Chronicle of Higher Education,* chronicle.com/daily/2008/02/1700n.htm

Pavela, G. (2006). *Questions and answers on college student suicide: A law and policy perspective.* Ashville, NC: College Administrators Publications.

Prochaska, J. O., Norcross, J. C., and DiClemente, C. C. (1994). *Changing for good: The revolutionary program that explains the six stages of change and teaches you how to free yourself from bad habits.* New York: William Morrow and Co.

Seligman, M. E. P. (1995). The effectiveness of psychotherapy: The *Consumer Reports* study. *American Psychologist, 50,* 965–974

Sharkin, B. S. (2006). *College students in distress: A resource guide for faculty, staff, and campus community.* New York: Haworth Press.

Soet, J., & Sevig, T. (2006). Mental health issues facing a diverse sample of college students: Results from the College Student Mental Health Survey. *National Association of Student Personnel Administrators, 43,* 410–431.

University of Michigan News Service. (2007). Students with symptoms of serious mental illness often don't seek help. Retrieved March 12, 2009, from www.ns.umich.edu/htdocs/releases/story.php?id=5913

271

Wilcox, D., Harper, R., & Herman, J. (2007). *College student mental health: Information and suggestions for academic advising.* (NACADA Webcast Series, No. 8). Manhattan, KS: National Academic Advising Association.

CHAPTER 14

Applying the Theories

Ruth Harper and Nona L. Wilson

The goal of this book is to demonstrate how counseling theories and skills can enhance student affairs practice. Chapters 1 and 2 offer overviews of theories from both student development and counseling. Chapters 3 through 12 apply those theories to a series of case studies. Chapter 13 describes how student affairs professionals can work with counselors to help students who are struggling psychologically. Pope, Reynolds, & Mueller (2004) say that "Case studies encourage consideration of multiple perspectives, allow simulation of real-life practice, and yet simultaneously reduce anxiety because the stakes are not nearly as high as in an actual work situation" (p. 183). If this book is successful, it will do just that, and you will feel encouraged to apply both student development and counseling theory to your work with students.

We hope the following scenarios help you rehearse how to respond to challenging situations, without the urgency or pressure that typically accompany them in real life. Many of the case studies in this book, including those that follow, were based on real-life situations. Details have been changed, and the descriptions of students are composites of aspects and circumstances of several students. None of the case studies is intended to reflect a specific, real-life situation or student, with the exception of statements in the Vaccaro case study (see chapter 12).

As you work with these scenarios, you may wish you had more information about the student, the institution, your role, or other factors that might affect your response. Feel free to adapt these situations to the setting(s) of your choice and to create additional circumstances or roles for reflection or discussion purposes.

In considering each student and his or her circumstances, strive to build your responses from both student development and counseling theories, as has been modeled in the previous chapters. Asssess which theories or strategies will work best for you, yield the richest conceptualization of the student's challenge or dilemma, and offer techniques that will be useful in your actual work.

Keep track of what else you need to learn to serve students most effectively. For example, which multicultural competencies are still challenging for you? How will you develop those competencies? Does being a Person-Centered (student-centered) or Solution-Focused ("not knowing") professional help you work with students who are different from you? Which Cognitive-Behavioral strategies do you feel comfortable using? Pay attention to your initial reactions to the students and situations presented in the cases. What do you notice? What do your responses reveal about you, your assumptions, possible biases, knowledge and skills, values, strengths, and insecurities?

The case studies presented here may be used by individuals, small groups, or entire classes. The questions posed are simply a starting place and should generate further lines of inquiry. For example, you might wish to add characters (e.g., other students, staff members, faculty members) to the scenarios, or examine a situation by focusing on a single aspect or characteristic at a time (e.g., ethnicity, sexual orientation, institutional mission). Try role-playing to generate fresh perspectives and to experiment with the ideas using your own language and personal style. What does working with the cases suggest to you about what you could read, what conversations you might want to have, what training you could pursue? To make the most of the cases, go beyond simply reacting to truly engaging the theories and strategies you have learned about in this text.

References

Pope, R. L., Reynolds, A. L., & Mueller, J. A. (2004). *Multicultural competence in student affairs*. San Francisco: Jossey-Bass.

CASE 1

Culture/Career Dilemma
Jennifer

Joy Hoffman, Lori M. Ideta,
Hikaru Kozuma, and Karlen N. Suga

Jennifer is a second-generation Chinese American student and a first-year student who lives in your residence hall at Poplar Hills College, a nondenominational liberal arts college in northern California. As the resident director, you see her at least once a week in passing or when she stops by your office.

In your first extended conversation with Jennifer, you ask about her background and learn that her father is an endocrinologist and her mother stays at home to care for Jennifer's two younger siblings, who are still in elementary school. Jennifer's older brother is a senior at Grove University, the most prestigious and competitive public research institution in the state, where he is excelling as an electrical engineering major. Both Jennifer and her brother attended a private high school, because their parents thought it would give them the best chance to succeed academically at the universities on their list of acceptable institutions.

As the year continues, you see Jennifer periodically and discover that her dream is to become a teacher. She loves to work with children. In high school, she was a second through fifth grade tutor for a local after-school program and sometimes volunteered with arts and crafts at the YMCA. She earned most of her college money by babysitting and tutoring. She enjoys participating in student leadership and was a board member for her high school's Asian Student Association and a student senator. She was also a member of the Kiwanis Club.

275

Her parents have made it clear that academics must come first, and have asked Jennifer to refrain from volunteer and cocurricular activities in college. They fear that student leadership and service opportunities, although commendable, may distract her from her studies.

Jennifer confides to you that her parents originally wanted her to attend Grove to become a pediatrician. They agree that she is wonderful with children but strongly prefer that she use her talents in a "better" profession than teaching. Jennifer applied to six schools, including Grove and Poplar Hills. She was accepted to four of the six, including those two. Both are within an hour of her home.

Jennifer's father told her that she could not live on campus if she attended Poplar Hills, because he wanted her to help with her two younger siblings. However, if she decided to go to Grove and chose the medical field, he would gladly support her living on campus to allow her to focus on her studies. Poplar Hills College was Jennifer's first choice; she decided to go there but agreed to pursue the medical field. Jennifer's father was not happy with her choice of college, but was pleased with her decision to pursue medicine. He reluctantly permitted her to live on campus.

During the fall semester, Jennifer becomes overwhelmed with coursework and homesickness. She confides in her roommate, who shares the information with you. You take Jennifer aside in the lobby one day to ask her how she is doing. Her eyes tear up immediately and she asks to talk with you privately. In your office, she hesitantly confesses that she is not happy with her classes because she doesn't really want to study medicine. She says that although she likes living in the hall, she is a bit homesick and especially misses her siblings. You talk with her and describe some of the resources available to her, including yourself, campus counseling, and the career and academic planning center.

In considering this scenario, place yourself in the various student affairs roles that bring you into contact with Jennifer. First respond as the residence hall director, then as a career counselor/academic advisor; add other roles that allow you to approach her situation from multiple perspectives. Pay particular attention to how you connect theory to an action plan for Jennifer. Also reflect on how your approach with Jennifer might be different from (or similar to) the way you would work with a student from another background, say, a White student with Western values or a fourth-generation Chinese American student whose parents are both professionals.

Discussion Questions

1. Which theories of college student development will inform your work in this situation?

2. Which ideas and techniques associated with Person-Centered, Solution-Focused, and Cognitive-Behavioral counseling might be helpful in responding to the student in this scenario?

3. What resources would you consider using to assist Jennifer with her challenges, and why? Which particular aspects of this case must you handle most carefully? How might this situation look with a student from another group?

4. What else do you need to explore or learn about to deal with this situation with confidence and professionalism?

CASE 2

Religion and Relationships
Ibrahim

Julie P. Baumberger

Ibrahim is walking on campus with a sad look on his face again, and people are noticing. His academic advisor, biochemistry professor Dr. Hermann, cannot understand how Ibrahim could express anything but sheer joy after scoring a 34 on the MCAT. Ibrahim's goal is to become a physician. With a 4.0 grade point average and strong MCAT score, he will almost certainly be accepted into a number of medical schools.

Ibrahim is a senior pre-med student, a Muslim from Hyderabad, India. He has been one of Dr. Hermann's most capable students and advisees for the past three and a half years at a small, residential private college in the southern United States. While he has worked closely on a number of projects with Ibrahim, Dr. Hermann readily admits that he really does not know him very well beyond his outstanding academic work. Dr. Hermann is concerned about Ibrahim's recent mood changes and wonders what is going on.

Ibrahim is well liked by other students. Dr. Hermann believes Ibrahim even has a girlfriend, Lisa, a young woman who attends Dr. Hermann's church. Lisa and Ibrahim are both in a class Dr. Hermann teaches. He has noticed that Lisa walks to and from class alone, but sits with Ibrahim and other Muslim students at the Student Center. What seems odd to Dr. Hermann is that Lisa and Ibrahim never sit together. It crosses Dr. Hermann's mind that Lisa's parents may not be thrilled that their daughter is dating a Muslim. It does not occur to him that Ibrahim's family may be even more upset than Lisa's regarding this budding interfaith relationship.

Ibrahim is a leader in the Muslim Students Association (MSA). He strongly believes in the underlying principals of the organization, embracing the ideas of unity, brotherhood, and sisterhood among Muslim students of different origins, nationalities, and ethnicities, with a single belief and faith in one god. Ibrahim is proud to be active in the organization and works hard to promote friendly relations with other students—Muslim and non-Muslim—on campus.

Dr. Aziz, assistant professor of computer science and MSA advisor, often remarks that Ibrahim is generous with his time and talents when community service opportunities arise. Ibrahim seems to accept and live out the responsibilities that come with being a faithful Muslim, praying five times a day and getting to the mosque well before sunrise most mornings. Dr. Aziz notes that Ibrahim helps new students, especially other international students, adapt to college life and their community while at the same time encouraging them to stay connected with others like himself—a faithful Muslim. Ibrahim is usually the first student in the association to volunteer to organize lectures, social gatherings, or study groups to introduce Islam to interested non-Muslims.

Dr. Aziz has seen Ibrahim on three separate occasions talking to a non-Muslim female student who has shown more than a passing interest in learning more about the Muslim religion. He wonders about the depth and sincerity of her interest in Islam; is her interest more in Ibrahim than in the faith? He has observed that dynamic before; sometimes it leads to problems, but sometimes it does not.

Dr. Aziz also notices how tense and preoccupied Ibrahim becomes when conversation turns playful among the young men and women in the group. Ibrahim seems most comfortable and confident when he is sharing the word of Allah; he can be somewhat self-conscious in informal, coed social situations. Dr. Aziz remembers his own youth, and how shy and uncomfortable he felt around women on the few occasions he was allowed to interact with them. He has made a few attempts to reassure Ibrahim that, with time, he will get past the awkwardness he feels, but Ibrahim cuts him off in such a way that a meaningful conversation never takes place. As MSA advisor, Dr. Aziz sees it as his responsibility to provide guidance and support on a number of subjects to young Muslim students. He would like to get closer to Ibrahim, to talk in more depth about the faith they share and, if possible, to learn what might be troubling him. Dr. Aziz makes a mental note to mention his concerns to the imam later today.

Ibrahim's hall director, Bob, has also noticed changes in Ibrahim's demeanor. Typically a positive, community-minded resident in the upper-class hall, Ibrahim has been acting out of character lately. In the past, Bob could always count on Ibrahim to be the voice of reason during any dispute. And when Bob needed someone to get the residents enthused about a campus event, Ibrahim was the man who could do it. Lately, however, Ibrahim does not seem to care about what is going on in the hall or on campus. In fact, he is rarely there. Ibrahim says he sometimes studies all night at the library, but Bob, who also frequents the library, has not seen him there. When Bob pressed Ibrahim about where he is spending his time these days, he got a "don't go there" glare in response. Bob believes that he is just trying to do his job: keeping an eye on his residents and making sure they are okay. He mentions his concerns to you.

As associate director of student life, you know Ibrahim fairly well through his leadership roles in many campus activities. You contact him and ask him to stop by. When Ibrahim does not respond to your invitation, you seek him out in the Student Center. He greets you cautiously and gives you a look you do not understand but agrees to come to your office for coffee after lunch.

When Ibrahim enters your office, you see that he is exhausted. He also looks sad and maybe even frightened. When you say you have not seen him for a while and that he is missed in his hall, he stuns you by putting his face in his hands and breaking down. Before you know what is happening, Ibrahim tells you that he is "a terrible, terrible person, a hypocrite, and a liar" who cannot live with himself. He blurts out a story of love and intimacy that sounds developmentally appropriate to you but clearly is not acceptable to Ibrahim, who makes his "confession" while choking back sobs. Eventually Ibrahim stops talking and puts his head down on his folded arms.

After a minute or two of silence, you say gently, "Ibrahim, let me make sure that I understand. You and Lisa have strong feelings for each other and it sounds like you two are in a committed, intimate relationship. But now you want to break up with Lisa because you believe you cannot control your physical desire and you believe this relationship is a sin?"

"That's right," he responds in a muffled voice. "I don't know why I even told you all this. I know it is wrong and I know what I have to do. I don't expect you to understand. I think that if I can just stay away from her, maybe these thoughts and feelings will disappear."

"It seems that it's really important to you not to think about Lisa in that way," you reflect. Ibrahim looks up and says, "You know how important my faith is to me. The Holy Qur'an is very clear about adultery and fornication. How could this happen to me? My father talked to me many times before I left for college in the United States. He warned me that I would be tested, but I never worried because I believed my faith to be unshakable. Now look what I've done. You know, I've tried to break it off with Lisa, but I always go back. Sometimes I hate her!"

Discussion Questions

1. Which theories of college student development will inform your work in this situation?

2. Which ideas and techniques associated with Person-Centered, Solution-Focused, and Cognitive-Behavioral counseling might be helpful in responding to the student in this scenario?

3. If the campus counseling center or an off-campus mental health professional will be consulted or involved, what will be the best way to make the referral? Which particulars of this case must you handle most carefully?

4. What else do you need to explore or learn about to deal with this situation with confidence and professionalism?

GLBT Issues on a Conservative Campus

Heidi Stanton

Larson University is a largely residential 100-year-old institution of 10,500 students that sits on a hilltop in the center of Farmington, a town of 25,000 people in the northwest United States. Farmington is a rural agricultural community in the most conservative part of an otherwise liberal state. The town is geographically isolated—two hours away from urban resources, shopping, and entertainment. Founded as a land grant college, Larson is now known for its veterinary medicine and communications programs and as a research university with specialties in agriculture, animal science, and bioengineering. Farmington residents have historically looked to Larson as the center of the community. The campus climate at the university has improved a great deal for gay, lesbian, bisexual, and transgender (GLBT) students and faculty/staff members over the past ten years. As a result, students are more comfortable being open about their sexual orientation on campus.

As assistant director of the GLBT center, you have been at Larson for just one year. You have a master's degree in literature from an East Coast university, and are still learning to navigate your new role. You are knowledgeable about Queer Theory and dedicated to working with GLBT (and other) students, but you have no related professional experience. You enjoy your work and have been talking with your director, Hannah Derivan, about restructuring the GLBT center; she supports your ideas and frequently requests your comments and advice. Hannah is active at the national level in a well-known professional organization.

Because of her association responsibilities, she travels a great deal and is relying on you to assume a leadership role at the center. Your goals, which she strongly supports, include directing more attention and resources to building relationships with academic departments, bridging the divide between social and political student programming, and developing supportive allies.

You have already been instrumental in revamping the Speakers Bureau, a program that sends trained GLBT students into classrooms, residence halls, and Greek houses to tell their stories and discuss GLBT issues. Nearly 40 students are involved in the Speakers Bureau, and you hope to further develop leadership within this group through a one-day retreat that is about to take place. The very full retreat agenda includes assessing the Speakers Bureau, setting goals for next year, identifying target audiences, and creating speaker panels to work together. Overall goals are to increase campus awareness and educate the community about GLBT identities, as well as to address leadership issues and skills.

Extremely busy preparing all the logistics and materials for the retreat, you receive a somewhat surprising e-mail from Sarah Burton. You have met Sarah in other campus contexts and know her slightly. She is a graduate student in molecular biology; you have heard through the grapevine that she comes from a conservative Christian family in the Midwest. So the content of her message is quite unexpected:

> I was given your e-mail address because of recent personal issues I have been experiencing. Within the past 6 months, I have realized that I like girls. After 20-some years of assuming I was hetero, this realization has rocked my world. In fact, I fell in love with a woman, told her of my feelings, and was soundly rejected. While I know there is no cure for heartache, I am hoping that you can help me connect with more people in the gay community. Meeting people who are going through some of the same issues I am may help me on my path. Are there any events coming up, or perhaps a support group for those of us new to Larson? I am new here and very busy with my studies and graduate assistant work. Thank you for any help or advice you can offer.

As you sit back and think about this graduate student and her situation, your phone rings. It is Dr. Krista Austin, Sarah's academic advisor. Sarah has just come out to her as well, and the professor says she was caught without an adequate response. Dr. Austin says she would like to be supportive; however, her personal and religious beliefs may interfere. To her credit, Dr. Austin asks if you have information that will be helpful to her. You agree to provide such information and to meet with Dr. Austin next week, after the retreat.

As you reflect on the situation, Erin Roberts, president of the GLBT student organization, appears in your office doorway. "Have you seen this?" she says in a voice of angry disbelief. She thrusts today's issue of the college newspaper into your hands and points. The *Larson Chronicle* carries an interview with members of a local fundamentalist Christian church. One of the parishioners is quoted as saying, "The university shouldn't provide funding or space or any resources to support homosexuality." As you scan the article, you are dismayed to find that the person being quoted is Dr. Austin. Erin is enraged and wants to gather all members of the GLBT group to demonstrate in the campus quad to show their support for the GLBT center.

Not surprisingly, your phone is ringing again. You answer and are relieved to hear your director's voice. Hannah wants to let you know that Dr. Austin has been to see her, very upset about the article. Dr. Austin claims she has been quoted out of context and says that her position and views were misrepresented. Hannah also states that Dr. Austin is very concerned about how this misquote will affect her relationship with Sarah.

You are reeling with the demands on your time, energy, and attention, yet you want to handle these situations sensitively and effectively. One of your most important tasks on this campus, you realize, may be to help those who want to become allies of the GLBT center and its students but who struggle with their religious and political beliefs in taking on such a role. Also, you are learning that the coming out process is different here, in this state and at this institution, than where you grew up and went to college. You are suddenly not so sure about things you thought you knew.

Discussion Questions

1. Which theories of college student development will inform your work in this situation?

2. Which ideas and techniques associated with Person-Centered, Solution-Focused, and Cognitive-Behavioral counseling might be helpful in responding to the students in this scenario?

3. If the campus counseling center or an off-campus mental health professional will be consulted or involved, what will be the best way to make the referral? Which particulars of this case must you handle most carefully?

4. What else do you need to explore or learn about to deal with this situation with confidence and professionalism?